Faces of Evil

Faces of Evil

Kidnappers, Murderers, Rapists and the Forensic Artist Who Puts Them Behind Bars

by
Lois Gibson
and
Deanie Francis Mills

New Horizon Press
Far Hills, New Jersey

Gibson, Lois and Deanie Francis Mills
    Faces of Evil:
    Kidnappers, Murderers, Rapists and the Forensic Artist Who
    Puts Them Behind Bars

Cover Design: Robert Aulicino
Interior Design: Susan M. Sanderson

Library of Congress Control Number: 2004108083

ISBN: 0-88282-258-6
New Horizon Press

Manufactured in the U.S.A.

2009   2008   2007   2006   2005   /   5   4   3   2   1

This book is dedicated to the survivors
of violent crime everywhere.
May you find sweet justice
and, at last, may you know peace.

"...it is a rare and shattering experience...to gaze into the face of absolute evil."

Carl Jung
Phenomenology of the Self

"One picture is worth ten thousand words."

Anonymous

Table of Contents

Authors' Note

This book is based on the experiences of Lois Gibson and reflects her perceptions of the past, present and future. The personalities, events, actions and conversations portrayed within the story have been taken from her memories, court documents, interviews, testimony, research, letters, personal papers, press accounts and the memories of some participants.

Although all the crimes depicted in this book are a matter of public record, the names and a few identifying characteristics of the victims have, in most cases, been changed in order to protect their privacy. Events involving the characters happened as described. Only minor details have been altered.

Acknowledgements

To my husband Sid and children Brent and Tiffany; you are my life.

Lieutenant Don McWilliams, Diane Denton, Captain Bobby Adams, Sergeant Douglas Osterberg, Chief Jerrie Stewart, Lee P. Brown, Judge Sam Nuchia, Captain Richard D. Williams, Lieutenant Thomas C. Jennings, Captain Dale Brown, Deborah Goldman, Marsha Johnson, Dr. Sheryl Green, Dr. Sharon Garner-Brown, Pam Holak, Lizzy and Tom Hargrove, Skip Haynes, Mark Vabulas, Priscilla and Angela, Liz Scardino, Christa Hardin, Lin Mills, Adonna, Laura, Mark, Brent and all the detectives with whom I've worked a case that you solved.

Lastly, to the savage criminal who attacked me, know that you didn't destroy me. In fact, you helped transform me into an artistic dynamo whose sketches have taken down over a thousand evil creatures like you and given the means to their victims to gain justice.

Preface

People often ask me if I have nightmares.

They wonder how I can possibly sit through the constant parade of murderers, rapists, robbers, pedophiles and swindlers who march across my drawing board each day without being haunted by their faces in the depths of night.

Of course, I don't just see evil faces. I also see the carnage their evil leaves behind, on the faces of their victims, in their eyes and on their bodies. Those of us who work in law enforcement often become what I call "secondary victims" of the violence we see each and every day of our lives.

And I see more than most.

As the only forensic artist for more than twenty-one years in one of the largest police forces in America—the Houston, Texas Police Department—I get the worst of cases—mutilations, murder, rape—an endless stream of misery that flows like tears through the various divisions of the department and pools at the door of my office.

Whereas a homicide detective may juggle three murder cases in a given week, I sometimes see that many in a *day*. I schedule them in with rapes, muggings, robberies and emergency cases that yank me out of bed in the middle of the night.

But when people ask me if I have nightmares, I say no. Not usually, anyway. The dead-eyed mug-shot stares of the killers and criminals whose faces I draw don't stalk my dreams, because I know that, as the Apostle Paul put it, "faith is the evidence of things unseen."

I've worked with the victims of those criminals and together we've taken something *unseen*—their tortured memories—and created *evidence*: a likeness of their attacker. I have faith, then, that law enforcement officers can take that likeness and use it to track down the bad guys. When they do, then I have empowered those victims and helped them to become something they never thought they would be: *survivors*.

Through my gifts and my labors, these survivors find, to their surprise, that they have been able to think what had been—up until then—the unthinkable and to take control of what had been uncontrollable. And when news comes that we've caught the bad guy, believe me, I sleep like the proverbial baby.

I haven't just done my job; I've fulfilled my calling.

However, there is one aspect of my work that does haunt me sometimes, especially when the job involves a child.

Sometimes, I am called upon to help identify a murder victim.

And there's only one way I can help with that task.

Many times, over the years, I've been asked to go down to the medical examiner's office—which is just a euphemism for a morgue—and do a portrait of an unidentified murder victim. Over time, I've grown strong when asked to do this, because the way I see it, this is my way to help someone who can no longer speak or even cry out.

In many cases, I've learned that if the unidentified victim is an adult or a juvenile, then they were probably murdered by an enemy.

If that victim is a nameless child and none of the available databases turns up anyone missing who fits that general description, then most likely this child was killed by someone he or she loved, someone the child trusted to take care of him or her, someone who betrayed that trust. And when you see what has been done to the bodies during their brief, tormented little lives, then you know that death has often come as a relief.

They bring me photographs.

Big, strong detectives looking sad and depressed bring me color crime-scene photographs of tiny children they have found brutalized unto death and thrown out like so much trash on the side of the road, in a ditch or mud puddle or crammed in a dumpster. Sometimes the bodies have been exposed to the elements and it has become almost impossible to make out a face.

They bring me photographs. They ask if I can use the pictures as references, and transform them into a portrait of a child, smiling.

"If the victim's smiling," they say, "then maybe somebody, somewhere will recognize your portrait and help us figure out who this child is and who did this terrible thing to them."

And so they bring me their grotesque crime-scene photographs and when it's a child, well, I've never yet seen a detective who could hand them over without tears welling up.

You ask me if my job gives me nightmares.

The British poet, Dylan Thomas, wrote a poem after the horrors of the blitzkrieg bombing of London during World War II called "A Refusal to Mourn the Death, by Fire, of a Child in London." In it, he eloquently told how overwrought outpourings of sentiment at such tragedies sometimes worked the opposite of what was intended, only cheapening the stark power of the event, which should stand alone.

Wordless, for there are no words.

He said, "After the first death, there is no other."

I know what he means. Every time I hold in my hands a sacred photograph of the remains of another mangled little life and the sweet young voice cries out to me from dumpster or ditch or whatever else passes for a grave, then I know it is not the time for tears and mourning. Not yet.

"Never until..." writes Dylan Thomas, "...the still hour is come...Shall I pray the shadow of a sound..."

Never until the ghastly photograph in my hand has been transformed into a portrait of a smiling child on my drawing board and from there into someone's heart, motivating them to go straight to their photo album, and from there to the police department... never until what's left of a body becomes a once-breathing child who loved and was loved... never until then do I let myself mourn.

Never until then do I let myself weep.

Part One:

My Life

Chapter One:

Angel Doe

Ibraced myself early one morning when a rookie homicide detective, Darcus Shorten, came to my office and asked if I could do a reconstruction of a little girl who had been found half-submerged in a watery ditch, her body wrapped in a blue fleece blanket decorated with happy little polar bears and reindeer.

Darcus, a young, vibrant African-American woman, had been teamed up on this case with Clarence Douglas, a seasoned veteran homicide investigator. Sergeant Douglas was the best partner a young detective could have. Kind and caring, with an intelligent, calm manner, he hadn't let the cynicism of the job creep in over the years the way some police officers do. I knew he would never quit until this child could find her name and be laid to peaceful rest.

Still, I ached for Darcus, whose initiation into working on crime cases would be so gruesome. Some investigators go their entire careers without ever having to gaze upon the horrors she and Sgt. Douglas came upon in the ditch that day. It was a trial by fire, but I knew she was strong. She could and would handle it.

"Some kids found her," Darcus told me. "And the patrol officers who responded to the scene figured she was about four years old, because she was so small. She only weighs forty-seven pounds and is less than four feet tall."

"But?" I prompted, though I knew what Darcus was going to say.

"Clarence thinks she may be older than that, but that she was starved."

"To death?" I asked.

"No." She shook her head and I could see the weariness this job can give reflected in her young eyes. "Medical Examiner says she was hit in the head with something that probably caused her death," she continued and after a short pause, added, "but you can tell from the bruises and cigarette burns and other old injuries all over her body that she suffered for a long time before she died." Darcus struggled hard to blink back the tears.

"I'm sorry you have to face such a tough case so early in your career," I said soberly. She nodded and left without saying another word.

I didn't tear right into the envelope containing the hellish photographs. For a while, I busied myself with other tasks. They needed to be done, but mostly, I was working up my courage.

Ask any cop or emergency worker and they will all tell you that when it comes to child victims, it's tough. Most of us have children of our own and it's impossible to gaze at a murdered child without thinking of your own precious ones at home.

But we steel ourselves to do what has to be done.

After a few moments to collect myself, I reached for the envelope, pulled out the photos and looked at them.

I gasped. I'd never seen anything more horrible.

The child had lain, partially submerged in fetid water, her little face upturned to the elements, in the Houston heat and humidity, for more than two days. Animals and the ravages of exposure had peeled away the skin from her face. Her eyeballs were missing, as well as eyebrows. Most of her nose had been eaten off. Her lips were pulled back in a grotesque death-grin. Several of her front teeth were missing and her tongue protruded, swollen, from what remained of her lips.

From the black, curly hair on her head, the parts of her neck and head that had not been submerged in the water and what remained of the skin on her body, I could see that she was African American. From additional photographs taken at the autopsy, I could also see the starvation, the bruising, the burns… the torture.

It was so overwhelming that for a long moment, I feared that I would not be able to go on.

But I had to. She needed me. She was *depending* on me.

Numbly, I pinned the ghastly photos onto the right-hand side of my drawing board, which rests on my aluminum Stanrite 500 easel.

The human brain, I have learned, has a powerful ability to block out things it's not prepared to handle. In some cases, this can be a blessed coping ability, but I knew I didn't have that luxury. I have to be able not just to *see* the grisly scene set before me, but to *look past* it, so that I can create something beautiful out of something horrific.

I have to do it. They're counting on me, those lost little souls.

And so are the detectives.

Through the years, I've developed certain techniques to enable me to handle the stresses and strains of my job. If I have to do a post-mortem drawing of an unidentified victim, especially one found exposed to the elements and particularly a child victim, then I turn on a television set and place the screen to my left as I face the paper with the gruesome photographs arranged to the right of it.

I try to find a compelling news program of some kind—not a tacky soap opera-esque talk show or one of those screaming cockfights between extreme points of view—but a reasoned, thought-provoking and informative debate on some issue or other that can hold my attention for at least a few minutes.

This serves as a distraction, a protection from the jarring emotional jolts that come with staring for a long time at faces brutalized beyond recognition.

I keep a small television set in my office. Normally in the mornings, even at home, I don't watch television. I prefer to eat my simple breakfast of fruit and juice in peaceful silence while I gear myself up for the day's stresses. (Just driving in Houston is stressful enough.) On that particular morning, I hadn't even listened to the radio in the car. I'd plugged in a Diana Krall CD and listened to her sweet, mellow tones instead.

Now that I had pinned the photographs to my drawing board, I reached for the TV set as if I were treading water in heavy seas and it was a lifeline tossed to me from a boat. Positioning it to the left of my drawing board, I glanced at my desk calendar and watch to remind myself the day of the week and thereby remember what program might be on television at this time.

The date was *Tuesday, September 11, 2001.*

Everyone remembers where they were on 9-11 when they first heard the news, when they first saw the awful, terrible images over and over, the planes crashing into the Twin Towers in screaming fireballs, people running, bodies falling from the sky.

I was transfixed in horror, not believing what I was seeing. I wished I could look at the images without seeing them or otherwise somehow will them to go away, to stop, to turn back the clock, to make it not happen.

People were dying in front of my very eyes and there was nothing, nothing, nothing I could do about it. Like many other Americans and people the world over, I prayed. At least, as best I could, not even knowing *how* to pray about the things I was seeing or what to say, how to form words out of the unspeakable.

I stared at the massive horror unfolding on the TV screen until I couldn't bear it any more. Then I forced myself to turn and face the smaller horror staring back at me from my drawing board.

This time, I wept.

As time passed, I sobbed awhile, prayed awhile, watched TV awhile, tried to concentrate on how I would do the sketch, watched some more TV, cried some more...

Then from a place so deep within me that it had no name, a still, small voice seemed to say, *You can't help them. You can pray for them, but you can't help them. But you CAN help her. You can bring her back home. You can give her a name. You can help her restless little soul find peace.*

It was a strange sort of comfort—for lack of a better word—that I just can't explain. The unbearable images coming at me from the television screen somehow enabled me to bear the ghastly image pinned to my drawing board.

On that terrible day in September, I realized that I had to take the negative energy that was unleashed in me as I watched the violent attack on our citizens and use it as a force of good. I could take all the power and majesty of my own grief, fear, rage and horror and USE it. I could funnel it into the task before me.

And so I did.

Cried awhile, prayed awhile, tried to draw awhile.

While black plumes of smoke from the north and south towers of the World Trade Center billowed skyward and news anchors scrambled to their desks, I tore myself away from the sight and studied the photos of the little girl whose tiny life had been so violently snuffed out.

What I had to do was basically a skull reconstruction, because most of the flesh on her face had already rotted off due to water damage.

Steeling myself, I began.

I started, as always, from the top. This keeps me from smearing the pastel chalks with my hand as I lean on the paper. Usually, I do my sketches in warm black and white, but I knew that for purposes of identification, it would be better to use full color on my rendering of the little girl. With a black-and-white sketch, I can usually complete the job in an hour or so, but since this was a full-color reconstruction, with little to go on, it would most likely take me half a day.

That is, under *normal* circumstances. But 9-11 was anything but "normal."

The top of the child's head was relatively intact and I could see from the photographs that she had short, black hair, so I drew that. I knew I could go back later if I wanted and give it more of a style. The forehead was visible, so I was able to match the color of her skin as I worked my way down to her eyebrows.

Before I got very far, the phone rang. It was Dr. Baker, the medical examiner who had done the autopsy on the child.

In a kind, gentle voice, he said, "I know you don't have much to work with there with those photos."

"That's true," I agreed.

"Would you like me to get you something, er, better?" he asked. In a sad but determined voice he went on, "I could give you a prepared specimen."

A *prepared specimen* is a nice way of saying that, in order to make my job easier, the good doctor was prepared to remove the child's head and put it through a process known as *maceration*. This involves immersing the skull into a solution of 60% hydrogen peroxide. (What is used for household purposes is a 3% solution of hydrogen peroxide.)

This high content solution dissolves the soft tissue away, leaving the skull clean and intact. For an artist, this is an ideal way to depict the contours of that particular person's face.

"It's so kind of you to offer," I said. "And you're right; it would make my job easier. But I think I'd rather do this as quickly as possible, for one thing and for another, well, she's such a tiny little girl. I'd really rather not this time."

It was a form of respect for the body that he understood. I thanked him though, because I knew his offer was made with the sincerest form of kindness. He was trying to spare me having to go through what I was going through now: staring at what used to be a face, trying to draw it as it was in life.

I turned back to my task and glanced up at the television just in time to hear the horrifying news that a plane had crashed into the Pentagon. For a while, I watched the TV compulsively, hoping for some fragment of news that would somehow make sense of everything. The president released a statement that we were under attack by terrorists.

What could I do? I cried, I watched a while longer...and then, glancing back and forth from the horror on television to the horror on my drawing board, blotting my eyes with a tissue, I picked up my chalk and went back to work.

Eyebrows lie on top of the bones of the skull in a specific way and since I could see her superciliary arch (the brow ridge), I was able to place the little girl's eyebrows just right. They would be fine, pre-pubescent hair and probably not very noticeable. Not much drawing, just some wispy child eyebrows.

The eyebrow follows the shape of the brow ridge. If people have a high, distinct arch to their eyebrows, it means that the bone is rather thick and takes a sharp curve as it travels downward. As I looked closely I saw this child had a small bone with a shallow curve.

Just as I was about to start drawing the eyes, Two World Trade Center, the North Tower, suddenly collapsed. It was... horrible? Terrifying? Mesmerizing? I searched in vain for words to describe what I was viewing.

There just weren't words to explain what I saw as I stared, transfixed, helpless, and watched people die. The grief, which I realized all who watched felt, was speechless, unspeakable. Heedless of the chalk I was holding, I clapped my hand over my mouth, cried, "No, no, no," and sobbed.

For a long time, I could not work. My eyes were too blurred with tears; I couldn't even see what I was doing.

I was still sitting, the chalk in my limp hand, when the South Tower collapsed.

Bawling, blowing my nose, praying, trying to compose myself, a few minutes later I heard the report about yet another plane that had crashed in rural Pennsylvania, southeast of Pittsburgh.

"The world has gone mad," I whispered.

For a long time, I was hypnotized by the images on television, but eventually, when reporters began repeating themselves and it was clear that nobody really knew anything new, I took a deep shuddering breath and turned my attention back to the little lost child whose image I was trying to capture.

The eyes of a person have specific places that attach to the inner corners of the eye socket. Since the flesh had decomposed and disappeared and the eyeballs were gone, I could clearly see the "landmarks" that told me how wide-spaced her eyes would be. The fold above the lid would be smooth and dark, since there would be almost no fat in the pad behind and the eyelids would be visible. (Lack of body fat lets that nictitating membrane curve over the eyeball.) So I drew tiny eyelids.

Meanwhile, it seemed as if our whole country was under attack and nobody knew where these evil monsters would strike next. I even glanced out my office window, picking out taller buildings, trying to assess if my own was at risk.

Then I scoffed at my own nervousness and went back to work, back to crying, back to praying, back to watching the TV, spellbound, like everyone else.

In police work, there is a peculiar phenomenon that occurs whenever there is a child murder, especially one so gruesome and emotionally wrenching as this one. When the detectives who "catch" the case "make the scene," meaning, they go to the crime scene before the body is removed and begin their investigation, other police personnel slowly begin to show up at the scene.

They may be office workers, supervisors and so on. What they are doing is offering mute moral support, quiet, steadfast presence. In many ways, it's like a silent memorial to honor this most innocent of victims.

But I wasn't at a crime scene. I was alone in my office, coping with the horrors both without and within.

The phone rang again. This time I recognized the voice of homicide Lieutenant Steve Arrington and I knew instinctively that he wasn't trying to intrude or check up on me or bother me.

He was hurting as badly as I was at what we were seeing happen to our country and to the tiny girl.

"Are you all right?" he asked. "Can you still work despite the horror of what's going on in our country?"

I assured him that despite my own shock I was working.

"Lois, can you make her smile, like when she was alive?" he asked, a bit embarrassed at making such a request at this moment.

He knew and I knew that I could. The phone call wasn't really about that and we both knew it, but I was so grateful for his support. "Sure I can," I said softly.

"Make her pretty," he said quietly, "like I know she was in life."

"I will," I said.

"I know you will," he said. "I know you can. Help us find her, help us nail whoever did this to her and pray for our country."

I promised that I would and we hung up. I felt as if I had been hugged. It gave me strength.

Once again, I went back to work.

In order to tell how to draw the "iris to eye opening" ratio right, I glanced at photographs I had in my office of my two children, Brent and Tiffany. They were teenagers now, but I had some pictures from when they were small children that I used as references. The iris, I found, would occupy more of the eye opening than it would in an adult, but less than in an infant. I worked out a good balance and gave the little girl nice eyelashes.

Her ravaged little face was beginning to come to life. It gave me hope. While the somber television news anchors tried to sort out what was going on in our country, I listened and kept working.

The nose, I decided, would be smooth. The bridge that I could see from the crime scene photographs was smooth and lay low to the facial plane. The outer edges of the bottom part of the nose would start about one-half to two millimeters outside of the nasal hole, which was visible through the last film of flesh that hadn't dissolved in the water. I gave her average-sized nostril holes.

The cheeks were easy. I covered those bones with the appropriate muscles and the smooth, brown, little girl skin.

It was time to draw her smile. Her alveolar ridge—the bony arch from which the teeth protrude—was wide as I faced her, so I drew it that way. The bottom teeth were arched so wide that I felt certain she would show them along with the top teeth when she smiled, so I drew the bottom teeth just above the full bottom lip as they would appear during a happy grin.

Of course, one thing an artist has to do at this point is depict the tongue peeking through as the light hits it, along with a glistening shine, because a live person's mouth is always wet.

The little girl was missing one tooth and the other was tilted. I needed to know a strong estimation of this child's true age. Height and weight would not tell the true story.

So I put in a call to the forensic dentist, Dr. DeLattre, who had examined the body.

Dr. DeLattre said, "Her front teeth were all adult teeth but the back teeth were deciduous or baby teeth."

That told me two things. One, this child was six or seven years old, not four, as Darcus had said the officers who found the dead child thought, due to her tiny, shrunken size. And two, she had not lost that front tooth naturally. It had been punched out and during the same incident, the tooth next to it had been jammed up back into the socket in a crooked way.

This was a sickening development that caught me by surprise. I'd assumed...well, it just hadn't occurred to me that this precious child had been punched in the mouth.

I asked, "How long before she died do you think that tooth was knocked out?" Dentists can tell by how much the bone has grown shut after tooth loss.

Her voice sad, she said, "About six weeks to two months."

Poor, sweet baby.

I decided to use the lost tooth as a sort of "gap-toothed grin" when I sketched her smile. I made her as pretty as Arrington had asked and I thought she once had been as I reflected on how much she'd been through.

After completing her smile and drawing the chin, I sat for a moment and stared at the blue plaid shirt she was wearing. It was only visible at a distance from the shot where she lay on the red plastic body bag on which she'd been placed by personnel from the medical examiner's office. I tried to reproduce it as closely as possible, because it was another clue to her identity.

Finally, I put some shadows on her neck under her chin and fluffed up her hair a bit, as if it had just been washed.

My sunny, windowed office is located on the seventh floor of the Travis building. Ironically, this houses the Robbery division of the Houston Police Department. Robbery detectives seldom see the kinds of violence I have to deal with all the time. Their work is usually not as emotionally wrenching as it can be for homicide detectives or those who work in Juvenile Sex Crimes. Sometimes the detectives are surprised at the dreadful things I often have to deal with and even on this frightening day in which there were so many horrible sights, as I worked, some of the detectives drifted by and commiserated on the shock and horror affecting our country and the shock and horror of the photographs pinned to my board.

One of the detectives said something I'll never forget. "They've checked all the area schools, looking for a child who has been missing from class and is unaccounted for or who would otherwise fit her description," he said. (In Houston, school starts in August, so a child absent for several days this far into the semester would be noticed.) "She's not been reported missing by a single school."

I looked up at him, as he leaned against the doorjamb of my office.

"You know what that means," he added.

Yes, I did know.

"It means that she has been deliberately kept out of school by somebody," he said. "She's been locked up someplace, hidden away."

Over the drawing board, our glances met.

"She's a closet child," he said.

They called her *Angel Doe*.

Police investigators searched databases for similar cases nationwide. In Kansas a little black girl near the same age had been found beheaded and discarded about four months before Angel Doe turned up in Houston.

Though investigators didn't find any connection, I found one difference truly heartbreaking. Kansas City police had been inundated with more than 800 leads when they first started investigating their own case. There had been a tremendous public outcry and a candlelight vigil.

But when poor Angel Doe was discovered in Houston, the entire country was reeling from the horrendous national tragedy of September 11. News outlets were dominated by that story and consequently, an unidentified little black girl found in a ditch full of water and old tires in southeast Houston drew little attention.

Not for lack of trying—Sgt. Douglas and Officer Shorten did everything in their power to keep the story alive and copies of my sketch displayed (what Officer Shorten called "foot-work," just walking through the neighborhood, posting copies of my sketch with pertinent information), but in those early weeks, they had little response.

An Internet search turned up several possible leads; another one in Kansas, one in North Carolina and one in Houston, but none panned out.

Houston's Child Protective Services caseworkers combed their files and the National Center for Missing and Exploited Children entered Angel Doe into their database... all to no avail.

Jerry Nance, a caseworker for the National Center for Missing and Exploited Children, was quoted in the *Houston Chronicle*, "Facial identification is the only thing that will solve this case," adding, "A child that young doesn't have fingerprints, a driver's license or DNA on file."

The detectives felt terrible about all this and I felt as badly as they did. By this time, we all had an emotional investment in this case. The way Sgt. Douglas put it was, "This case is deeply imbedded." He meant, in our souls.

"Not knowing who she is has really been trying to me personally," Officer Shorten said. It bothered her deeply that the police could not put a name to this child. She even pinned a copy of my composite drawing on the bulletin board behind her desk.

Sergeant Douglas wanted, more than anything, to identify Angel Doe and give her a decent burial before Christmas, but as time passed with no new leads on the case, it was looking unlikely.

In Kansas, concerned citizens paid for a funeral and buried their little nameless child. They had been searching for her identity for seven months and they wanted at least to give the tiny child a proper burial.

Slowly, the country began to recover from the initial shock and horror generated by the events of 9-11. Rescue efforts evolved into body recovery. Our national grief was nowhere near healed yet. But as New York firefighters, police and steel workers—and, down in Washington, D.C., soldiers and firefighters—combed through smoking wreckage for the remains of the lost, the rest of us slowly returned to the vestiges of our normal lives, even as we knew that things would never be quite the same again.

A somber Christmas came and went.

Houston never has much of a winter and the days began warming up. In early March, local and regional events once again began to creep into city newspaper and evening news headlines. In that period, Sgt. Douglas and Officer Shorten renewed their efforts to publicize Angel Doe's case.

A police spokesperson released a statement to newspapers: "The worst part is that no one has come up to say this child is missing. No parents or friends or relatives," he said. "It's as if she never existed."

That week, police, assisted by Crimestoppers Child Watch of North America volunteers and other civic leaders, printed up numerous flyers with my sketch on it and posted them throughout the neighborhood where Angel Doe's body had been found. They released a photograph of the blue blanket that had been used to wrap her body. They held news conferences and redistributed my sketch to news outlets, patiently answering repeat questions, doing all they could to get the word out.

I felt as frustrated as they did.

"How will this case get solved?" I asked Clarence.

"A grandmother will have to call it in," he said. "It will have to be a grandmother who solves this case."

He was right.

It was the child's grandmother, Alice Curtis, who finally recognized my sketch. Alice says that she does not watch television other than religious programming and (we can only assume) does not read the newspaper. This is how she explains the fact that, although my composite sketch of her granddaughter LaShondra was televised and printed in the paper, off and on, for six months, she did not see the sketch.

When detectives held the press conference in early March of 2002 and, once again, displayed my composite drawing of "Angel Doe," Alice says that day she was "flipping channels" when she came across the news conference. She says she "knew right away" that it was her granddaughter.

She called the police. "That's my child," she told Sgt. Douglas. He says she insisted on meeting with him that very night; he could not convince her to wait until morning. After several extensive interviews with Alice and two of her other grown daughters, Sgt. Douglas believed they had finally identified Angel Doe.

Although prosecutors would refer to her as "nobody's child," this was not really the case with LaShondra.

To my way of thinking, a "nobody's child" is one who is never loved and is shunted around from foster home to foster home until he or she either winds up in juvenile lock-up, becomes a streetwise runaway or turns up dead at the hands of a drug dealer or pimp or suffers some other tragic fate. It's deeply depressing to me when I think how many, many children fit that description in this, the richest country in the world.

Although LaShondra's brief little life started out tough, she was not unwanted. She was born to a crack-addicted mother who already had four other children. Though the infant was treated for drug addiction at birth and put into foster care as a newborn, her grandmother, Alice Curtis, wanted to raise the child. Once Child Protective Services decided that LaShondra would have a good home with her grandmother, Alice took custody of the baby. LaShondra's birth mother, Connie Knight, did not object.

LaShondra was a jolly, bright baby who was the light of Alice and her husband Roger's lives.

"She was the kind of child, you could not help but love her," Alice told a newspaper reporter later. But when LaShondra was just a year old, Alice had a sudden stroke that rendered her incapable of taking care of an infant.

Still, LaShondra had family who cared. Living in another state was one of Alice's sons and his wife. They did not have any children of their own and gladly took the baby into their home.

When Clarence and I spoke of these things later, he always had to blink back tears. "She never wanted for *anything* there," he kept saying. Her new parents adored her and LaShondra began calling them Mommy and Daddy. The child, who was known to be bubbly and sweet, thrived.

But back in Texas, three years after LaShondra's birth, Connie claimed to be drug-free and she began to pressure her mother to let her have her daughter back. She started calling her brother and sister-in-law frequently, demanding that they allow her to take LaShondra. She even called local police where the couple lived, claiming that they had stolen her baby. Finally, when it was time for LaShondra to start school, her grandmother offered to take her back and the couple reluctantly agreed.

But it wasn't Alice who came to pick up the child. It was Connie.

Since Alice Curtis had custody of LaShondra and since she did not object, there was nothing the heartbroken couple could do, legally, to keep the little girl. Alice Curtis never notified Child Protective Services of her decision to allow Connie to take LaShondra back. If she had, CPS case-workers would have visited the home, made reports as to the condition of the child and evaluated her new home. But they never knew.

Time and time again, I have seen cases where unworthy, uncaring parents demand the return of their children and I don't believe it has anything to do with love. Some people regard their children as possessions and often don't rest until that "thing" has been returned to them. Whatever Connie Knight's motives for yanking LaShondra away from the home she loved and dragging her back to Texas, one thing is certain: from that moment on, LaShondra's life became a living, bloody hell.

Soon, she disappeared from sight.

Alice Curtis claims she phoned her daughter frequently, asking to speak to LaShondra, and visited the house. Apparently, she was easily manipulated by the former drug addict, who convinced her elderly mother, time and again, that LaShondra was out of the house, staying off and on with a distant relative of her stepfather's.

When Alice became naggingly persistent, Connie allowed her to speak with LaShondra—briefly—on the phone. "I never got any signals anything was abnormal," Alice said later.

What the old woman didn't realize at the time was that she wasn't speaking to LaShondra at all. Connie had put up one of her other daughters to pretend to be LaShondra whenever her grandmother called.

"I never got alarmed, because I saw the other children and they were fine," Alice said.

Yes...the other children. What *about* the other children?

In the June 30, 2002 *Houston Chronicle*, Dr. Curtis Mooney, president of DePelchin Children's Center, which provides counseling for children and families in the Houston area, including those suffering abuse, stated that it is not unusual for a parent or parents to pick one child out of a family to use as the family's "scapegoat," which means that child will suffer more serious consequences for misbehaving—even being locked up.

"That child becomes the one everything is blamed on...Such a victim can be targeted because he or she is seen as a 'problem child,' or perhaps has a more aggressive personality than the other children," said Mooney.

Whenever Alice called Connie and asked why LaShondra wasn't there, Connie would always tell her mother that the little girl was uncontrollable and that other relatives had better luck with her, saying, "She has mental problems."

It's hard not to judge Alice Curtis. Most of us who have children feel, when months and months have gone by without a sign of a grandchild who was supposed to be living only a couple of blocks away, that we would be hugely concerned, we would do something—especially if we knew that this same child's mother had had drug addiction problems in the past.

But Alice, whose health was not good, was caring for her own dying mother during those days. Distracted, unwell and manipulated by her daughter, she let herself believe that LaShondra was being taken care of somewhere by someone who loved her.

As I said, the human brain is capable of blocking out things it's not prepared to handle.

Even so, a mother's instincts can be a powerful thing. Alice claims that, around the first week of September, 2001, she became almost frantic to find LaShondra. When she insisted on seeing the little girl, Connie told her that she'd put LaShondra into a psychiatric facility. Alice demanded to visit LaShondra and Connie agreed.

But on the day they were supposed to visit the facility, Alice pounded on Connie's door and found the house completely empty.

The family—Connie Knight, her common-law husband, Raymond Jefferson, Jr. and her children—had fled in the night. No one in the family had heard from them. No one knew where they were. At that point, Alice's own mother passed away and she didn't have time to worry about a daughter who tended to pick up and leave whenever things got too hot for her.

Using Jefferson's employment records, Sgt. Douglas traced the family to Louisiana, where they had been living since LaShondra's death.

All three of the surviving children, ages four, thirteen and sixteen, who lived in the home with Connie and Raymond, denied ever even having seen LaShondra. When Sgt. Douglas showed a photograph of LaShondra in happier days to the thirteen-year-old, she started to shake—violently—from head to foot, but maintained that she had not seen LaShondra. The children each swore, adamantly, that they *did not even have a sister.*

Raymond swore he didn't even know the girl and for several hours, Connie maintained LaShondra was still in Georgia with relatives.

So Sgt. Douglas showed them Jefferson's employment records, in which he'd claimed LaShondra as a dependent, and witness statements from Houston neighbors that there had been "another child" who was not allowed outdoors. He showed them photographs of the blue fleece blanket and he showed them photographs of the closet from their house in Houston, the one with human feces smeared on the walls and floor.

Finally, Connie cracked. At first, she confessed that she had been responsible for LaShondra's death and she was arrested. The children became hysterical and refused to speak, not to police, not to social workers, not to counselors, not to anyone. In his calm, reassuring way, Sgt. Douglas left word that, when they were ready to talk, he was ready to listen.

After several weeks, Sgt. Douglas's patience was rewarded. He was contacted by family members who told him that the girls were finally ready to talk. They admitted that, although both parents had been horribly abusive to their sister, it had been Raymond who had killed her.

Confronted with her children's truth-telling, Connie changed her story. Although he continued to deny even knowing LaShondra, ultimately, Raymond Jefferson, Jr. was charged with injury to a child, failure to stop her mother from abusing her and denying her proper medical attention. Connie was also charged with injury to a child. They were both jailed in Harris County.

Family members, filled with shame, rage, guilt and grief, buried the tiny girl, giving her, at long last, the funeral that Clarence Douglas and Darcus Shorten had so longed for. The detectives attended the service. On the funeral program, above a smiling and happy picture of a younger LaShondra, were printed the words from the Twenty-third Psalm: "Yea, though I walk through the valley of the shadow of death, I will fear no evil..."

Weeping relatives said a few words about how LaShondra had to die because "God needed another flower in His garden."

But little "Angel Doe" did not have to die; nobody should ever have to die the way she did.

The rest of the story, when Clarence and Darcus finally pieced it all together, was grim.

Because she'd been ripped from the only home she'd ever really known, where she was loved, and thrown into a house full of strangers thousands of miles away, LaShondra did not behave like the adoring daughter her mother and Raymond thought she should be.

So they threw the little girl in a closet.

And left her there.

She was not permitted to leave the closet to go to the bathroom, but when she soiled herself or used the closet floor, she was terribly, horribly punished. And she was starved by her morbidly obese mother.

The other children were told that LaShondra was "crazy" and to leave her alone, but at night or when her parents were out of the house, the thirteen-year-old daughter would sneak LaShondra out of the closet and feed her or creep past and throw parts of her own meals into the closet—LaShondra's only food.

Sometimes the girl slipped her brother's training potty into the closet to help out her sister. On cold nights, she let LaShondra slide in under the covers and sleep with her, but they had to hurry her into the closet very early the next morning, because if Connie found them out, she would beat LaShondra.

LaShondra was never enrolled in school. She was not allowed outdoors. She was repeatedly hit, kicked and burned with cigarettes by both her parents.

When LaShondra's sister asked her mother why LaShondra had to stay in the closet, Connie only said, "Because she doesn't know how to act," or, "because that's where I want her to stay."

All the children were forced to keep the secret from their grandmother.

On the night of September 7, 2001, little LaShondra said or did something that Raymond didn't like and he kicked her so hard that she fell back onto the heater, cracking her skull, and began "to shake all over," said the sisters in trial testimony. Raymond went to the store and brought back some ice, but nothing helped. Finally, he and Connie told the children that they were taking LaShondra to the hospital.

When their sister did not return, Raymond ordered the children never to speak her name again or "I'll take you to the same place I took her."

During her testimony at the trial, the closest sister suddenly put her face in her hands, threw back her head and keened with grief so wrenching that District Judge Mary Lou Keel stopped the proceedings.

In a dull monotone, Connie testified that Raymond made her drive him and the blanket-wrapped child to a secluded spot. While she waited in the car, he took the little girl into his arms and walked some distance from the car. "Then," Connie testified, "I heard a splash."

Other than that, the only other things she would say on the stand were, "I don't know," or "I don't remember."

In an agonizing jury deadlock, the first trial of Raymond Jefferson was declared a mistrial. Eleven of the jurors wanted to convict him, but one was not entirely convinced that Connie had not killed the child herself, as she originally claimed.

But prosecutors Casey O'Brien and Sylvia Escobedo would not be deterred. Within a few weeks, they mounted a second trial.

After all we'd been through with our little Angel Doe, I couldn't stand not being there myself this time. When a witness canceled a composite sketch appointment and rescheduled it for later, I grabbed my purse and headed for the courthouse.

At the trial's final proceedings, as I sat in the spectator gallery, I could see Raymond Jefferson in profile and I studied him. He was a big man, six feet tall and weighing more than 200 pounds. He had fists like cement blocks. I kept thinking about what those brutal fists had done to that child's face and it was all I could do not to throw up.

But his face? His face was bland.

The thing is, when you see a monster like him in court, you expect him to look, well, like a monster.

But they never do.

The prosecutors were rewarded for their determination and I was quietly pleased when this trial resulted in a conviction for Raymond Jefferson, Jr. It took that jury less than three hours to pronounce justice for little LaShondra.

On August 22, 2003, LaShondra's stepfather was given the maximum sentence—life in prison. (As of this writing, his attorneys have filed an appeal with the Fourteenth Court of Appeals.) He will be eligible for parole in 2018, when he is sixty-five years old. Connie Gazette Knight pled guilty and was sentenced to fifty years in prison.

Later, I asked Clarence whether Connie herself might have been a victim of Raymond's abuse, which could have contributed to her own abuse of her daughter.

Solemnly, he shook his head. "Connie Knight would never put up with any abuse from anybody," he said firmly. "She's plenty big enough to take care of herself," and added, "No...The truth is, she's just plain *mean*."

A few months before Officer Shorten brought me the death photos of little LaShondra, I read a *Newsweek* cover story in the May 21, 2001 issue on the nature of evil. In it, psychologist Michael Flynn of York College in New York was quoted, "I spent eighteen years working with people who everyone would call evil—child molesters, murderers—and with a few exceptions, I was always struck by their ordinariness."

I know what he means. If you want to know what the face of evil looks like, well, it looks like your neighbor, or your boss, or your lover.

I know, because I've drawn more than three thousand evil faces and most of them did not "look" evil. When I see them in court, these murderers and rapists, they always have what I call a "shark-eyed look."

Just blank. Like they're there and yet not there.

At least, that's when they're in court or standing in front of a mug-shot camera. But when they're in the process of raping and murdering, that bland expression can change dramatically.

I know, because I've seen it for myself. I've looked right into the eyes of a man who was trying to kill me and I know what the face of evil *really* looks like—right *then*—not later, all cleaned up for court.

I know what it means to feel like a helpless victim, to feel caged in the terror and powerlessness of one day, one moment that can change you forever, an endless, heart-stopping moment when you are fighting for your life, sense it draining out of you as you choke for breath... when the world goes dark and you're all alone... facing evil.

Chapter Two:

"We'll Have to Date Again"

Never in my life had I looked into the face of evil until the day I found myself being killed.

There are some crime victims in this world to whom violence comes as no surprise. They've grown up with it, both at home and in their neighborhoods, in so many ways that they don't know anything different. I once heard an account of a woman who was kidnapped by a brutal serial murderer who had killed all his other victims, but when he put the gun to her head, she simply nodded in weary recognition and said, "Go ahead. Pull the trigger. You'd be doing me a favor." He was so surprised that he actually spared her life and let her go free.

I wasn't like that.

The picturesque, homey setting of the old television series, *The Waltons*, starring Richard Thomas, would, if you've ever seen it, give you a pretty good idea of what my childhood was like. It's the kind of lifestyle seen in nostalgic Hallmark Christmas specials and I've got a lot of brothers and sisters who could back me up. I was born on a farm in Missouri on February 25, 1950, to Eva and Don Herbert, the second of five kids. When it came time for Mama to go to the hospital, they took her in a horse and carriage. Mama was college educated. She had been a school teacher before she got married and Daddy had a gift for carpentry, so they moved their growing family to Kansas City, to a house with only one bedroom, where he soon found all the work he could handle. All my growing-up years, Daddy was building on to that house. The sounds of hammering, sawing and Daddy whistling *Tennessee Waltz* was the soundtrack of my childhood.

We lived at the top of a hill on a dead-end street and in wintertime, Daddy climbed onto a big sled he'd fashioned and piled as many kids on his lap as he could fit and down the hills we went, screaming with glee in the sun-sparkled cold.

There was so much love everywhere I looked. Artistically gifted and (like most creative types) a very sensitive child, I was what you might call a "goody two-shoes," always trying to please, doing well in school, making my parents proud. My sister Adonna was two years older than me and, like Mama, a born teacher. From the time I was a toddler, Adonna made it her business to teach me whatever she had learned that day. When I started school, everyone thought I was precocious because I seemed to know my lessons before they were taught. But for years, I suffered from bouts of self-doubt, fearing that the only smart one in the family was my older sister. I didn't know if I was really intelligent or just well-trained, like a good dog.

In high school I twirled baton with the marching band, but I wasn't what you would call "popular." I tended to rely on my sisters to be my girlfriends and, though I dated boys, I wasn't really aware of the fact that others felt I was turning into something of a beauty.

I wanted to go to college, but there was no way my parents could afford it, especially since they still had three young children at home. After struggling to take classes at Wichita State University and Kansas University while working part-time, I decided that there had to be a better way. Even though I'm an artist, I have a very practical nature and I knew that even entry-level jobs in a city like Los Angeles paid a great deal more than those same jobs did in Kansas City. I figured I could find work out there and, if I lived very frugally and saved my money—something all us Herbert kids knew how to do—I could come back to Kansas after a year or so and be able to afford at least a year or two of college without having to work part-time while going to school.

It was a good plan, actually. I got a job fairly quickly working for Prudential Insurance Company on Wilshire Boulevard and found a nice apartment near the UCLA campus. It was a secure building; you had to have a card to get your car into the garage, a key to get into the front door of the building and then a separate key to get into your own apartment. Young professionals and college professors lived there and I felt very safe.

Of course, I knew that if I ever forgot my key to the building, I could just slip in behind someone else who had just entered, but it never occurred to me that so could anyone else who wanted to get in. As I said, I didn't know evil. Not then.

A guy I dated suggested I apply at a modeling agency in town, but I didn't take him very seriously. I'd been to "Career Days" back in high school and modeling representatives there had always said you had to be tall—at least 5'7"—and I was only 5'5". But I took the dare and gave it a shot and before I knew it I was going out on all kinds of jobs during my off hours from the insurance agency.

I worked part-time as a model and made quite a bit of money doing it. If people don't know me very well, they assume I was one of those proverbial starry-eyed milk-fed Midwestern girls who get off the bus, big-headed with dreams of fame and fortune on the silver screen. The truth is, I was paid $100 an hour—which, at that time, was real money—and although the guy who ran the agency thought I'd have a big career because of my looks, I was never swayed by that kind of talk. To stake an entire career on looks that were doomed to fade eventually made no sense to me at all. Even worse, I found modeling to be a mind-numbing occupation and I wanted a career that was more challenging than standing in front of a camera all day long. Still, I got to pose for *Playboy* and that was fun.

The modeling led to a stint as a "go-go girl" on one of the popular L.A. television shows of the day, *The Real Don Steal Show*. Don Steal was a popular disc jockey who based his show on Dick Clark's *American Bandstand*. At the beginning of the show, he introduced one other girl and me as "The Real Don Stealers" and we came running out in our hot pants and knee-high go-go boots looking all jazzed and excited to be there. We climbed up on raised platforms above the crowd of mostly high-schoolers and we danced for an hour and a half.

It was like jogging in high heels for an hour and a half, but it was fun. I loved to dance and, I must admit, I loved the attention. The show was filmed at the old Fox studios on Beverly Boulevard, where I met and dated a few celebrities of the time, including the handsome Max Baer, who played "Jethro" on the popular TV show, *The Beverly Hillbillies*.

With all the fun, there was also an undercurrent of violence. The Vietnam War still raged out of control on the TV evening news and movie heroes like Clint Eastwood in *Dirty Harry* and Al Pacino in *The Godfather* glorified macho, violent manhood. At the Olympic games in Munich, terrorists turned a sporting event into a bloodbath when they murdered eleven Israeli athletes.

I was aware of all those things, of course, but they seemed far away, in places that didn't affect me. I was having the time of my life, a single girl in L.A., making money, dating successful, good-looking guys and being told all the time how beautiful I was. My life was full and busy and I was saving money to go to college. I missed my family terribly, but I was home (at my apartment) so seldom that I didn't even own a television set.

The thing is, when you are raised surrounded by love and security, you assume that the world is a good place, full of good people. I always expected the best out of people and I had a loving nature. When I met someone, I usually liked him or her; when I loved, I loved unconditionally. It was what I had known and it was what I expected.

And then one day, my calm, happy life exploded.

Anyone who has ever experienced a tragedy knows that nothing will ever be quite the same again.

It was about six in the evening and I was in my peaceful apartment, lounging around in jeans and a T-shirt. I'd quit my job at the insurance company and had not found a new one yet, but I had plenty of money in savings and was glad to be able to relax at home for a while.

There was a knock at the door.

"Who's there?" I called.

I heard a man's soft-spoken voice, "Uh, hi. You don't know me—my name is Jim Hutchinson. I live right down the hall and I've seen you come and go and I thought, hey, we're neighbors, why don't we get acquainted?"

As I said, when you're brought up loved and safe, you expect the best in people. I didn't know anyone named Jim Hutchinson, but I had met so many nice people in the building. Right away, I trusted him.

I opened the door to see a thin white man with a goatee.

In a heartbeat, powerful hands closed around my throat, thumbs pressing against my larynx and out of the corner of my eye, I saw the door to my apartment being kicked closed.

In that one moment, my own home became a torture chamber.

The chokehold on my throat was so tight that I literally went blind. As I was shoved backward onto my sofa, I struggled to breathe.

Did you ever have a nightmare where you strive with all your might to scream, but no sound comes out and you wake up heaving and sweating, too scared to close your eyes again from fear the nightmare will return?

This was my nightmare, only there was no waking up.

He ripped at my jeans with such violence that it felt as if my leg was being torn off. The pain was so intense that, in my oxygen-deprived panic, I thought I might really lose my leg, so I twisted my body to enable the pants to come off and, in so doing, managed to free my throat just enough from his death-grip that I was able to gasp for air. I felt like I was in a swimming pool or lake, under water for far too long and, finally breaking to the surface, I gulped for life. At least I tried to, but as soon as he noticed, he squeezed more tightly again.

Air. Sweet, blessed air. How we take it for granted. How we breathe, in and out, in and out, without giving it a thought.

Air was all I could think about as I fought and pushed against his chest, his arms, his face, fighting for my life, but it was all in vain, because the harder I fought, the tighter he squeezed until finally, I blacked out.

But that was all part of the game. He'd been waiting for me to black out, so that he could loosen his grip and watch for me to regain consciousness. When I came to, I took a couple of ragged gasps for air and as I did he began to choke me again.

Again I fought. Again he squeezed the life out of me. Again I blacked out.

This time, when I came around again, I was weaker and for the first time, the clear thought came to me: *He'll never let me get out of here alive.*

When you're facing death, I learned, time doesn't have the same properties. A second no longer feels like a second, because seconds are all you have left. So a second seems to last more like a half-hour—everything slows way, way down, as if you are moving through water or slogging through a swamp. I felt myself detach from myself and stand aside, like an observer, watching myself being strangled.

Then I blacked out a third time.

When I woke up, I actually flashed on that old cartoon image of a drowning man going under water; he puts up one finger, comes up for air, goes under again, then puts up two fingers, comes up a second time, but then, when he goes under and holds up three fingers, you know that he's not going to come up again. I had been strangled unconscious three times and I didn't know how long I'd been under each time, but I knew my brain had been seriously deprived of oxygen. I wondered how much brain damage I could stand before it would be better if I didn't wake up at all.

He choked me unconscious again. This time, when I came to and saw him glaring over me with a strange smile on his face, I thought, *I'm going to die! I'm not ready! I haven't had children yet! I didn't get to go to college! I haven't LIVED!*

And my next thought was of love, of those I loved and I only had time to think about my favorite person—my baby brother, Brent, who was about fourteen, when "Jim Hutchinson" started to kill me for real.

When the life is being choked out of you and you feel you only have seconds to live, all you have left in the world are your thoughts. In many ways, it's like being instantly paralyzed—all you have is your intellect, your mind. You are trapped. All you have is NOW, this moment, and suddenly, everything in life becomes relative to that one fact.

There is something else both shocking and surprising. In an act of violent crime, when your life is literally held in the hands of another, you have, during those brief but seemingly endless seconds, a *relationship* with your attacker. And as death narrows the perimeters of your existence and you begin to detach and look at the situation from the distance of approaching annihilation, it all becomes relative.

Now, I looked straight into his face—really looked. After all, I was going to die anyway, I reasoned and I wanted to look my killer in the eye. His complexion was pasty white. He had a bluish five o'clock shadow around his goatee and dark eyebrows. His expression was amazing to me, because he appeared to be thoroughly enjoying himself.

What I actually saw was a pitiful, awful, *monstrous* man who had taken what should be a supreme act of love and tenderness between two people who care deeply for one another and had twisted and perverted it into an act of hatred and violence and death.

What kind of person needs to watch someone die to have fun? I thought.

I've always been a spiritual person and my faith has always had a powerful impact on my life. I believed that I was probably bound for heaven in the next few moments and I also believed that, when his own time came to die, this man was going straight to hell.

And something about that thought struck me as funny. Not that I could have laughed, if I'd wanted to, because his chokehold on me was tightening again, but I felt my body relax and I guess I laughed in my eyes because whatever he saw drove him into a rage. He grew more vicious. Still holding me by the neck, he began to shake me like a rag doll, my head snapping back and forth.

"Say you love me!" he growled, his voice angry, agitated and demanding.

How stupid, I thought. *How the hell am I supposed to say anything when my throat is completely closed?*

I guess my expression was defiant, because he yanked me back and forth by the throat again, my head flopping like a balloon.

"SAY 'I LOVE YOU!'" he shouted, his voice almost inhuman in its fury.

Death was there, *right there* and it drove me to panic. Somehow, some way, I managed to squeeze out something that sounded like, "dgll LLODSOVE DGOO."

My compliance seemed to calm him a little, but it wasn't enough. A few moments later he started to choke me even more violently and I knew that this time, I would not wake up. In a raw terror, my instincts took over, pure animal fight-for-survival instincts that were telling me to act as if I was enjoying it.

So I moved my hips, trying to get him to climax so he would be *done*, so he would get *off me*, so he would *go away*, so I could live.

It worked. He ejaculated and immediately rolled off me, pulled up his pants and headed for the door. I got up too and tried to get there first so that I could run, but he anticipated that and hurried to block the way, walking backwards toward the door.

Suddenly, he put his hands up in front of him, almost in a pleading gesture and said, incredibly, impossibly, "We'll have to date again."

We'll have to date again. The words resounded in my ears.

But he wasn't finished. Reaching into his pants pocket, he withdrew a little silver and tiger's eye jeweled, oval pillbox and handed it to me.

A gift, a present...from our "date."

Still moving as if in a nightmare, I put my hand to my throat and realized that I was actually bleeding *inside* my throat. I stood there shaking in front of him, still naked from the waist down, bleeding inside, holding the pill box. In the next moment, he was gone.

It took one rapist less than half an hour to rip apart my life.

I remember looking at the clock because I was worried about how many minutes my brain had been deprived of oxygen. He knocked on my door at 6 P.M. and was gone by 6:25.

In that brief time frame, everything that had made me, *me*, had been crushed; I was consumed by fear and traumatized.

My family was a couple of thousand miles away and I was alone.

The first thing I did after he left my apartment was bolt for the bathroom, where I took a glance at my reflection in the mirror and almost fainted again.

The whites of my eyes were no longer white. They were blood red.

Gagging, I staggered backward. I no longer recognized myself. I was so shocked that I did not look into a mirror again for days.

Then I crawled into the shower and scrubbed my whole body with vinegar and then shampoo and then soap and other stuff. Scrubbed until my skin nearly bled.

I thought about calling the police, but I couldn't bring myself to do it. What if they said that, by opening my door, I had willingly let the guy in? Plus, I'd modeled for *Playboy* and I'd danced on television in hot pants and go-go boots—what if they said I had somehow brought this on myself?

If any cop says anything like that to me, I caught myself thinking, *I'll kill the son of a bitch.*

The state of mind I was in, I could easily picture myself lunging across the desk of some smart-ass cop and bodily attacking him.

Gone was the sweetly trusting, loving, naive little Lois from Kansas City. In her place was this raging, filled-with-frustration, devastated and distrustful...*thing*.

I just wasn't me anymore and I wasn't sure what the new me would be capable of.

I slept.

For twelve hours, I slept.

And then I realized I needed food. I was out of almost everything.

But I looked like a monster, bloody-eyed and fierce. And I didn't even own a pair of sunglasses to help me hide.

So I hid in my apartment.

In the kitchen were one egg, one piece of bacon, one limp stalk of celery and half a bag of flour.

I lived on that. I cut the bacon into eight little slices. Once a day, I fried up one of the small pieces with a handful of flour and ate it.

Otherwise, I slept and waited for the blood to drain out of my eyeballs so that I could look human again before venturing forth into polite society. I lived like that for two weeks.

Starvation finally drove me out. I deliberately planned my visit to the grocery store less than a block away. I would go at 2 P.M., which I deemed to be the safest time of day and also the least crowded.

When I finally skulked into the market, I refused to get a cart and start down the aisles until I looked around and could be reasonably certain that there were no men in the store.

Once I had done this I rushed to grab a few modest but necessary purchases. Gratefully I found a female checker.

So far, so good.

I paused at the magazine rack in front of the store, bag of groceries in hand and was browsing the periodicals when a little boy—no more than six or seven—came over and stood beside me.

ATTACK HIM! screamed a voice inside my incredulous brain. *KILL HIM STRIKE HIM SMASH HIM HURT HIM!!*

Blinking in shock at the savagery of my own thoughts, I forced myself to breathe deeply, told myself, *For heaven's sake, he's just a little boy!* while I broke out in a sweat and began to back away.

From some dim distance I heard a man's voice say, "Come on, son. It's time to go," and it was all I could do not to whirl around and scream, *You idiot! He could have been hurt!*

With that, I rushed out of the store, my vision so blurred with tears I could barely find my car.

It was then that I realized just how messed up I really was.

In the blur that passed for the next few weeks, I spiraled downward and downward into a depression so severe I began to question my own sanity.

When I had to go back to work, I chose to work for a temp agency, because it allowed me to be basically anonymous, as the jobs afforded little time to make friends. Somehow I managed to function, more or less, in a way that didn't arouse any suspicions from anyone around me, but inside, I was screaming.

"Justice" isn't a word that we normally think about in our day to day lives, but it preoccupied me to the point of obsession. More than anything in the world, I wanted that awful pervert to be caught and made to pay for what he had done to me, but how could that possibly happen if I wouldn't go to the police?

So then I obsessed about making a police report, but my thoughts kept swirling round and round themselves and always came out the same: *They'll take one look at me, find out I'm a model and a dancer and blame me.*

And I still had all this rage inside me, this wild animal clawing against the cage and howling at the moon. I was truly afraid of what I might do if I did talk to the police and they did doubt my story in any way. I actually worried that I would attack somebody at the police department and they would arrest *me* and put me in jail.

I was terrified and filled with fury and I wanted to die.

In all fairness to the Los Angeles police, I have to say that since I *didn't* make a report, I really have no way of knowing what they would have said or how they would have reacted—these were fears, among the many terrors that roamed around the black desperate corners of my mind—and nobody ever said there was anything logical about fear. So I never did go to the police, but that didn't stop my own unreasonable obsession that the guy who had raped me somehow, some way had to be punished for his crime.

Six weeks or so after the rape I left work early one day so that I could beat the traffic. I got in my car and was traveling down a busy boulevard, not thinking anything in particular, when suddenly, as if driving itself, my car turned into a parking lot. I sat, somewhat befuddled and stared at the shop in front of me. It was a high-priced clothing boutique where I never shopped because it was far too expensive for me, but there I was, for some reason.

I got out of the car and, like a zombie or some extra from the movie *Night of the Living Dead*, walked into the store. There, hanging on a rack in front of me, was a splendid full-length purple velvet skirt that had been marked down to less than twenty dollars.

Maybe I'm supposed to buy this, I thought, but I was still confused. Why had I driven here? What weird thing was happening? I paid for the skirt and got back into my car, determined to drive home this time.

But my car seemed to have a mind of its own and without my consciously doing so, I found myself turning the car up a steep, winding, two-lane street next to the parking lot.

I couldn't turn around, I didn't know where I was, I didn't know where I was going and my eyes welled up with tears because I was beginning to think I'd entered the Twilight Zone.

It was one of those times when I was truly afraid that I might be losing my mind.

After all, I was terribly scared of everything after my traumatic attack. The last thing I ever wanted to do was find myself in unfamiliar territory. All I'd done for two months was go to work, buy groceries and stay cloistered in my apartment. Why was I doing this? I didn't want to be here!

I just wanted to go home. Yet I couldn't.

Finally, the road leveled off and I spotted a graveled area where I would be able to turn my car around and get the hell out of this place. I pulled into the small area and glanced up—

Right into the face of my attacker.

He was just emerging from the second-floor doorway of a shabby, run-down apartment complex and seemed to be heading straight for my car.

A soul-chilling scream gathered at the back of my throat, but before I could open my mouth, two other men appeared in the doorway, one on each side of the man who had tried to kill me.

Police officers.

The man who had forced his way into my apartment, tortured and raped me was being led out of the building in handcuffs!

His thin, pale face was twisted, enraged and desperate. He was fighting and struggling against the cops the same way I had fought with him.

I stared in profound shock as the police dragged him down the stairs and slammed him face-down onto the hood of the police cruiser. My mind was so stupefied at the sight that I don't think I even breathed.

Something about this strange, horrified woman sitting staring from her car at the scene must have caught the attention of one of the officers, because I was startled from my stunned disbelief by a cop banging his hand down on the hood of my car.

I fumbled to roll down the window.

"Do you know this man?" he asked.

Now, I'm a very honest person normally and I felt like every thought I had in my mind at that very moment was plastered all over my face, so I tried to tell myself that, actually, I *didn't* know the man since, obviously, we had never been formally introduced.

"N-no," I stammered.

Of course the cop knew I was lying, because they get lied to all day long and they know a liar when they see one, so he asked me to get out of my car and requested permission to search the vehicle. Naturally I said yes and when he had satisfied himself that I didn't even have a pack of cigarettes, much less contraband, he relaxed a little.

"Why has this man been arrested?" I asked breathlessly, my heart hammering in my chest so hard I thought it would jump out of my mouth. My knees were so weak I had to lean against the car for support.

He said, "Six keys of cocaine."

I didn't know what a "key" of cocaine was. In many ways, I was still an innocent little girl from Kansas City and I struggled to get my mind around a picture that flashed into my head of a piece of cocaine, shaped like a key.

With a little smile, he added, "That's six kilos of coke."

Timidly, I said, "Is that a lot?"

"Yes," he said and to his credit, he didn't laugh at the question. I guess he'd figured out by then that I wasn't one of this guy's drug customers or something.

"He'll get a lot of jail time," he added kindly.

Numbly, I crawled back into my car, turned on the ignition, stepped lightly on the gas pedal and somehow managed to steer to the bottom of the hill, where I pulled into the first parking lot I could find, stopped and burst into jagged, tearing sobs. For a while I wept and then suddenly, I broke out laughing. Then I cried some more. And laughed some more.

It was so incredible. So unbelievable. My bruised and battered heart had cried out for justice, just simple, sweet justice and it had all seemed so impossible. I had never reported the crime and I didn't see how this guy would ever get caught.

Los Angeles is an enormous, sprawling city with millions of people. The way I see it, there is no other explanation for what happened to me *other* than a miracle and, as I mentioned before, my faith has always played a powerful role in my life. What else could it be? What are the odds that I would be driving down that unfamiliar road at just that time, when I would usually be at work, but that day I would leave early and would happen upon the evil man who had attacked me being taken into police custody right in front of me?

As long as I draw breath, I will never forget that sight: that twisted, angry, wicked face emerging from the dark doorway into the light, followed by two big strapping cops.

That feeling, that amazing, jubilant, triumphant feeling I had at that moment—the relief and joy that, at long last, justice had indeed been found...is a feeling that I want to give to every victim of violent crime.

I know now that the way I behaved after my attack is perfectly normal for anyone who has been the victim of a violent crime; however, I also know that if it happened to me now, or to someone I love, I would encourage completely different steps following an attack.

In order to understand why I behaved the way I did after my attack, it is necessary to turn back the clock more than thirty years. Before the women's movement. Before rape crises counselors. Before victim's advocates. Before sensitivity seminars and modern laws and DNA evidence analysis and "post-traumatic stress disorder" counselors and even before women law enforcement officers (other than meter maids and undercover prostitutes). It was a different world back then for women who were victims of violent crime.

I have a friend who is a fine law enforcement officer now for a major metropolitan police force. When she was nineteen, she was attacked and raped by a stranger while walking to class on her college campus one night. She called the police and the male detectives who interviewed her not only acted as if she had somehow invited the attack or was otherwise being untruthful about it, but actually snickered and told jokes at her expense.

She vowed from that day that she would become a cop, "Because I knew then," she told me, "that I could do a better job than that."

Even if a woman showed clear signs of a beating or knifing when she reported the rape, she was very likely to be brutalized all over again when called upon to testify in court. Her past sexual history could be brought up and used against her, as well as whatever clothing she might have been wearing that could be construed as "seductive."

For these reasons and many more, only one rape in ten was even reported and very few actually went to court.

Nowadays, thank God, the public is much better informed and educated about sexual assault. We know now that this is not a crime about sex at all, but about power and dominance and humiliation. If it were a crime that had anything to do with sexual attraction, then eighty-year old women and five-year-old children would not be raped.

A woman who is sexually assaulted now—especially in a major metropolitan area—is more than likely interviewed by a sympathetic detective (a female, if possible) and at the hospital during her examination will usually be accompanied by a rape crisis counselor, who will walk her through most of the judicial process. Her sexual history is off-limits to defense attorneys and she is treated with far more respect, in most cases, than could be expected thirty years ago.

At the very least, even if she chooses not to report the rape, she will have crisis hot lines she can call and someone to talk to, anonymously and free of charge, from anywhere in the country, at any time, day or night.

But none of those resources was available to the young Lois.

Over the years, I have since interviewed hundreds of rape victims and have found that certain things I did during the attack may have saved my life. For instance, moving my hips to force his ejaculation. This is not an unusual tactic for a victim to use in order to survive. It can cause unnecessary guilt later, making them fear that somehow they were encouraging the attack, but rest assured, it's nothing like that. It's pure survival, nothing less.

Some of the other things I've learned through the years of working with rape victims have, when I think about my own attack, made my blood run cold. Like significance of the fact that the whites of my eyes turned red.

I've now seen this several times in strangulation victims. I have to add—some of those victims were dead. (I'm sometimes called to the morgue to do sketches of unknown crime victims.) Whenever I see some poor girl who didn't make it out alive, stark-staring eyes blood red, it just brings home to me all over again how very close I once came to death.

I now know the phenomenon is called *petechial bleeding* and what it means is that the force of the pressure on the veins and arteries in the throat is so powerful that the tiny blood vessels in the eyeball actually burst.

I didn't know any of this, of course, back in 1972.

I also made plenty of mistakes following my attack. The first was not reporting the assault to the police. The second was the fact that I bathed away all the evidence of the crime.

Nowadays, of course, victims are urged not to bathe until they have had a chance to be examined by a doctor, so that semen and other evidence can be collected in a "rape kit" and saved for trial. So valuable is this evidence that it is crucial that a victim go to the hospital even before being interviewed—preferably in the company of a police officer who can secure the evidence and preserve the chain of evidence for trial.

But what I did is a very common reaction. The first thing most rape victims report is feeling "dirty." But what they don't realize is that the stain is not on their bodies but in their *souls*. This is a violation of the most private, most personal, most essential part of what gives a woman her sense of identity and once that secure wall has been breached, she can never again feel safe.

The man who attacked me in my home may not have killed my body, but he killed me, all right. He killed the *me* that I was and for the next couple of months, I was a dead woman walking. Now that we understand so much more about post-traumatic stress, my behavior was understandable. But of course, I didn't know that then. In fact, even the term "post-traumatic stress" was not coined until a few years after my attack, by psychologists working with Vietnam veterans.

Still, my healing started on the day I saw justice done. That day, I came alive again.

This is what I want to give my witnesses: new life.

It would be a while, though, before I would be able to find my life's work.

First I had to figure out what I wanted to do with my life. And then...I had to come out of hiding.

But before I could do that, I had to do some hand-to-hand combat with my own demons.

Chapter Three:

"If I Can Just Get off That L.A. Freeway without Getting Killed or Caught"

I owe my career path as an artist to an obscure seventeenth-century Dutch master painter by the name of Johannes Vermeer.

I say "obscure," because the name "Vermeer" is not usually the one mentioned by most people as the Dutch artist with whom they are most familiar. They're more likely to say "Rembrandt," for instance. Art lovers, of course, are well aware of the artist who brought to light everyday life in the city of Delft in the Netherlands in the 1600s. Thirty-six masterpieces of his work survive today.

After the rape I was still living in Los Angeles but growing increasingly disgruntled with it. I had begun dating Mark, an attorney who loved Vermeer and had a book of his paintings.

One day he proclaimed, "Vermeer is the best artist ever!"

I shrugged. "I don't know about that. Van Eck is probably better technically," I said, "and anyway, I prefer Rembrandt."

Surprised at my argument, he attempted to convince me of the error of my ways. Suddenly I said, "Shoot, I could paint as good as Vermeer."

"Oh don't be ridiculous!" he scorned. "There's no way in the world you could paint that well. You don't know what you're talking about. You wouldn't even know where to start." Calmly, I persisted in my assertion that I could paint every bit as well as Vermeer and he grew so incredulous and insulting that he threw a dare at me that was intended to shut me up for good (and prove his superior knowledge).

"You think you can paint as well?" he demanded. "Okay, fine. I'll take you to an art supply store, buy you whatever you need and you do a reproduction of one of the paintings in this book."

So I did.

I spent hours in my apartment, painting a copy of "Girl With Pearl Eardrops and Turban." While I painted, I listened to my tapes of George Harrison's *Everything Must Pass*, Sly and the Family Stone and *Cheap Thrills* by Janis Joplin and Big Brother and the Holding Company.

And I loved it. Loved every minute of it. And I realized that listening to music and painting was as close to bliss as I was ever likely to get in this life, that I loved doing it so much more than I had enjoyed going to discos, L.A. parties and all the rest of the Hollywood scene.

This is what I want to do, I decided. *For the rest of my life.*

The rape was never very far from my mind and I remembered well those terror-driven moments and my thoughts, when I'd despaired that I was going to die before I finished college. I made up my mind right then that I would find a way to go to college and major in art.

Eventually, I finished the painting and called up Mark to come and pass judgment.

He was astounded, incredulous.

Of course, he couldn't just compliment my work and let it go. This was the 1970s and like many men he believed that most women should be at home keeping house and making babies. He kept saying things like, "Did you *really* paint that?"

As my cheeks began a slow burn, I said, "What do you think? That I had some guy come in here and paint it for me?"

And he said, "Maybe."

I was furious, but it was only the beginning. He insisted that I paint in front of him so that he could be reassured that I had indeed done the work.

So he watched me and I painted, thinking, *I will never see this ego-maniac jerk again EVER.*

When he was satisfied that I had indeed done the work, he then demanded that I give him the painting.

"Are you kidding?" Now I was incredulous. "There's no way I'm giving you this painting."

"But I bought the art supplies," he replied, as if that was all there was to it.

I didn't know if he was ignorant that good replicas of Vermeer paintings could go for $6,000 to $8,000 on the open market or if he was that big of a jerk—that sixty-five dollars' worth of art supplies was somehow an even trade for my talent and my labor.

I crossed my arms over my chest and stood in front of my picture. "I'm not giving you this painting," I said.

Sputtering, near apoplectic, he left, slamming the door so hard that it rattled things on the walls.

As soon as he got home, he called and screamed at me for more than twenty minutes, because I wouldn't give him that painting.

I set the receiver down on the bed and sat there, listening from a distance while he ranted and raved and screamed.

And I thought, *I want a man like my daddy. A man who's not afraid to work hard, get his hands dirty, stay the course and take care of his family.*

While this jerk kept screaming, I contemplated the men I'd known in the Midwest. *A real man*, I thought, *or at least the kinds of men I grew up with, would call you up and let you know that he was angry in deep, calm tones.*

And so I hung up and started making plans.

My decision to leave Los Angeles didn't happen right away. I talked to some people, although not about the attack, which I still kept locked inside, and while I thought more about things, I continued to date men who neither were sensitive nor had deep values. I certainly do not mean to imply that all California men have something wrong with them, but, still slowly recovering from my rape and growing more homesick all the time, I began feeling that the lifestyle I was seeing was patently phony. Ambitious men on the fast track to make it in Hollywood cared deeply for superficial things that I didn't care about at all and seemed to think that projecting an image was more important than being real.

Even so, I wasn't ready to go back home to Kansas. I would have felt too defeated, too much like I had failed at something and I wasn't even sure what. So one day I sat down and drew myself a map of the states of Oklahoma, Texas, Louisiana and Arkansas.

Then I stood up, closed my eyes, twirled around and put my finger on the map. I opened my eyes and saw it landed on Texas.

I did the exercise again. And again. In all, I twirled around blindly seven times. Five out of those seven times my finger landed on Texas.

It seemed to me a sign. Everyone I had spoken to who came from Texas loved it. I'd heard stories about riding down rivers on inner tubes, taking trail rides, exploring mountains and caves, deserts and forests and the Gulf of Mexico.

One way or the other, I was being guided to Texas.

Later I looked at a real map. Dallas appeared to be a sprawling metroplex where I figured jobs would be plentiful and I knew the University of Texas had a branch campus in the Dallas suburb of Arlington. I called the Dallas Chamber of Commerce for information and the woman who answered the phone was warm, friendly and sweet; she even offered to send me brochures on all the college campuses in the area. The brochures arrived, as promised, within two days and I was sold.

It didn't take me long to pack my modest belongings into my little car and hit the road.

And as I was driving out, over the radio came the hit Jerry Jeff Walker song, "If I Can Just Get off That L.A. Freeway without Getting Killed or Caught."

Turning up the volume, I sang along and headed for Texas.

Sometimes things happen from time to time in my life which seem to be signposts. They let me know that Someone greater and smarter than me is guiding my path. I call them mini-miracles, because I don't know how else to explain it.

If I tried to write the story of my life as a novel, most editors would probably reject the story, claiming it was just too unbelievable. But it's my life; it happens and, in truth, it can be pretty remarkable sometimes.

Once I had moved to Arlington, I found a nice duplex home not far from the University of Texas at Arlington campus, got a job and enrolled in classes. A couple of months into the spring semester of 1973, I was sitting in class, waiting for the professor to show up. Suddenly I commented aloud, to no one in particular, "I wish I knew if they had a place at Six Flags Over Texas," (located in Arlington) "where they let you work doing live portraits like in Disneyland. Because I draw faces really well and it would just seem like the most fun way to make money."

The young woman sitting right next to me almost fell out of her seat. "Are you *kidding?*" she cried. "I'm the business manager of the portrait artists' concession there and they do! They've started training already, but if you're really talented and you really want to do it, they'll take you anyway."

Like I say. A mini-miracle.

I started out as a watercolor portrait artist, making from $10-$12 an hour, which was really good money at the time. Learning to do quick portraits in watercolor on live subjects—many of whom are wiggling children—is a real trial by fire. You can't make mistakes, you can't cover up and the paint dries in about sixty seconds. You can't even use white paint for details like the gleam in someone's eye. What you have to do is paint *around* that little point and leave the white paper to stand in for white paint—and pray that none of your other colors "bleed" into it.

You have to have just the right touch of wetness, not just of the paints, but of the wash for the illustration board—too wet and all your colors run together; too dry and the watercolors don't work. And you have to do all this with squirming subjects or kids who just can't sit still but who are so cute you want to hug them, with dozens of people standing around, staring at your work over your shoulder.

Most artists aren't daredevil enough for such torture, but I loved it. The more portraits I did, the more I could feel myself getting faster, smoother, *better.* I painted tourist portraits all summer long and it was superb introductory training for my life's work.

However, after one semester at UTA I realized that I needed to find a school that had a more extensive art program. Though I had little money I was determined to get the best education I could for my future art career, whatever that would be. Looking at other nearby schools I liked the one at the University of Texas at Austin, Texas's capital, and transferred there. Austin is a beautiful capital city filled with cold spring-fed creeks, walking and biking paths, trees and rock formations and more bookstores, per capita, than any other city in the country. It's a music center famous for launching talent and Sixth Street near the university is crammed chock-a-block with music clubs and quirky shops.

However, I didn't get many opportunities to enjoy very much song and dance during the three years I lived there while finishing my degree. My life was a blur of day-long art classes and laboratories, followed by waiting tables well into the night, falling into bed for a few brief hours of sleep, then getting up and riding my bike to the shuttle bus to start classes all over again. Somehow I managed to survive on less than $5,000 a year, furnishing my place from garage sales, buying marked-down, on-sale clothes and subsisting on beans, soy, cheese, water and whatever else was cheap.

In my last semester of art school, just before getting my degree, I learned a painful lesson on how to watch for those "signposts" from God.

Call it a "still, small voice" or a gentle nudging, or whatever, but I believe that God sends us guidance in clear ways if we pay attention. I was dating a guy whom I thought I loved. He lived in San Antonio. On weekends I went there to see him. On the way home one Sunday night, I was planning to drop in on a girlfriend for a chat before returning to my place. Suddenly I got this powerful urge to keep on going straight home.

But I didn't want to go straight home.

The urge grew stronger, more persistent. It was so strong that I actually argued with myself out loud, saying, "No, I'm not going straight home! I want to visit Donna and I'm going to."

So I did.

Later that night, when I drove down the street leading to my house, I saw a fire truck in my driveway and smoke pouring from my living room!

Later I found out a careless roommate had thrown a rug my sister had hand-made for me over a heating grate and gone out. The rug had caught on fire and burned up my easy chair and hassock (which I sank into every night after exhausting hours waiting tables) and a painting I had just finished as a final major project for my last art class.

My kitty Blackie's paws were also scorched.

The only reason the whole house didn't burn down was that the fire station was *right across the street* and firefighters lounging on their front lawn had quickly spotted the flames.

I had loved that painting, a surreal, romantic work that depicted a lush jungle landscape suspended in mid-air in a blue sky with a waterfall cascading down into a cloud. Now it was almost unrecognizable.

I also loved my cat, whom I spent the night nursing. Heartsick, the next day I dragged my charred canvas to class for my final grade.

Though I explained to my oh-so-sympathetic classmates what had happened, they critiqued the painting anyway, saying things like, "The black velvety structure is so intense!" And, "The blackening actually becomes part of the art..."

I got a "B" on my burnt-up painting.

It was a good lesson, though. I learned never to ignore my inner promptings again. And I never have.

After graduation I moved to San Antonio to be closer to my boyfriend, who was a dental student. San Antonio is a city rich in cultural and historical significance to Texans. It boasts the start of the Texas Revolution, in which a small band of "Texians" held out for thirteen days in the tiny Mission San Antonio de Valero—known throughout the world as "The Alamo"—against overwhelming Mexican forces led by General Antonio Lopez de Santa Anna. The famous defeat inspired other Texians to "Remember the Alamo" and eventually win their independence from Mexico.

The influence of the Mexican culture can still be seen all over the city and through the years, San Antonio has become a mecca for tourists, offering such attractions as Sea World, Fiesta Texas, historical restored theatres, cultural centers and the River Walk.

Strange as it may seem, I actually enrolled at the University of Texas Health Science Center at the San Antonio Dental School.

I wasn't studying to be a dentist, but rather a maxillo-facial prosthesis technician who makes artificial eyes, noses, ears and other facial parts for patients who've lost them due to trauma or surgery. (I didn't realize it then, but that training would later enable me to draw even the most complicated jaw and teeth structures when doing forensic sketches. If someone tries to describe, say, an unusual overbite, I understand immediately what they are talking about and can draw it with little trouble.)

The first time I saw San Antonio's beautiful River Walk, my emotional reaction to it was so powerful, so visceral, that my eyes filled with tears and I became almost physically ill.

The San Antonio River ribbons gently in and out of the downtown area and throughout the city. Located one flight below the downtown streets, the River Walk is like entering another world. Lined by softly swaying cypress trees, the banks of the river are dotted with sidewalk cafes, hideaway clubs, live music and shops of every kind. River taxis cruise slowly past and the sights, sounds and colors are, to an artist, like walking into a kaleidoscope.

But it wasn't the beauty of the place that overwhelmed me. It was one of those nudges from God again, only this time, it was more like a sledge-hammer to the side of the head.

I've got to do portraits here! I thought and the impulse was so strong that, for a moment, I wondered if I'd said it out loud.

I had to. That's all. Period.

Girls growing up in the fifties were taught to be pleasers, "nice girls," to hide our intelligence from men so that they could always feel smarter, to be ladies, to have, as the Bible says, "a sweet and gentle spirit."

That's pretty strong conditioning to overcome and I sometimes wonder what drove me to be so stubbornly independent. Somehow I mustered the courage to approach various businesses located on the River Walk and requested permission to set up my easel and two chairs and sketch tourists for money. I always offered the manager a percentage of my income. But even though I worked at four separate businesses, not a single one took any money from me.

For I always attracted business for them and me.

The first couple of years, I worked mostly weekends, but it became clear to me that I was making so much money that I didn't need to do anything else. In fact, I didn't *want* to. Eventually, I dropped out of dental school and spent most of my time along the River Walk doing portraits and I loved every minute of it.

In all, I did more than three thousand portraits in that milieu.

But then something stopped me in my tracks and sent me to Houston, something more than the doomed romance that was petering out, something more than my restless heart's desire for a fresh start.

My body.

Nowadays, "repetitive motion injuries" such as carpal tunnel syndrome are widely understood, but at that time, I never gave a thought to the thousands and thousands of times I turned my head back and forth like someone watching a ping pong match—subject to canvas, canvas to subject. I developed an inflammation of the muscle connections that run from the sternum—or breastbone—all the way up my neck to the mastoid process, which is the bony protuberance on the skull behind the ear. So severe was the inflammation that the skin over my breastbone turned purple.

I could barely move. Simple motions such as tying my shoes, rolling over in bed or reaching my arms out in front of me were so intensely painful that I screamed. When my hard head finally gave in enough so that I was forced to go to the doctor, I learned that my condition had a name: *costra condritis*.

The doctor told me to quit doing portraits.

Instead, I ate aspirin like candy, used heating pads until my skin blistered, swathed my neck in scarves and turtlenecks. It got so bad that I couldn't turn my head to check the entrance of the freeway—I'd just jam down the accelerator and pray.

Finally, because of my physical condition, I couldn't do portraits anymore. I had to quit.

Defeated, scrunched up in pain, dispirited, depressed and alone again, I packed up my paints and moved to Houston.

What I didn't realize when I left San Antonio was that the only way I was ever going to have a future was for me to face, once and for all, my past.

Little did I know that it would be in Houston that all my carefully pent-up demons would come swarming out of their hiding places and all my running from myself would come to a soul-crunching halt.

Recently, medical science has begun to take a second look at what eastern and Native American traditions have long known to be true: that our bodies, minds and spirits are intimately connected, a delicate, intricate web. Touch one strand and the entire web shivers.

I've spent some time looking into this matter and now I find it not so surprising that it was the "shield" covering my battered heart that eventually began to show the bruises on the outside that I felt so acutely on the inside.

The fact that my neck stiffened up and was intensely painful was partially because I did put considerable strain on it in my work doing riverside portraits; there's no question about that—but it's also true that I had nearly lost my life when someone evil put his hands around my throat and that I kept this attack a secret from everyone around me.

It causes tremendous stress to the physical body when it's being held in an emotional straitjacket by the mind. It requires great energy to pretend on the outside that everything is well on the inside when it's not. Since my attack, I'd tried to run from what had happened to me by working myself almost to death, burning up every single waking moment of every single day and never letting anyone know the turmoil that I was trying to hide even from me.

However, busy-ness may keep us from thinking very deeply, but it can't fool the subconscious.

I was a performer on stage, covering my true self with a mask while singing and dancing so furiously that my body was beginning to break down. But I have an almost unimaginably strong willpower and when I first moved to Houston, I was still not yet ready to confront those demons. I did all I could to keep them caged up.

However, it was getting harder and harder all the time.

If you were to consider Dallas, Austin, San Antonio and Houston as siblings in one big Texan family, you'd have to think of Dallas as the society doyenne, a bit snooty, dismayed that her bawdy cowboy brother, Fort Worth, lives so close by. Austin would be the spoiled little rich girl, the wild child who gets away with a lot but whom everyone loves anyway. San Antonio would be the historian, the keeper of the family scrapbooks, always wanting to be taken seriously.

Houston? Houston would be the *nouveau riche* step-brother, too busy buying and trading, back-slapping and cigar-smoking, to care much what anyone else in the family thinks. Compared to the others, Houston is shiny and new and proud of it and thinks there's no such thing as "wretched excess."

When I moved there in 1979, Houston was booming and jobs were plentiful. It was a good place to get lost in, like a film extra in a cast of thousands.

In a grand gesture of supreme...what's the word? *Ignoringness?* I chose to ignore what my body was trying so hard to tell me and before long, I started doing portraits again, this time at Houston's Northwest mall.

One sunny day in May of 1980, I was in the process of setting up my easel and preparing to begin my Saturday afternoon work, when suddenly, my vision focused upon, quite simply, the most beautiful man I had ever seen.

His blond hair shone as if backlit and he walked with a dancer's grace, carrying his tanned and muscled body with ease, like a tool he well knew how to use. It seemed to say, *I could pick up a car if I wanted to. Thing is, I just don't want to right now.*

I'm nothing if not a fast thinker and before he could get away, I hailed him and asked if he would sit for me to help me "warm up." I offered him a huge discount (though Lord knows I would have painted him for free). Actually, this is a common practice when doing candid portraits. If an artist just sits there with a blank easel, people will hurry past as if they're afraid you're going to ask for a donation. But if you are doing a portrait, natural curiosity will draw them 'round and once they see how good the painting can be it isn't long before you can attract quite a bit of business.

It wasn't business I was looking for that day, though.

My intention was to make casual conversation, get to know the man, toss in some flirting and see if I could snag a date.

But I had no idea just how shy Sid Gibson really was.

The minute he noticed people hanging around gawking, he turned crimson, hung his head, dropped his shoulders and mumbled answers to all my friendly questions. To this day, I couldn't understand what he said, but the truth is that I was so smitten I probably wouldn't have heard anyway.

In fact, he was making such an effort to disappear into the floor that I thought he was short. It wasn't until we actually did have a date that I realized he was built like a body builder.

The day God brought Sid to the Northwest mall and into my life was the day I truly began to live again....though it didn't exactly seem that way at first.

After he stumbled and mumbled off from the portrait session, he suddenly re-emerged from the crowd, grinning at me like a little kid. He handed me a small, torn-off piece of white paper.

It turned out to be the corner of a deposit slip, containing his name, address and phone number. In spite of the fact that I found him enormously sexy and attractive, I wadded up the piece of paper into a little pea-sized ball and tossed it into my coin purse. After all, I'd been hurt plenty by men in recent years. I didn't know how to trust anymore.

A couple of weeks passed and then a girlfriend who worked nearby started complaining that this "gorgeous, muscle-bound guy" kept coming by and asking about me and was I going to do anything about it or not?

That was the first clue I had that Sid Gibson had apparently been as attracted to me as I was him, so I called him and arranged to meet him at a local restaurant.

Disaster.

Getting him to talk was about as easy as getting children at an amusement park to sit still for a watercolor portrait.

"So, do you have any brothers and sisters?"

"Yeah."

"Oh? How many sisters do you have?" (I'd found that my relationships with men tended to work better the more sisters they had.)

"Not too many."

"How many?"

"Just four..." (lengthy pause) "...and there were two cousins who lived with us who were like sisters to me."

It's a wonder we ever got together at all. It took two such miserable dates for me to learn that the man hated restaurants, which, of course, he had neglected to mention to me. That's when I asked him to come jog with me and *that's* when the magic started to happen.

It was during that afternoon that I told him my dream of being able to paint for a living and to my astonishment, he said, "Why don't you let me pay your rent and buy food and that way you could just paint full-time? You could still live by yourself."

Of course I was way too proud and independent to take him up on that offer, but I knew from that point on that this was a man who knew how to love—unconditionally.

The youngest of seven children, Sid grew up with four older sisters and it gave him a perspective on life that was unique among men I'd encountered. He knew how to talk to a woman, how to treat her, how to care for her. Though a man's man in every way, Sid was a *nurturer*.

I'd been working so hard, being so independent and brave, that I didn't realize how much I needed nurturing. In relationships, I tend to be the giver and so many men I'd known had been only too happy to be takers. Sid knew how to take love but he also knew how to give it.

Almost as impressive to me as his ability to love unconditionally was that he had worked hard to build a career in construction plumbing, he was proud of what he did and not the least bit pretentious. (The muscles came from hard work, not from some elite fitness club.) I was so used to dating guys who lied about their incomes and tried other tactics to impress me that I fell in love with Sid's honesty and genuineness as much as anything.

When we first started dating, Sid was living with a lovely young couple named James and Diane Denton. Diane was a stay-home mom, taking care of their first baby and Sid helped out with the rent and household expenses. Sid has always loved kids and he was terrific with their daughter, Amy—an energetic one-year-old—and it made me joyful, watching him with her. The four of us got along wonderfully well and when I was over at their house, I felt at home.

Let down my guard a bit more.

It was nice, not feeling so alone for a change. Feeling like part of a family. Being in love with a gorgeous guy. Within three weeks we knew we would be married. In fact, there wasn't even a romantic proposal. It was just a fact that we accepted almost from the beginning.

I had found the love of my life and I was looking forward to happiness with him...but it was complicated. There were still all those demons to contend with.

With Sid, I lowered my shield a little and let myself be vulnerable. That's when the demons get you.

Everything was just fine until the day Diane turned on the evening news.

I never watched the evening news. *Never.* Of course, I know now that this is one way in which some victims of violent crime deal with their attacks—they avoid news of anyone *else's* violent attacks. And that's all the local evening news is—murders, rapes, fires, violence.

I had found that watching the evening news and hearing about those violent crimes triggered all sorts of uncomfortable feelings I did not want to deal with, so I just avoided the subject altogether...until the day Diane turned on the television and I was trapped into watching with her.

That's when I heard that a dance instructor had been raped at gunpoint *in front of her students—little girls, eleven and twelve years old.*

Suddenly, as if some underground cave deep inside me yawned open, out swarmed clouds of bat-like demons, driving me to an almost unrecognizable rage. All my carefully-controlled emotions burst loose in a torrent of outrage and pain and I didn't know what to do except scream at the television.

I wanted to chase that animal down and run him over with my car. I wanted to parade him in front of that poor woman and those traumatized little girls and say, "See this? They're gonna put him in *jail*, in a *cage* like the animal he is!"

Diane kept her composure, but she must have wondered what in the world was going on. I hadn't been dating Sid all that long at that point, but long enough for her to know that this was just not like me.

I didn't know, of course, that everything I was feeling was completely normal, that in fact, it was long overdue. This kind of white-hot anger is necessary for the healing process, or else it will fester inside a victim like pus in an infected sore and, like an untreated infection, can poison over time. I wasn't just filled with rage for this poor dance instructor, I was filled with rage for *me*, for *anyone* who was forced to suffer unjustly because of another.

The announcer was droning on with a generic description of the attacker: "male, 5'10", brown hair, brown eyes."

At that, I found myself giggling, but it was mirthless, cynical laughter. "That's just *laughable!*" I cried, almost hysterical. "They're describing half the men in Houston—you're talking a million guys."

They'll never find justice for her, I anguished. *She'll be alone and afraid and lost just like...*

Just like me.

I felt something building inside my chest, a physical burning, a sickness just like what I had felt that day years before after I had been raped.

Remember that Bible story about how the blind apostle Paul was walking along on the road to Damascus, when suddenly, "the scales fell away from his eyes" and he could *see*—not just literally, but also figuratively?

That's what happened to me, in a manner of speaking.

I *knew*, just like that.

It was as if all that tumultuous, chaotic energy that was colliding within my heart and mind had suddenly focused itself with all the concentrated power of a laser beam.

All the scattergun restlessness that had driven me from city to city and job to job and man to man since the rape, the force that had pushed me almost over the brink of sanity, that had pressured me until my chest turned purple from the pain...all that energy suddenly compressed itself into one powerful lightning bolt: a knowing.

Whirling toward Diane, I said, "I could sketch that guy."

Although I had never done a sketch of anyone based on descriptions alone, I *had* done thousands of portraits and I knew—almost without hes-itation—I knew I could do it.

If Diane was having trouble keeping up with the thunderstorm of emotions she was observing passing over me, she kept it to herself. I still had not told her about the rape, nor was I ready to discuss the attack I had suffered at this point. But Diane seemed to accept what I was saying at face value and said, "Okay, call the police. Tell them you can do a sketch of the guy."

In my mind flashed an image of what the police would have to say about some artist approaching them out of the blue with such a suggestion and I shook my head. "No. I'm not ready. I have to practice first."

She nodded. "All right, then. Let me describe my mother to you and you can draw her."

"No." Pacing the floor, I said, "You know her face too intimately. I need to do a sketch of someone who's a stranger to you."

At this point, the energy was burning a hole right through my chest, or at least it felt like it. I knew that I would do *anything* to make this work. Instinctively I knew that if I could use my gifts and talents to help other people get justice, it would also soothe my own pain.

"Go pick out someone, anyone," I instructed a bemused Diane. "A gas station attendant. Anyone. I'll stay here with the baby. You come back and tell me what the guy looks like and I'll see if I can do a sketch."

Though she did comment that the idea was "weird," Diane was nothing if not game. She gathered up her purse, car keys and left.

Almost immediately, I burst into tears.

I'd never seen anyone do anything like what I was proposing before. I had no idea how it was done or even where to begin.

Why did I let myself get into this? I agonized for a few moments. *Why did I let these demons loose?*

However, though I couldn't articulate it at the time—not even to myself—somehow I knew that if I was able to do the sketch, it would heal me.

But if I didn't...it would destroy me.

If I can't do it, I found myself thinking, *I really don't want to live anymore.* All of a sudden, no other job in the world seemed as worthwhile to me. I began to grieve in advance, knowing that a failure at this point would make me feel worthless.

At that point, as I continued to agonize, Diane's baby started to get fussy. I struggled to pull myself together before Diane returned. That little ten-minute trip of hers felt as if it took an hour. When she got back, I went to fetch my drawing materials, which I always kept in the trunk of my car, and returned, sitting down at the kitchen table.

"Okay," said Diane, clearly into what was for her a cool game. "I saw a black guy. He had a round face."

I stared at the blank sketchpad I'd laid flat on the table—which I soon figured out was a mistake—and I couldn't visualize what she was saying.

How do you start? *Where?*

Eyes blurred with tears, I shoved back from the table. "I can't do it," I said. "This is too hard. It's impossible."

But Diane knew how to get things done. She was relentless. She simply would not let me quit. She bossed, pushed and would not take no for an answer. "You can do it," she insisted. "Keep working. It'll come to you."

I'll always be grateful to her for that.

She described the guy's hair and eyes, nose and ears, constantly making me rework and make changes. By the time I'd worked my way down to the mouth, I was completely drained.

"He's the kind of guy who never stops grinning," she said.

"Mouth open or closed?"

"Open."

"Does he show his upper teeth and his lower teeth?"

Surprised, she said, "Yeah!"

For the first time, I felt a smile creep across my face. The eighteen months I'd spent in dental school were going to come in useful after all. One of the things we'd had to do was memorize the placement of teeth.

I drew the grinning mouth, even showing a touch of tongue behind the teeth.

Diane threw up her hands and said, "That looks like him! That's him!"

My heart was beginning a slow thud in my chest. "Don't say it looks like him if it doesn't," I said solemnly. "I mean, don't flatter me. This is too important." She had no idea the emotional investment I had in this one drawing.

"No! I'm not just saying it. It really looks like the man at the gas station." She grabbed up her car keys and the baby. "C'mon, let's go down to the gas station and I'll show you."

It was three blocks from Diane's house to the station and I turned my face to the passenger-side window, eyes squeezed shut, willing myself not to cry. The short trip was almost unbearable.

We drove up and got out of the car. I pulled out the 18" by 24" piece of drawing paper on which I'd drawn the portrait. The attendant walked out of the little office.

A total match.

It looked as if he had posed for the portrait.

Handing the picture to Diane, I placed my hands on the top of the gas pump, hung my head between my shoulder blades and sobbed, *wailed*, in joyous relief.

While my tears poured out and Diane stood, dumbstruck, I stared at the oily concrete of the gas station tarmac and saw my whole future laid out for me.

I will catch them, I realized. *All the killers and rapists and thieves and haters like the one who attacked me and the one who assaulted that dance teacher. I will give crime victims back their lives and, in so doing, they will give me back mine.*

At this realization, I laughed a little and looked up to see the gas station attendant, staring at the drawing. He recognized Diane from her earlier visit and asked, "Did you do that?"

Grinning, Diane shook her head and pointed at me. "She did it."

He glanced from me to the drawing. At first, his expression was one of disbelief and then, amazement, followed by genuine anxiety. He said, "But you weren't here!"

I could see that he was spooked. In fact, he began to inch backwards away from me, holding up his hands as if to fend off a curse. Narrowing his eyes, he said, "Why would you want to do *that*?"

I couldn't begin to imagine how weird this whole thing must have seemed to this man, if for no other reason than because of my own behavior, which must have seemed bizarre to him. But I could also understand how it would worry him that someone he'd never seen before could appear out of nowhere with a dead-on drawing of his face.

I didn't know how to answer him without going into the criminal angle of the whole thing, so I just said, "C'mon Diane; let's go."

It was a profound, powerful, energizing moment in my life. All I had to do now was contact the police.

When I realized that I could draw people's faces without looking at them, from descriptions alone, I guess I thought the hard part was over.

Little did I know that it was only just beginning.

Chapter Four:

"Total Failure"

"Houston Police Department. How may I direct your call?"

"Um...hi. My name is Lois Gibson. I'm an artist, and I can draw faces really well, just from descriptions, and I was wondering..."

"You need to call the television stations. They set up courtroom artists."

"No, no. I'm not a courtroom artist. I mean...I'm offering to draw faces of suspects from witness descriptions."

"You need another department. Why don't you try Homicide? Their number is..."

"Thank you."

"Homicide."

"Hi. My name is Lois Gibson. I'm an artist and I can draw faces really well, just from descriptions and I was wondering..."

"Well...hmmm...I'm not sure who you should speak with about that. Have you tried Robbery?"

"Okay. Would you mind giving me the number?"

"Sure. It's..."

"Thanks."

"Robbery."

"Um, hello. My name is Lois Gibson and I'm an artist who can draw faces really well. I could do drawings of suspects from witness descrip—"

"You need to call Homicide."

And so it went. Basically, nobody seemed to know what to do with me and so everyone wanted to get rid of me as quickly as possible. Most said they had never heard of using an artist. One detective with whom I spoke said they did use an artist but couldn't describe what he or she did and didn't want to let me speak to the person. The thought of spending *money* on anything that they did not regard as essential was considered a ridiculous waste of scarce and valuable resources.

And hiring some flaky woman artist to come draw criminals was, to their way of thinking, absolutely not essential.

I was sure they were missing out. Following my emotional meltdown in my friend Diane's house and my drawing of the gas station attendant, I was glued to the evening news, night after night.

Rapes, murders, kidnappings, robberies and assaults flashed across my television screen with nauseating repetition. Houston was now one of the most crime-ridden cities in the nation. There were more homicides than there were days in that year. Every night I watched and waited to see if any of the news outlets would display a forensic sketch of the suspect, but they never did.

Over and over again, monotone-voiced newscasters reeled off what sounded like the same description of the same criminal: *white male, 5'9" or 5'10" tall, brown hair, brown eyes...*or *black male, 5'10" or 5'11" tall, black hair, brown eyes...*blah, blah, blah.

It blew my mind, the sheer number of crimes that were committed in full view of horrified witnesses who, no doubt, got a clear view of the suspect—not to mention rape victims who, more often than not, certainly saw the guys who were raping them.

If the police would only let me speak to the victims, I could draw those creeps—*I knew it!*

It was all I could do not to scream at the television—this time in sheer frustration—as I had done at Diane's that day.

Meanwhile, one upbeat thing occurred. I moved into a one hundred-year-old duplex with sixty-foot pecan trees domed over the back yard, ceilings ten feet high, tall windows and a cast-iron bathtub with claw feet. The wood frame house was set up on blocks, like all the houses in that neighborhood, to protect it from hurricane-driven floods. Behind the house was a three-car garage that had a great little apartment upstairs.

The plumbing in the old house was state-of-the art—thirty years earlier. I'll never forget the first fight Sid and I had. He slammed out the front door and I went to bed fuming. Early the next morning, there was a knock at the door.

"Who is it?" I grumbled.

"It's me."

Growling under my breath that he would have the nerve to wake me up so early when he knew good and well I was mad at him, I flung back the front door and there he stood, a big old grin on his handsome face, clutching in his arms...a brand-new, snowy-white toilet! He had it installed in about twenty minutes, like some kind of voodoo magic, and his ploy worked like a charm on me.

From that point on, whenever Sid and I had a fight, he fixed something. Once he installed a shower over the old claw-foot tub, complete with a ring to hold the shower curtain. The next fight we had, I wound up with a garbage disposal in the kitchen sink.

Soon we got married.

I had never told Sid of my seething passion to break into the world of forensic sketching that lurked just beneath the surface. Of course I had told him, eventually, about the rape, but unfortunately, the poor guy reacted as most men in the early eighties would: he asked me what I had been wearing. He didn't even understand his insinuation that I might have provoked the attack. He didn't realize he was trying to "blame the victim."

And as I said earlier, though my husband was usually sensitive, those were the prevailing attitudes at that time. Sometimes, even today, crime victims are subjected to these kinds of questions. People forget that a predator watches for an opportunity to strike at his prey and it doesn't matter how the prey is dressed.

A predator is like a hunter, sitting up in a deer blind, seeing a doe stray into his line of fire; he doesn't stop to think how beautiful her big brown eyes are or how gracefully she stands: he just aims his weapon and fires.

It's the same way with predatory criminals. They're just looking for an opportunity to strike.

When Sid asked me what I had been wearing that terrible day of my attack, I screamed at him.

"I had on *my apartment!*" I shrieked. "*That's* what I was wearing! My *home.* He didn't *know* what I had on when he decided to come crashing through the door and kill me!"

Sid apologized, of course. He felt awful, because he just didn't know what to say.

I had no one at that time to help me process my still-simmering rage over the attack, no idea what to *do* with it and the sweet man who adored me was clueless.

We never spoke of it again.

So I kept all that emotional turmoil bubbling just beneath the surface, but by then, I'd grown skilled at living an outwardly normal, even happy life, in spite of it.

And Sid tried to help me launch the career I dreamed of. Whenever he came home and said that a new guy had started work, I asked him to describe the man for me. He did and I created a sketch. The next day, I dropped Sid off at work and waited in the car. Soon he emerged from the building with the new guy—coffee cup in hand—in tow. Then I held up the sketch and made a comparison.

Time and time again, the guy was a dead ringer.

And at night, I kept watching the news programs. But I saw only one sketch displayed and it wasn't a sketch at all. I realized it was an Identi-Kit composite. With an Identi-Kit, the witness would begin with a generic face shape and the detective would then overlay facial features imprinted on sheets of clear acetate until a reasonably close facsimile to the witness's description could be reached.

But those kit-faces never look real and the one I saw during that period on the evening news was no exception. The face looked flat, a clumsy depiction that bore no subtle shadings to give the face its shape and texture. It didn't resemble a real person you might see on the street.

That's when I knew that the Houston Police Department did not have a forensic sketch artist, even though one person with whom I spoke said that they did. What they had was a harried and hurried detective, doing the best he or she could with what was available, and it wasn't much.

Sometimes, detectives were interviewed on the evening news concerning this crime or that. They were usually taciturn and jaded. They seemed to be always tired and discouraged and had dark circles under their eyes.

My heart went out to them. It seemed to me that they had an impossible job. The crimes kept coming, wave upon wave, and they were doing the best they could to hold back the overwhelming tide.

More than anything in the world, I wanted to help. I *burned* to jump into the fray. It ate at me, day and night. I knew my talents could be of some use. I *knew* my sketches could help them.

If I could just get someone to give me a chance.

When our son Brent was born, he came out looking like a manly little man, muscular, trim and square-chested. He was not a cuddle baby. He did not want to be held, rocked and lulled. Almost from the beginning, he fought to get up and *go*, as if he wanted to try his hand at rock climbing or join the Marines.

I tried to rock, to nurse, struggled to keep him from crawling out of my arms and watched the daily litany of crime goose-step across my TV screen. The politicians droned on about how something had to be done about this relentless crime wave and the newscaster offered up yet another dazzling description of the perpetrator: *5'9" or 5'10" tall, brown hair, brown eyes*, etc., etc.

In one bloody twenty-four-hour period, nine murders were committed in Houston and many of the crime scenes included eyewitnesses. And yet, as always, all they had to offer the media was the same generic description.

"Momma Nadine," my dear mother-in-law, who had come to live with us and was a wonderful help with the baby, noticed that part of the reason Brent was so restless and wouldn't sleep through the night was because the kid was hungry. Even with supplemental bottles, I couldn't keep him comfortable. Before the pediatrician got a clue as to what was wrong, Momma Nadine showed me how to mix up rice cereal and formula and feed it to Brent on a spoon.

Immediately, he was satisfied and slept all night from then on.

After that, I was able to get some sleep and have a little time to myself. I started giving some serious thought as to how I could break down this concrete wall that was the police department.

One day, after about twenty fruitless calls, I remembered something my daddy had said to me when I was a skinny, shy little girl about to enter the terrifying arena of selling Girl Scout cookies. I was eight years old at the time and absolutely mortified at the idea of knocking on people's doors and trying to get them to buy cookies.

Pulling me down beside him as he sat at the breakfast table, my daddy said, "Lois, do you think that when someone buys a box of your cookies, they're doing you a favor?"

I nodded. Shoot yeah, they were doing me a favor.

And he said, "No, no! You're looking at it all wrong! You see, *you* are doing *them* a favor, just by going up to their door!"

"I am?" That sounded doubtful to me.

"Well, let me ask you something. Are those good cookies?"

"Yes, sir," I said. "They're real good. They taste better than any cookies I ever had!"

"All right. They're great cookies. Let me ask you this. Do they have to pay for the cookies right then?"

I shook my head. "We take their order and they don't have to pay until we deliver the cookies."

"Uh, huh." Nodding, he glanced over at me and asked slyly, "Do they have to pick up the cookies?"

"No!" I cried. "We take the cookies right to them, to their door."

"That sounds pretty good. Do you think these people might buy cookies anyway, say, at the grocery store?"

I agreed that yes, most people did buy cookies at the grocery.

Taking me by my little arms, he said, "Honey, I want you to remember this for the rest of your life. Don't think that these people are doing you a favor just because they buy these cookies from you. Remember, they would be buying cookies anyway and these are delicious cookies. They don't even have to pay for them right away and you will deliver them right to their door! You see, *you* are doing *them* a favor, aren't you? Now, here is what I want you to say when you go up to someone's door."

I leaned closer.

"Say, *This is your lucky day!*"

He told me that I should use that approach for everything from a job interview to getting ahead in life.

I did just that and I sold more cookies than any other rookie Girl Scout in Kansas City.

Now, sitting in my rocker, watching my active infant son scramble and scoot around on the floor (trying to find a way to bust out of the joint, no doubt), I thought about what my dad had said. I decided that I needed to change my approach. I needed to convince the police department that this was, indeed, their lucky day.

So I made another call to them.

"Robbery," I said firmly.

This time they put me through.

"Hello. My name is Lois Gibson. I am a portrait artist and I can draw the faces of suspects from witness descriptions," I rushed on. "I'd like to offer—"

"Well..."

"I'll bring all my gear down to HPD myself. I'll set it up in your office. All you have to do is send somebody down to the jail, look at someone there, then come back and describe the person to me."

"Hey," interrupted one detective before I could finish my rehearsed speech, "We'll fix you up with a guard and you can go down to the jail yourself and draw all the perverts you want!"

I heard him laughing as I hung up.

Sometimes I sat in my rocker, stared up at the ceiling, cried and talked to God. I told Him that I understood, now, why I had been attacked and that I knew what my purpose was on this planet and how I could use such a terrible thing for good, to help others. And I prayed for His help in breaking through the hard shell of a major metropolitan bureaucracy. But there were a lot of times when it just seemed impossible.

Every day, when I put Brent down for his long afternoon nap, I got on the phone and went through my rehearsed speech.

"If my drawing is good," I said as persuasively as possible to a reluctant cop, "then think what a wonderful thing that would be to help with your investigations. And if I'm no good, then hey, I'm just a housewife, right? You guys are armed, after all. I'll leave. What have you got to lose?"

One day, I launched wearily into my act, to a lieutenant. And when I was done, the policeman said, "You need to call Lieutenant Don McWilliams."

Okay. Fine. I'll call the damn detective, I thought and redialed the police department, hoping the big sarcastic sigh I was heaving couldn't be heard over the phone.

Finally I had the name of the right person.

"Lieutenant McWilliams," I said. "Hi. My name is Lois Gibson. I'm a practiced portrait artist and I am positive I can draw a good resemblance from a description given by a witness who has seen a face," I recited. "I can prove it to you. I'll bring my gear down to your office. You send somebody over to the jail and have them look at anyone they want. Have them come back and describe one of the inmates to me and I guarantee you I can draw the guy just from their description."

And without hesitation, Lt. McWilliams said, "Well, come on down, girl! Let's see you do it!"

I almost dropped the phone. I wasn't even sure I had heard correctly. Had he just said *come on down*, like some kind of game show announcer?

I was so flabbergasted that I didn't say anything for a moment or two.

Lt. McWilliams went on to set up a date and time and when I offered to drive there myself, he said, "Nah, no problem, I'll send someone to come pick you up."

And just like that, I got my first opportunity to perform.

I was nervous on the sunny afternoon when I handed the baby over to Momma Nadine and got ready to leave for the Houston Police Department. I was just so *ready* to show what I could do. After all, I'd been doing it in my head for more than two years and not only that, but with Sid's help, during that time I had been practicing on unwitting "suspects," drawing their portraits using only Sid's description—and that didn't even count the thousands of quick portraits I'd done with watercolors and pastels along the River Walk and in malls all over Texas.

I was ready, I told myself. I could do it. All I had to do was convince a bunch of hard-nosed cops that they needed me and that this was their lucky day.

Officer Howard White picked me up and helped me load my cumbersome easel and my drawing supplies into the squad car. He was funny, entertaining and personable on the drive to the police department. He acted as if he did this sort of thing every day and it helped me to feel as if it was something I did every day, too.

The Robbery Division was housed in a 1950s-era building that was spartan but serviceable and Lt. Don McWilliams worked in a small office. When I first met McWilliams—whom I've since come to love and refer to, like everyone else who knows him, as "Mac"—he reminded me of the actor Wilford Brimley in his younger days. He had large, powerful legs, a firm handshake and a soft-spoken, homey demeanor. There wasn't a great deal of room to set up my easel in his office, but I was not deterred. I made myself a little corner studio adjacent to the open doorway.

Years later and still grateful, I asked Lt. McWilliams what had motivated him to take a chance on an unknown like me—a female artist.

His answer was pure cop: "Aww, my captain didn't want to deal with you. He told me to let you come on in just so we could get rid of you."

We laugh about that even now.

When I was ready, McWilliams said, "Why don't we send one of the detectives down to lockup and he'll come back with a suspect description for you?"

I shook my head. In an act of almost brazen chutzpah—since this was clearly the biggest test of my life—I said, "No, I'd rather you not use a detective. Detectives are trained to be keen observers and they would notice details that most crime victims and witnesses would not."

I paused, then said, "I want you to pick out the ditziest dingbat you can find. And don't tell the person what we're trying to do. After all, most people don't plan ahead of time to pay attention during a crime, do they?"

Oh Lord, what a brassy dame I was.

You've heard that expression, "be careful what you wish for"?

I should have known better than to present any kind of challenge to detectives, because believe me, they went out of their way to find the spaciest space cadet they could round up.

They took the young woman to the jail and when they returned and she found out what I intended to do, she let out a cat-like holler, put her hands over her horrified face and cried, "Ohhhh NOOOOO! They didn't *tell* me we were going to make a drawing! No, no! I can't *remember* enough to do a *drawing!*"

Great, I thought through a frozen smile, *you had to ask for a dingbat*.

I learned a valuable lesson. Never give a cop a chance to get one up on you. It's just too much fun for them.

In a soothing voice, I got the blond to admit that she had noticed that the guy was a white male, in his twenties. Starting at the top of the head, I said, "Okay, what kind of hair did he have?"

"Uh...uh...I don't *knoooow*," she whined, growing more befuddled the longer she spoke. Holding her hand up to cover her forehead, she said vaguely, "It was just all dark up here. Just all...dark."

Trying not to grind my teeth, I did my best to depict generic dark hair covering the perpetrator's forehead and asked her to describe his eyebrows and eyes.

As I worked, I was well aware that various Robbery personnel who were passing in the hallway were stopping and leaning into the doorway to see what was going on. Eventually, there was a small crowd congregated, craning their necks to see.

As we began to concentrate on the nose and facial structure, I could hear them exclaiming in awe and amazement at how good I was.

This was just what I wanted to hear. And after so many years of doing portraits in front of an audience, it didn't bother me in the least.

Then we got to the mouth. The young woman said, "He had these really weird teeth...I don't know...I can't describe it."

Eighteen months of dental school were not wasted.

After a little gentle prodding, I figured out that the man had what is known as "spaced maxillary laterals" and that these teeth were slightly rotated, so they would appear as "pegged laterals" and so I drew that.

For the first time, I felt a grin tugging at the corners of my mouth. I knew I'd nailed him.

When I was finished, the detectives showed me a dark Polaroid snapshot of the guy, but I couldn't tell much except for one thing: he was wearing a baseball cap. No wonder she couldn't describe his hair! It was my first lesson in how to direct a forensic sketch session.

However, the really frustrating thing about the Polaroid was not the baseball cap, but the fact that the guy wasn't smiling.

There was too much riding on this for me to take a chance. "Lt. McWilliams," I asked, "Would you mind terribly having this man brought up here so that we can see his teeth?"

Surprised, but game, McWilliams sent a detective to bring the man from the jail. They corralled him in the small office, next to where I had placed the drawing and I asked him to smile.

He did.

And there were those lovely little pegged laterals.

Everybody gathered around the sketch was wildly impressed, but like most artists, I wasn't really satisfied with the likeness I'd made. But if there was one thing I'd learned by then, it was to pretend otherwise. So I acted as pleased as they were.

They took the guy back down to the jail, the dingbat soon left and Lt. McWilliams asked for my phone number.

I gave it to him and another detective was summoned to drive me home.

And for the first time, I felt petrified. What was going to happen next? Would they drop my number in a drawer and forget about it? Would I get a *real* chance to prove what I could do?

Was I on my way or just on my way home?

One of the things they don't teach you in *Trailblazer 101* is that when you are the very first person to do a thing, to beat down a door and open up opportunities for others to follow, there aren't any textbooks to read, no courses to take, not even a mentor to guide and help you. You're on your own, baby, and every single lesson you learn comes the hard way.

It only took a couple of weeks for my first "hard knocks" lesson.

I got a call from the Robbery division to come in and do a witness sketch for a robbery case. (Years later, I learned from Lt. McWilliams that he'd been so impressed with my work that very first time that he was sold, "from then on.")

I didn't know that then, of course. I was excited, but this time, I was really nervous. Although I'd done thousands of portraits and had done many sketches of persons described to me by other people—I had never actually sat down with a crime victim before.

This was *it*, the real thing.

It wasn't so much that I wanted to impress the detectives, although that was certainly part of it, because the better I did, the more likely they would call me back; but as a victim of crime myself, I really, *really* wanted to help this witness. I believed that God had put me there for this purpose and I wanted to do the best I possibly could.

But there was nothing, *nothing*, easy about that first crime sketch. For one thing, I didn't yet have a parking permit, so I had to park six blocks away. Six blocks is no big problem—unless you happen to be hauling more than fifty pounds of gear. And in Houston, sweat is a way of life. So I arrived at my first appointment sweating like Michael Jordan in the third quarter of the play-offs and feeling pretty much like it, too.

The detectives were glad to see me and everybody was expecting to handle my time with the witness as they had our trial run, so they were surprised when I told them that I needed to be alone with the witness. Still, they were agreeable, although they didn't really have anywhere to put me. I wound up in what turned out to be, basically, a storeroom that was about the size of two phone booths.

I squeezed in and set up my easel. *You can do this,* I whispered to myself. *Show 'em what you can do.* By the time they brought me the witness, a slender, small-statured man of Middle Eastern descent, I was ready.

However, there was one tiny problem.

He spoke Farsi and I didn't.

LESSON NUMBER ONE: When dealing with a non-English speaking witness, start by asking him for the words in his language that designate such things as "nose," "eyes" and "hair." This is a charming icebreaker and also facilitates the sketching process.

LESSON NUMBER TWO: Have a small sketchpad and pencil ready so that, if the witness still has trouble communicating, he can draw the part of the face he wishes to describe.

LESSON NUMBER THREE: Don't freak out.

No, I didn't freak out, at least, not to the guy's face, but I also didn't know lessons one, two or three, either. Not then. The upshot of it all was that the witness grew so frustrated and discouraged that he finally put his hands over his face, shook his head slowly and silently looked away.

All of which would have been devastating enough if I hadn't had to endure the door swinging open every ten minutes and a confused detective saying, "Oh! Sorry! I didn't know anyone was in here."

LESSON NUMBER FOUR: Crime files are the same size as any other business-related files: 8.5" by 11". Therefore, it's real handy to the detective if the sketch you present to him is, well, 8.5" by 11". Of course, I didn't know that. I was used to using a sketchpad with the dimensions of 18" by 24", so when I turned over that first awkward and, eventually, useless sketch—it was huge. They probably had to fold it over twice to cram it in the file.

They paid me for my work from the coffee fund.

After that first experience, I didn't think things could be much worse in terms of a crime sketching session, but I was young and naive. I didn't realize they could be *much* worse.

A couple of weeks later, I got a call from a detective in Sex Crimes to come in and do a witness sketch. The victim had been picked up by a marked cab, but rather than being taken to her destination, she was instead taken to a remote location, where the cab driver repeatedly raped her. This galvanized me to get over my earlier failure and help a fellow rape victim find justice. I was thrilled to get the opportunity and lugged my stuff back down to HPD.

The detectives showed me to an interview room in the Homicide division and soon brought in the rape victim and her best girlfriend.

LESSON NUMBER FIVE: Never let anybody sit in on a sketch, not the cops and definitely not a best girlfriend.

From beginning to end, that gal never shut her mouth. Running chatter continued the entire time I was setting up my equipment and thanks to her, I never was able to get any sort of description from the victim herself.

Every time the victim said something like, "his hair was curly and dark and kind of long," her friend piped up and claimed loudly, "but you said it was straight and short." When the girlfriend wasn't changing the witness's description, she was distracting her and inhibiting the witness's focus— actually upsetting the witness more than helping her.

More than once I wanted to scream at the girlfriend, "SHUT UP! You weren't there, were you? Don't offer any opinions on *anything*, all right?" But of course, I didn't.

By the time I got back out to my car with my gear, my hair was sweat-soaked to my scalp and my spirit matched my appearance. I plopped down in the front seat of my car, leaned my head on the steering wheel and thought, *What a complete waste of time.*

However upset I was by two failures in a row, it did not seem to faze the detectives.

I will be forever grateful to those detectives who kept calling me even when my sketches led nowhere. They trusted in my talent even when I didn't, even took time to sit down with me and offer encouragement when I was ready to give up.

Because I wanted to give up. Many times.

In early July, 1982, I got a call from a Detective Douglas Osterberg in Homicide. When we met I saw Osterberg was huge—6'4" tall, with a shock of curly blonde hair. Later I learned that his appearance had earned him the nickname of "Big Bird." I also found out later that he had once played football at Wichita State University, where I had twirled baton during my early collegiate years, before I moved to Los Angeles.

But we didn't know what we had in common when we first met and Osterberg was not particularly pleased when I told him that I wanted to work with the witness alone. After all, I was a civilian and he was protective of his case, but I must say he respected me enough not only to grant me my wish, but to set me up in a lieutenant's office, which was spacious and well-lighted.

He didn't tell me much about the witness, other than that the man had been bicycling in Houston's Memorial Park when he had come upon one man stabbing another man to death. Osterberg warned me that the witness was "hysterical" and "freaked out," which was about as emotional and descriptive as Osterberg was likely to get. Ever.

The young man who had seen the crime was in his early twenties and clearly, this was the first time he had ever witnessed a violent act. The more he described what had happened, the more upset he became. "Hysterical" was not an exaggeration.

I decided to take some time just to soothe him and let him calm down before we went to work on the drawing.

Eventually, he told me that he had been riding his bike in a thickly wooded section of the park, which is located in an upscale area of the community, when he heard a disturbance. Something about it caused him to slip off his bike and sneak a peak over some bushes. There he saw one man face-down on the ground and another man straddling him, his fist up in the air, clutching a large knife. As the horrified witness looked on, the attacker brought his fist with the knife down *smack*, over and over, into the other man's back. In his shock, the witness made a rustling noise. The killer whirled around and looked straight at him before leaping to his feet and running away.

The bicyclist hurried over to the victim and the one detail that kept repeating itself over and over in his horrified mind was that every time the poor man breathed, dark blood from the wounds in his back bubbled up and out in a macabre fountain.

And then, he saw the victim had stopped breathing.

My distraught witness scrambled down the pathway, screaming for help. To his astonishment, he stumbled upon a man who looked exactly like the killer, only he was wearing different clothes. The witness recoiled and almost screamed again, but even in his panic, he instinctively knew that this could not be the killer, since the attacker had no time to change clothes and furthermore, this man didn't *act* like he'd just killed somebody. The witness asked the man to call the police.

Now, sitting with me at the police department, the witness kept obsessing about this other man. "I know it wasn't the killer," he kept saying, "It couldn't have been the killer, but I'm telling you, he *looked just like him.*"

"Look," I said finally. "Let's not worry about that right now, okay? The thing is, this man you saw looked like the killer, so let's just see if we can draw that *look*, all right? And we won't worry about who it is. We'll let the police take care of that."

"But I really didn't see him all that long," he kept insisting. "I can't really describe him to you."

LESSON NUMBER SIX: Witnesses often say they didn't get very good looks and can't describe the suspects. What most crime witnesses don't realize is that their subconscious took better snapshots of what they saw than they can consciously recall. A good forensic sketch artist can almost always get a usable sketch from the most reluctant witness.

I know that now, of course. But I sure didn't know it then.

To further complicate matters, the witness insisted that I somehow capture the same expression he'd seen on the killer's face during the moment of murder.

LESSON NUMBER SEVEN: Don't worry about capturing the same homicidal expression remembered by the crime victim. Most people don't look like serial murderers. The people who recognize suspects by forensic sketches displayed in the newspaper or on the news are usually friends who normally don't see that expression anyway. A standard expression is one that will most often be recognized.

At that time, I struggled with the witness for more than three hours in a vain attempt to capture the expression he so vividly remembered.

LESSON NUMBER EIGHT: Don't hesitate to use visual aids. For one thing, I didn't have an *FBI Facial Identification Catalogue* to help this witness. For four years, in fact, I worked without one. When you work without the catalogue to help you, the witness has to find some way to come up with descriptions that they can communicate as to how a suspect's eyebrows or nose looks. It's laborious, tedious and needlessly difficult. I can't emphasize enough how much easier it is just to flip to a page of eyebrows and say, "Select a pair that most closely resembles what you remember." It does not "contaminate" a witness's memory. On the contrary, having a number of choices facilitates it.

But with our witness that day, we were on our own and by the time I'd rendered a likeness that received my witness's tepid approval, I was absolutely, completely drained. Nothing I had ever done—physically or mentally—had been more exhausting and I was convinced the sketch was terrible, one of the worst I'd ever done.

I couldn't get out of that place fast enough.

As I handed over the sketch to Detective Osterberg and dragged my easel out of the building, I was convinced that I was a total failure.

I drove down Houston Avenue, turned down White Oak Street and when I came to a vacant lot, I pulled in, parked the car and burst into tears. Wailing and beating my hands on the steering wheel, I screamed, "I'm never going back there again! Never, ever again! I can't take it anymore."

All I had wanted to do was catch *one* person, just ONE, who had committed an evil act against another person. I'd been so certain that this was something I could do, so sure of it and now here I'd worked a robbery, a rape and a murder and what had I accomplished?

A big, fat zero.

"Quit torturing yourself," I sobbed. "You just wanted to catch someone who was like the guy who hurt you and you couldn't even do that! You're just a silly, tired housewife. Go home. Be a full-time mommy to your baby and let the big boys catch the bad guys."

Snuffling, wiping my eyes, I put the car in gear and headed home, utterly and completely convinced that I was, most definitely, a total failure.

A few days later, as I was standing at the kitchen table, trying to get Brent to sit still long enough to swallow a bite or two for lunch, the phone rang. An almost jubilant Detective Osterberg said, "You did it, girl!"

"Did what?" I grouched. So convinced was I of my own failure at that point that it didn't even register.

"You helped us find the guy!"

"What?"

I guess Osterberg could sense that my frustration ran deep. He suggested that I come down to the HPD so that he could talk to me.

"Is tomorrow all right?" I murmured. He said it was fine.

As I hung up the phone I grabbed Brent, who was attempting to stand up in his high chair. I was so shocked by Osterberg's call that I was actually afraid to believe what I had heard. I didn't even tell Sid; in fact, I barely even accepted it myself. Could it be true that I had actually had a success?

I didn't know how to feel successful. I showed up the next day like a kid who's been ordered to the principal's office. The detective greeted me with a huge smile on his face. Then he sat me down, opened up the police report and explained what had happened.

The morning after they had released my sketch to both newspaper and television media outlets, Osterberg had received a phone call from a man who was completely unnerved. "Listen," he'd said urgently, "there's a picture of me in the paper this morning. Spittin' image."

Osterberg had said dryly, "Well, are you my man?"

The distraught young man, actually yelling over the phone in his distress, assured Osterberg that no, he wasn't the guy, but he knew who was. He went on to explain that he and his roommate bore an uncanny resemblance to one another. He and his roommate (the suspect) and a couple other guys had been at Memorial Park the day of the murder and after they'd driven home, the suspect went to bed.

The informant was watching the 10 P.M. news when the murder was reported and the sketch displayed on the television screen. He'd been so flabbergasted by what he'd seen—basically a picture of himself as a murder suspect—that he'd stayed up until 2:30 A.M. to watch a rebroadcast of the news report.

If that wasn't bad enough, the next morning, he'd started getting phone calls from buddies saying things like, "Hey, man, did you kill somebody in the park?"

The whole situation had shaken him up so badly that he'd called the police himself and agreed to meet Osterberg at a coffee shop. "I couldn't believe it," the detective told me, "when I first saw the guy, it looked like someone had taken a photograph of your sketch."

Furthermore, the informant agreed to take the detectives back to his house where they found the knife and a pair of underwear the killer had used to clean the blood off the knife.

"We brought the guy in," said Osterberg triumphantly, "and no lie, those two could be brothers. Anyway," he said with a huge grin, "he confessed, Lois. We got him!"

Osterberg went on to explain that, although the suspect claimed self-defense, the killing was actually a sexual thrill-kill. The seventeen-year-old had seen a movie called *Cruising*, where a homosexual serial killer was stabbing his victims to death while they were performing fellatio on him. (Later, in the trial at which he was convicted and sentenced to life in prison, the movie was shown to the jury.) Had he not been caught for this murder, this evil young man most likely would have killed again.

I guess Osterberg could see the self-doubt in my eyes, because he went out of his way to claim that they would not have been able to solve the case without my sketch. Though "Big Bird" isn't much of the cheerleader type, he said in his own calm way, "You did good, girl. You did good."

I thanked him and, trying not to act too gushy and excited, I left. I drove down the same street I'd driven down just a few days before, when I'd sobbed and sworn to myself that I would never do this work again, that I was a total failure.

And I realized three very important things. One, that if, as the detective said, this guy could have killed again, then I had helped to save some future victim's life. This was an incredibly powerful realization.

Two, I had helped to capture a sexual thrill-killer—someone who was very much like the same monster who had attacked me.

"I got you!" I shouted and I realized that it wasn't just *this* killer I had "gotten," but in a way, the one who had tried to kill *me*, as well. It was an enormous, satisfying victory.

I was no longer a victim.

In some spiritual, visceral, emotional way, I had reached back in time and put my arms around that younger, terrified Lois. I was telling her that everything was, indeed, going to be all right. That nothing that had happened to her had been in vain. It was an incredibly powerful moment. It worked a healing on my soul and my spirit that can be described as nothing less than magical.

And three, I realized that if a drawing that I'd done was worse, to my way of thinking, than anything I'd done in high school and yet had still somehow become a valuable investigative tool, instrumental in catching a bad guy...then this was something I could do for the rest of my life.

This gave a heft to my work, a genuine importance, that I had never felt before. Instead of painting a landscape or a portrait that was meant to be beautiful, exciting and inspiring to the beholder, I had turned out a sketch I considered to be just pitiful, sloppy, poorly-done...and yet, the results it had produced made *me* feel beautiful, excited and inspired.

As I drove down the street and into my future, a great smile of joy stretched across my face. And I thought to myself, *They can't hide their faces with me around*.

For the next few weeks, I floated around in a whole new world, a smile on my lips, my heart afire. I was ready to jump into the fray and make my mark. The days of fear and trembling whenever the evening news came on were over. My attitude toward the bad guys I saw paraded on the news and in the papers now was more like, *Just let me at 'em!*

And if it had been left up to just me, my sketchpad, an empty room and a crime witness, I could probably end my story right here. But the real world doesn't work that way, unfortunately. In spite of my eagerness to tackle the bad guys and bring 'em down, I had a couple of little things standing in my path that I had to figure a way around first.

Like cops.

Chapter Five:

Breaking and Entering

In *Breaking and Entering* (Pocketbooks, 1997), a book which had a profound influence on me, Connie Fletcher interviewed more than one hundred female law enforcement officers who had broken new ground in the early days of the women's movement. Through grit, persistence, hard work and valiant spirits, they had forged new paths for all women who would follow them in the law enforcement field. Included in the book were such trailblazers as the first woman Texas Ranger, the first woman S.W.A.T. sniper for the Los Angeles Police Department, the first woman Drug Enforcement Administration agent, the first female bomb technician on a major metropolitan force and others. Many of these women had gone on to achieve great distinction in their careers, some even climbing to the rank of Chief of Police.

They all described how extraordinarily difficult it was for women to break into such a tradition-bound all-male bastion, how they endured sexual harassment, ostracism, loneliness and even danger—in some cases, male officers would not respond to a female officer requesting back-up. They had to put up with office walls papered with pornography, isolated and cramped quarters for changing into their uniforms (since most departments didn't have separate locker rooms yet) and many other indignities. Again and again, female officers and agents from all branches of law enforcement used the same word to describe how they felt: "outsider."

They explained what they had to go through to gain the respect of their male peers. Many of them told with wry amusement how, once they had shown their willingness to leap into street fights, fists flailing, they were instantly accepted by their male brethren.

Others detailed how they learned to parry back-and-forth with rude banter to gain acceptance. Some described responding to sexual harassment, not by filing grievances—which always resulted in instant and career-long ostracism—but by "knocking him on his ass."

Basically, they had to prove themselves.

Proving herself—that is what each and every one of those brave women had to do to "break and enter" into "the brotherhood" of law enforcement officers—she had to prove herself. Not just once, but over and over again.

I kept thinking to myself as I read about them how, though it was hard for women who had stood side-by-side with their male counterparts at the police and agency academies, had ridden patrol with them, fought with them, risked their lives with them...it was for even harder for *me*, a civilian, to break through that same barrier.

And not just as a civilian—that was hard enough. And not just as a woman.

But as an *artist*.

Ask most any cop what they think of artists and they'll use words like "flake" or "weirdo" to describe their ideas of what an artist is. Add to that the fact that I was a young mother, a *housewife,* and the task before me when I first started to work my way into the Houston Police Department was immense.

And if that wasn't enough of an obstacle, there was that other delicate little matter...how to pay me.

While it's true that I had a burning passion to do this work and would have gladly done it for free if I'd had that luxury, the truth of the matter is that my husband and I were struggling to raise a growing family. I needed to help support that family as best I could with what talents I had to offer. At that point, I was making most of my income as a portrait artist and I was busy enough at it that I actually was able to put my child (eventually, children) in day care during the day so that I could work without interruption. There were times when all that kept us from running out of diapers and baby food was a portrait commission.

When I got a call from the police department to do a forensic sketch, I had to drop everything, pack up fifty pounds of gear into my ten-year-old car, navigate downtown Houston traffic (paying for gas myself) and find parking (again, at my own expense). Then I sat down with a witness for what was, since I was still learning, a session that was likely to run more than two hours. Afterward I packed everything up again and hauled it home.

Every time I had a forensic sketch to do, it took half a day from my calendar—time I could have spent at home, finishing up a portrait. (And of course, there was day care for my children to pay for.)

I couldn't do my work for free and, anyway, if I *had* done it for free, I felt I never would have gotten any respect at all. I was a professional, this was my profession and I told myself I deserved fair compensation for it.

None of this detracts from the passion I had for my work—and still do—but working as a forensic artist created quite a problem in the beginning, because cash-strapped police departments everywhere operate on very tight budgets that are set for them by the city council and there was no budget in the HPD for an artist. For several years, I had to be paid out of petty cash.

Also, there was the matter of…What should I charge?

As with every other aspect of my work, I had no guidelines to follow and had to make the rules up as I went along. And that is exactly what I did. My husband was making twenty-five dollars an hour as a construction plumber. I decided that I should be able to earn at least as much, so that is what I charged. As my husband's fees went up, so did mine. When I was finally put on a regular salary seven years after I started, I made seventy-five dollars an hour—the same thing Sid would have made if he installed a water heater.

Since I couldn't fight with cops or ride with them to prove myself, I decided what I needed was a series of dazzling successes, and as luck would have it, that's exactly what happened.

Houston was teeming with crime, but if Homicide detectives thought they were overworked with 300 to 600 murders a year, Robbery was worse. Houston was riddled with about 18,000 robberies a year. That averaged out to 1,500 a month, or fifty a day—roughly two robberies every single hour of every single day.

Needless to say, the detectives in the Robbery division were swamped, shorthanded and eager to try anything that would give them some help, so most of my calls in the early days came from Robbery. As my friend Lieu-

tenant Manny Zamora pointed out to me once, robbers tend to keep rob-
bing until they are caught or killed, so composites work well at catching
robbers.

At one point there was a rash of Radio Shack hold-ups. The perpetrator was always stereotypically described as an early-twenties black male,
medium to muscular build, 5'10" tall. Yet when I sketched for three different witnesses I came up with three distinctly different men. One even had
a large mole over his left eyebrow.

A few weeks later, they ran a raid to serve a warrant on a warehouse
that was found to be loaded with stolen Radio Shack stuff. They arrested
five men at the site, but when they brought them in, the men refused to
give their identities. (This is a common tactic to hold up the police investigation and avoid, or at least postpone, being charged with a given offense.)

However, once I had done my work, the Robbery detectives armed
themselves with copies of my three sketches, went into the holding cells,
pointed to the guys who resembled my sketches and said, among other
things, "You robbed the Radio Shack on Long Point Ave, and you—back
there with the mole—you robbed the one on Forty-third and T.C. Jester."

Each of the stunned robbers, assuming the detectives must have actual
photographs of them, confessed—or rather, to be specific, snitched on each
other.

Thus almost from the beginning, Robbery "caught on" to the significance of my work and called me in.

Sometimes robbery cases spilled over into sex crimes. An old man,
watering his lawn, spotted a young man driving down the street who
looked like a sketch of mine he'd seen; he wrote down the car license number and called it in. Not only was the man identified as the assailant of the
sexual assault victim I had interviewed for the sketch, but it turned out he
was also known as the "bandana bandit." Wearing a sort of "old west" disguise, he robbed entire church congregations, patrons of restaurants, groups
at ball fields playing softball—turns out he'd perpetrated hundreds of robberies, but the only victim who'd seen his face was the one he raped.

In another, even more high-profile case, women joggers were being
assaulted and raped while frequenting a popular jogging trail in Memorial
Park. There was a great outcry throughout the city for the police to catch
the criminal. Luckily, one of his victims gave me a good description for a
sketch, and the police set a trap.

They outfitted Paula Franks, a beautiful, athletic female detective, with a wire device and waited in a white van near the park, keeping a watchful eye out while Paula jogged up and down the trail. Each one of the officers in the van had a copy of my sketch and before every pass down the trail, Paula took another hard look at the composite.

After one long, fruitless day, as rain started to fall, the detectives urged Paula to come in, but she said, "No, I wanna take another pass." Almost immediately, a man passed by her on a bicycle. Moments later, he ran up behind her, and glimpsing his face, she recognized him as the rapist. Just before he grabbed her, she shouted, "It's that son of a bitch! NOW!"

But as he gripped Paula in the crook of his elbow and began choking her, she realized that the rain had disrupted her radio signal. The detectives in the van could not hear her. But as she fought him, one of the detectives spotted the struggle. Instantly they all piled out of the van and onto the attacker.

It was a particularly satisfying arrest for me.

Another rapist, known as the "San Felipe" rapist, was turned in by his own father when the older man recognized his son from one of my sketches. Detectives provided corroborating evidence when the disheartened father realized that the various vehicles described by victims matched trucks and cars belonging to him that he had loaned his son at different times.

As word of these cases spread, a number of officers were very grateful for my help and became supportive of my work. They said encouraging things about me within the department, urging other detectives to try me out. Lieutenant Don McWilliams—the officer who gave me my first opportunity—and Captain Bobby Frank Adams of Homicide, as well as Deputy Chief Charles McClelland, were three of the most encouraging. They will always have my affection and gratitude.

Of course, from the beginning, Robbery detectives were happy to have my help and I also received tremendous support from the Juvenile Sex Crimes division. Children who have been sexually assaulted can't give detectives the make of a car or its license tag number, have no clue as to how tall someone is or how much he weighs and so on, but children do make superb witnesses as far as describing a person's face. I usually got very good sketches from child witnesses and Juvenile Sex Crimes was always grateful and quick to call.

But for every detective who saw the potential in my work and encouraged me to keep at it, there were ten more who thought a woman civilian had no place in law enforcement and that any kind of art was a waste of time and money.

One cop was particularly obstructive. Word trickled down through the grapevine that he was telling other detectives that if they wanted to use me on a case they would have to pay for me out of their own overtime fund.

Since cops are never paid well, to make extra Christmas or vacation money they depend on overtime pay. Sometimes, during times of particularly tight budget constraints, they are told that there is no more overtime pay available. This is particularly awful for detectives working homicides, because when their shift is up, they have to turn over the case on which they are working to the next shift—an almost impossible situation. The new detectives have no way of knowing what witnesses have already told investigating officers; traumatized victims have often developed rapport with the detectives on the scene and may not want to talk to the new guys and so on.

When an officer refused to be fair about using me, it shut down any chance I might have had to work with crime victims who could have been helped by my skills. Sometimes their cases went unsolved, because one hardheaded old so-and-so didn't like having a woman civilian around his police division.

Outsider.

No matter how hard I worked or how many successes I had, I was still an outsider, still struggling for respect, still trying to prove myself.

After two years of this, I decided that I needed—no, was *starved for*—some extra training to help me do better the most difficult work I'd ever done. But I also knew that I needed some criminal justice polish on my resume—something that would certify me in a legitimate way, be instantly recognized and respected by law enforcement professionals.

And I knew just the place to get it.

The FBI Academy.

Now, being a housewife artist trying to prove herself to a bunch of macho male cops in the 1980s was tough but it was *nothing*—a merry-go-round ride at the playground—compared to trying to break through the concrete wall that was and is a major metropolitan bureaucracy.

The first cement block I ran into came when I inquired into enrolling in the FBI Police Composite Artist Training Course at what is technically known as the National Academy at Quantico, Virginia.

I was told that I had to have a legitimate job at a law enforcement agency.

So I asked several times at Homicide if they would consider creating a full-time job for me with the division, but I was told again and again that they didn't have it in their budget. Neither did Robbery or any of the other divisions I asked. The economy was down; crime was up; city hall had fiscal problems.

With a constant stream of portrait commissions, a toddler at home and another baby on the way, I let it ride for months that turned into years. But there was never enough work freelancing at the HPD to replace what I was earning by doing portraits. Of course, everyone wanted portraits for Christmas presents, so every December I worked night and day painting—forget little Christmasy joys like decorating, baking and shopping—I was too busy painting portraits.

But I didn't give up. After my daughter's birth in 1985, I started asking again about being hired on to the department so that I could attend the FBI Academy training course in forensic art.

Robbery sent me to Homicide and Homicide sent me to Robbery— a familiar pattern that was getting harder and harder to take as my successes mounted and more detectives began to call for my services.

In her book, *Breaking and Entering*, Connie Fletcher interviewed one female officer who commented that, in the beginning, she never got eye contact from male officers. In a sense, they would look over the heads of the female officers, excluding them from the conversation.

In my case, it was phone calls I never got. Not phone calls asking me to do sketches—*follow-up* phone calls, telling me that we'd had a hit, that a case had been solved, at least in part, because of one of my sketches. If I called the detectives myself to inquire, they never answered my voice mails. I had to show up at the departments where they were milling around the offices. As soon as they *saw* me, they would tell me we'd had a hit.

But I had to be there.

And of course, I didn't have an office at the police department or even a place to stash my things, so I just had to show up from time to time and walk through the offices to find out how things were going with a particular sketch or case. Which meant making a special trip downtown…

One day, on an elevator ride up to Robbery to see how things were going, the doors opened up onto Homicide and I thought, *What the hell.*

I wandered down the halls, and as he always did when he spotted me, Captain Bobby Frank Adams called out to me. Capt. Adams has always been a favorite of mine at the HPD. Tall, angular, with a cowboy drawl and cowboy sex appeal, he is immensely popular with the detectives in his command. He told anyone who asked that he thought I was a genius, and he even told one television reporter that he thought I was "psychic."

I stepped into his office and, after a moment or two of small talk, I blurted out, "I need to get a job here if I'm going to be able to go to the FBI Academy. The federal government pays for it and I need the training, but they won't take me unless I'm employed by a law enforcement agency."

Capt. Adams' eyes widened, "Did you hear about that meeting I was at this morning?"

Of course I hadn't heard about any meeting. How would I hear about meetings? I didn't even hear when my own cases had been solved.

"No," I said. "What are you talking about?"

He folded his arms across his chest. "You knew about the meeting."

"No."

"You had to."

"I did not."

By this point, we were both getting annoyed, but when he finally realized that I had no clue what he was talking about, he explained that the new Chief, Lee Brown, had called a big meeting of division heads and had told them that if they wanted to start any new programs or positions, they were to take those requests straight to Cindy Smith.

After carefully copying down her name and phone numbers on his Rolodex, he handed me her card as if it were a velvet pouch of diamonds.

My heart pounded. Suddenly I had the name of a faceless bureaucrat who could make or break my whole career in forensic art. I knew I couldn't just bluster into a meeting with her unprepared.

So I went home. As if I were studying for a final exam in college, I gathered together facts and statistics and arranged photo comparisons of my best work: mug shots of captured suspects next to my sketches. Then I planned my wardrobe—actually waiting until I'd lost the baby-weight from my daughter Tiffany's birth so that I could fit into my nicest suit.

My biggest fear was that I'd do all this, make my pitch, only to have this faceless bureaucrat nod blandly, say, "thank you," and then do absolutely nothing while my life hung in limbo. When I was finally ready to make my pitch, I wanted an answer and I wanted it *then*, not six months later. If the answer was no, then at least I could appeal—to the chief or the mayor or God, if I had to, *somebody*—but I couldn't just let things hang. I'd been twisting slowly in the wind for years and I was growing weary and frustrated, sick of people like the cop who said detectives would have to pay me out of their overtime.

Just before meeting with Ms. Smith, I called up my sister Adonna, the family genius, and asked her what I could say that would force Cindy Smith to give me an answer on the spot, without necessarily sounding rude or belligerent.

Adonna thought for a moment, then said, "Say this: *What is your determination on this matter?*"

Okay. Got it.

I called for an appointment. On the day of the meeting, gripping my papers and trying to stand as tall as my 5'5" frame would allow, I entered a large, empty boardroom. Taking a seat, I carefully laid out examples of my many successes on the polished table, putting together as impressive an array as I could.

Then I waited.

And waited.

Finally, the door opened and Ms. Smith came in. Slender, well-dressed and attractive, she gave me a tepid handshake.

She did not sit down.

Instead, she stood, her back turned halfway to me, her head in profile, arms folded tightly across her narrow chest and listened while sliding sideways glances at me from time to time as if I were some unpleasant reptilian creature plopped on her garden wall.

She scarcely looked at my artwork and mug shots. Her face was impassive.

After briefly detailing a number of my successes and mentioning the number of solved cases directly attributed to my work, which amounted to one out of every three, I ended my little presentation by saying, "Detroit, Michigan has *five* artists available, yet they are *one-third* the size of Houston. Cleveland, Ohio has *three* artists on hand for their detectives to use, yet they are *one-fifth* the size of Houston.

"At the very least," I concluded, "Houston should have *one.*"

My passion for my work, the driving desire I'd had ever since my attack to make my life *matter*, infused every word. I was breathless by the time I was finished, my cheeks hot with anticipation. Normally, I have a very confident demeanor—especially where my work is concerned—but this woman's cold indifference unsettled me.

And with good reason. Abruptly turning her back square to me, she headed for the door, saying only, "We're finished here."

I had no idea what I had done or said that had offended her, or why she seemed to dislike me. But this was my greatest fear and I could not stand by and let it happen.

I sprang to my feet and hurried over to trap her before she could leave the room. Looking her straight in the eye for the first time, I said, "What is your determination on this matter?"

Clearly, my reaction had caught her off-guard. She could no longer dismiss me like a fly beneath the swatter. I could see her mind racing behind her imperious expression. Finally, in an arrogant tone, she said, "Just because there is a position created does not mean that you'll get it!"

WHAT?

I could not believe what I had just heard. For five years I had worked so hard trying to break through the barrier of the HPD, using my talents, gifts and my own life tragedy to help crime victims, all alone with no one to mentor or help me, and she had the *unmitigated gall* to even *suggest* that they might, at long last, create the position I had begged for...*and hire someone else to fill it?*

"No!" I cried. "*I'm* the only one doing this work! There's no confusion about that! I'm the only one—"

By this time, Ms. Smith had brushed past me and walked out the door. My last words echoed down the hall to her receding back, "—the only one in this whole area who's doing this work!"

By the time I reached to gather up my papers, my hands were shaking, no, *I* was shaking, from head to foot. In my entire career—my entire life—

I had never encountered such rudeness, not even from those male cops who didn't want me around.

The rudeness, though, I could handle. I was a big girl, after all. But the thought that I had done all this work and agonized for so long just to have my golden opportunity handed over to someone else made me sick.

But there was nothing else I could do that day.

I went home, occupied myself with my babies and tried not to obsess about it. After two endless days, Ms. Smith called me to say that an officer would create a "study of the situation" and get back to me.

Weeks crept past. I took care of my children, painted portraits, answered calls from the HPD, tried to hold on to my fragile sanity.

Finally, I got a call from a female police officer who said that the city council had agreed to create a "line of funds" that would be dedicated to my freelance fees when I did composites. It wasn't a job with health insurance and benefits, but it was enough.

Enough to get me into the FBI Academy.

Although when I applied I was told there would be at least a three-year wait to gain admittance to the forensic art course, I tried to have confidence. After all, I felt by this time I'd had enough experience and enough success to know my drawings were at least as good as other artists' and better than most. Despite their words about delay, I was accepted almost immediately.

I was excited to have this opportunity; the FBI represents the best of the best, not just in this country, but in the world... but to tell you the truth, one of the things that excited me most was the chance to run away from home for a couple of weeks.

After all, my son was four years old and my baby girl eighteen months. I'd been in a frenzy of non-stop activity from the time my son was an infant, between running back and forth to the HPD, trying to prove myself and build a reputation at the department, painting portraits portraits portraits for extra money, keeping my marriage strong and caring for two toddlers. Now, though it was hard to leave them, I knew I had to. I loved my children and husband more than life itself, but if I was to be the police artist I wanted to be I needed this.

And to make it sweeter, here I was going to get to climb on a plane and fly off to this Wonderful Land of Oz—a place where, all day long, I'd be surrounded by *grown-ups*; and not just that, but grown-ups *who did the same thing I did!*

I was elated to think that for once—for the first time, actually—I'd be spending time with *other forensic artists.*

For the very first time, I would not be alone.

I was so eager to learn and to share experiences and just to soak up the atmosphere of my chosen profession without having to explain to some-one what I did, or how I did it, or why. I wouldn't have to sugar-coat it the way I did with my civilian friends (hiding the more gruesome and heart-wrenching details of some of my cases) and I wouldn't have to hold back, trying not to be too pushy, the way I usually did with my cop colleagues. (With every difficult case, I always wanted to help, but was afraid that if I imposed myself on the investigation, they would think I was trying to tell them how to do their jobs—or worse, was indulging in the worst sort of ambulance-chasing. So I usually hung back and waited for them to ask me, which could be terribly frustrating sometimes.)

This was a chance just to be myself, surrounded by people who under-stood completely. Even my beloved husband really did not fully compre-hend the kinds of things I saw and heard each day at the police department and our closest friends were, well, civilians. And at this point, though I was still technically a civilian myself, the truth is I didn't feel like one. But at the same time, I was still not buddy-buddy with the cops who called me in to do drawings, either; we didn't socialize, or invite one another over to each other's cookouts.

So it was a lonely, in-between kind of feeling in those days, before I went to work full-time at the HPD, and I was really looking forward to the camaraderie I hoped to find among the other police artists.

I flew into Washington, D.C. and a large bus picked up all the atten-dees. There were eighteen of us. It was December, 1986 and it was snowing.

We arrived at the Academy, which was laid out much like a college campus. Classrooms were separated from the two seven-floor dorm towers by what were affectionately known as "gerbil tubes"—rounded plexiglass corridors between brick buildings that resemble a maze in a gerbil cage.

In many ways, the dormitory rooms at the FBI Academy were pretty much made for men. The ceilings were high and the furniture had been crafted with six-foot males in mind. The built-in drawers were so high that I could barely see over them—and *that's* where the mirror was located. The *only* mirror. On university campuses, most women's dorm rooms have a full-length mirror on the back of the door. Not here. (Apparently, men don't have to check and make sure their slips aren't showing and their pantyhose don't have a run.)

No bathtub, either. Only showers. Two rooms housed four people, who all shared a single bathroom and shower.

Female attendees said never to leave your curtains open, because across the way, male trainees were learning all about high-tech zoom photography. The gossip was they had amassed quite a little collection of photographs from the women's dorms.

We didn't know if it was true or not, but nonetheless, we all dressed well away from the windows.

The dining hall was legendary—the feds really knew how to feed you. Every meal was an all-you-can-eat cafeteria-style spread, complete with an ice cream machine in the middle of the room with every kind of topping imaginable. If you preferred, you could pile the ice cream onto your slice of pie or cake—a dangerous temptation for those of us who were only going to be there for two weeks, but those who were staying for a full thirteen-week course in law enforcement worked those calories off big-time. It really was "Oz," because there was a grueling obstacle course (featured in the opening scenes of the movie *Silence of the Lambs*) that was known as the "Yellow Brick Road." All attendees of the long course had to complete it—even if they were in their fifties. There was also an Olympic-sized swimming pool, a weight room, a sauna and a hot tub for relaxing after a workout.

Then, of course, there was "The Boardroom" where everyone went at night after a hard day at the Emerald City and where beer and simple mixed drinks were served until about 10:30 P.M. (what my daddy used to call "preacher son's time"). You could take the elevator from your dormitory floor straight to the Boardroom.

On the weekends we all went into D.C. to see the sights, the museums, monuments and landmarks of our democracy.

But it was in class that I really blossomed. Any instruction at the National Academy is top-of-the-line; experts in every discipline are brought in to share their expertise. We watched as an anthropologist put on a demonstration in skull reconstruction. A photo-retouch person gave us an airbrush demonstration. A forensic artist who'd been highly effective in the business for some time provided some suggestions for success. We also learned child age-progression.

One of the most useful skills I picked up was the ability to do a full-frontal drawing of someone's face that you've only see in profile. This is extremely valuable, since so many witnesses say, "I only saw him in profile," or, "I just caught a glimpse of the top of his head," or whatever. All of us who attended the forensic art course at Quantico learned to extrapolate a full face from a partial, side-only photo.

Another very valuable skill I learned was how to use visual aids, such as the *FBI Facial Identification Catalogue*. Developed in the early 1960s by forensic artists in what is now known by the unwieldy name of the Investigative and Prosecutive Graphics Unit of the FBI, the catalogue is divided into facial features such as eyes, nose, lips, and brows, but the examples shown (many of which are taken from mug shots) divide each feature into more specific categories, such as "flared nostrils," "squinting eyes," and "protruding ears." There are around 180 examples of each facial feature. Each feature has its own number and other features on the face are blanked out.

This is especially great to use when you are working with children, who may lack the verbal skills to describe a feature of a person's face, but who can instantly recognize it when they see it. Learning to use this catalog was a particular joy to me, because I'd labored along without visual aids like it for nearly five years. Getting information for an accurate sketch was difficult and time-consuming for me, exhausting for the witnesses and not nearly as effective as using the catalogue. Gaining this aid made my work much, much easier.

I adored our instructor, Horace Heafner. He said later that he remembered me, because I had "unusual intensity."

If he only knew.

I think one reason the instructor took to me was that I was the only one in the class who had done thousands of portrait-sketches in places like the River Walk, Six Flags and city malls. So I was by far the fastest artist there. He liked that.

"Okay, class," he'd say, "Draw a hook nose."

Then he'd mosey over to my desk and say, "Lois, are you done yet?"

Usually, I was.

But there was one more thing that set me apart from the rest of the class, and it was not a good thing: I was the only one there who did not have a full-time job working as a forensic artist for a police department. To make matters worse, the others in the class—all of whom were being paid to be there by their departments—came from much smaller cities than Houston.

Everyone in the class was so mystified that I did not have a job with the HPD that, at one point, they actually had a class discussion about it. As we talked they opined on such topics as how much my salary should be.

Little did they know the sacrifice I was making just to be there. It was December and for the full two-week time period of the course, I was unable to paint portraits. Therefore, while everyone else at least maintained their salaries during the schooling, I *lost* more than $800 in income.

By the time I packed my bags for home, I had made up my mind that, come hell or high water, I was going to find a way to be hired on full-time by the Houston Police Department, but it took more than my decision to get the task done.

I returned home to find that every aspect of my work had improved—except my status. I did more and more cases for the department. In fact, I had a number of high-profile successes. In one case, I even managed to get a successful composite from a five-year-old witness and we were able to put away a dangerous pedophile.

Whenever the police telephoned me, I dropped everything to do the case. One night, well past midnight a detective called. A Fort Bend County sheriff's deputy had been killed by a burglar. For forty-five minutes, I drove through the woods to get to the location where the witness, an elderly man who wore thick glasses, was waiting. The old man swore adamantly that though the suspect was more than thirty feet away, in a car going at least forty miles per hour, he had seen the man. When I finished the sketch, the deputies rushed out with it and as I was loading my gear into my old car, I saw an HPD helicopter lift off. They were flying my sketch to the media for the quickest possible release. (Meanwhile I had to find my way back home through the woods at three in the morning.)

Not long afterwards, they got a hit on the composite and caught the cop-killer.

Through the months that followed, I kept asking again and again to be hired full-time; again and again, I was told that there was no money in the budget. But by then, I was working so often as a forensic artist that I was finally making a living at it.

Still, since I didn't work "full-time," I was considered to be a "vendor." Vendors are companies who sell office supplies or vending machine supplies or whatever, to places like the police department and then bill the city. Houston often took months to pay its vendors, who had to absorb the delay as the cost of doing business.

But I wasn't a large company and I was struggling to survive for months at a time while I waited for checks from the HPD. Because I had to wait so long to be paid by the police department, I continued doing portraits, while at the same time raising two pre-schoolers.

By Christmas of 1988, the Houston Police Department owed me $11,350.

Broke, desperate, overworked, exhausted and a little bit crazy by then, I decided to drive down to the police department and see if *somebody somewhere* could, at the very least, advance me a couple of hundred bucks. I packed up examples of my most successful sketches into a portfolio, prepared my worn-out speech, dropped the kids off at the sitter's and headed downtown.

On the way, I was astonished to glance up and see red lights blinking in my rear-view mirror.

Inside my head, I was screaming. *I can't believe I'm going to get a ticket NOW!* It was too much and, when the officer walked up to my window, I burst into tears, bawling.

He asked for my driver's license and through my sobs, I broke out laughing.

This was a bit much for the young officer. His body tensed and his hand inched ever so slightly toward his gun. In the kind of voice one uses with those who are hysterical, he said, "Ma'am, do I need to get a mental health professional for you?"

Slowly turning my head toward him, I looked him full in the eye and said calmly, "You owe me eleven thousand, three hundred and fifty dollars."

Now he knew I was crazy.

Raising his hands as if to ward off a blow, he cried, "Now, wait a minute! I don't owe you eleven—"

"Not you!" I yelled, as tears once again streamed down my face. "The police department! I am your art squad! I do all your composites! I've got the invoices right here, and all the work I've already done!"

He paused. "You're the one who does those?"

Scrambling through the stuff on the seat behind me, I grabbed up an example. "Look at this sketch of the man who killed Deputy Heiman." Yanking up a receipt, I waved it in his face. "Look, here's the invoice. I did the sketch in February; it is nearly Christmas and I still haven't been paid!"

I could see him relax, even smile. "Damn those downtown bureaucrats," he said with sympathy. "They do take forever to pay." He asked if he could see my portfolio and I showed it to him.

We wound up having a lovely visit. I didn't get a ticket that day...but I also didn't get the money owed me until after Christmas and I didn't get hired full-time.

During the next year I met with the newly-appointed Chief of Police Lee Brown. My presentation to the Chief was almost the same one I'd given Cindy Smith years before. I was becoming further frustrated when Chief Brown suddenly interrupted me as I was giving statistics about all the other police departments in the world who employ sketch artists, my success rate, blah-blah and he said, "Have you ever thought about a full-time position?"

I stared at him. Blinked. Wondered if I was losing my mind for real this time.

"Uh, well, sir, yes I have. I've been asking about it for years. I was always told that we didn't have the money in the budget."

"Who told you?" he demanded. He wanted heads to roll.

So did I, but I didn't want to decapitate most every division head in the department, so I just mumbled, "Er...everybody...sir."

And then, almost before I could say, *We're not in Kansas anymore, Toto*, I found myself with an office, a salary, health insurance, benefits, and, best of all, *legitimacy*.

I started work at the Houston Police Department as full-time staff on

September 18, 1989. But it wasn't the office, the full-time hours or the pay that made me feel—*finally*—accepted as "one of the boys" at the PD.

It was one of those moments that feminist trailblazer Gloria Steinem refers to as a *click* moment—that instant when a personal truth hits home for you and changes your life.

I was standing by the copy machine in Homicide one random, wearying day, next to a detective who had just been given a case where a man had been murdered in a restaurant in front of a number of witnesses.

"I'm sorry to bother you," I said in my usual non-threatening way. "You've probably already got the case solved, but from media reports, it sounds to me as if you have plenty of witnesses to this crime and if you need or want one...I could probably do a sketch for you."

I backed away, so used to not intruding on their turf, when Capt. Bobby Adams suddenly walked up to me and drawled, "What're you being so shy about, Lois?"

I explained that I didn't want it to look as if I was telling an investigator how to do his job or acting like he couldn't do it without my help, or anything...

Putting one arm around my shoulders, Capt. Adams turned to the room at large and in a very loud voice, announced, "Ms. Gibson has the right to ask any detective anything she wants about any case they're working! You guys listen up, all right. She's well worth the time and trouble. She can ask anything! UNDERSTAND?"

Giving me a squeeze, he looked me in the eye and, in a softer tone, said, "I meant that, Lois." And he walked off, as if he was in the business of changing lives every day.

Until then, I had felt so *alone* and thought there was nobody who could do anything that would have made me feel, for lack of a better word, *respected*.

From then on, I was *home*.

At least, in a figurative sense. In more literal terms, I was still very far away from my childhood home, my loving parents and family back in Kansas. Since the summer of 1987, I had regretted that while my children were in their sweetest baby years (Brent was four and Tiffany eighteen months), my parents were missing all of it. I was missing them, too.

At that point Sid and I were only able to scrape together the money for all four of us to fly home once a year and it broke my heart that my mama, especially, who loved babies more than anything else in the world, could so seldom hold my children in her arms.

When I finally got my full-time job and the respect of my peers, the only other thing I wanted in the world was to be able to fly home to Kansas for a visit, so I could show off my darling baby girl to my folks. Tiffany was our own private version of Shirley Temple, complete with cheeks like cotton candy, eyes the color of the sky and curly blond hair. Unlike her hyperactive big brother, she loved nothing better than to be cuddled and cooed, which meant that she and Mama were made for each other.

So I hatched a scheme to approach the Wichita, Kansas police department and see if I could trade my skills for a free plane ticket home.

Having set up the appointment, I got the plane ticket so I could visit with my folks, but little did I know I would also get one nightmarish day, crammed with horrors.

Chapter Six:

WANTED: Dead or Alive

When I got to Wichita and Tiffany was safe in the arms of her grand-parents, I went to my meeting with all the Wichita Police Department's detectives, their supervisors and Captain John Dotson, head of investigations. The PD was located along with other city government buildings in a shiny glass and steel building in the center of town—much more modern than the forty-year-old Houston Police building.

I made a quick presentation of my sketches, detailing cases in which witnesses as young as five years old had provided descriptions, demonstrating how the sketches had helped to solve the crimes. In the beginning, they were very skeptical, but as they passed around the composite/mug shot comparisons, I could see that they were impressed. I decided to quit while I was ahead. (Cops are trained to be decisive; you don't want to ramble on too long or they'll start to wonder if you're a snake-oil salesman.)

My proposal was simple. After explaining that most of my family still lived in the area and I wanted to be able to see them more often, I added, "For the price of a round-trip flight, I will work on your case. You will not have to pick me up at the airport, put me up in a motel or feed me. My family will gladly do all that." I went on to mention that my usual rate for free-lancing cases was around $225 and added, "Since that's about the price of a flight, you'll get the going rate."

Ever mindful of tight budgets, the captain asked whether, if they flew me up for a murder, for instance, I could work on some rapes while I was there.

"Absolutely," I said. The question didn't surprise or offend me. Nobody understood bureaucratic spending restraints better than I did.

The officers seemed receptive, but not particularly enthusiastic. While they treated me with courtesy and respect, I still came away from the meeting feeling frustrated.

I didn't think they were ever going to call.

But it only took the length of a summer for those same detectives to feel their backs up against the wall, willing to try *anything*, even fly a flaky woman artist up from Texas to do a sketch, if it would help crack a collection of sexual assault cases that had left them frustrated and deeply disturbed as June bled into July and July into August.

When I answered the captain's call that September, I was trying to keep one eye on Tiffers (our little girl's family nickname), who was determined to run, not walk. In a resolute attempt to keep up with her race-around big brother, she'd sort of fling her body forward a few steps, topple to the ground, chew herself out in baby talk, then stagger up and do it again. She had so many cuts and bruises on her soft little body from ramming into furniture that I sometimes worried that she resembled a victim of child abuse. But she would not be deterred from her goal. I admit, I was pretty proud of her hardheaded willpower, though of course, I have absolutely no idea where she came by such a trait!

Back then, phones still had cords, which put me at a distinct disadvantage as I tried to prevent Tiffers from plowing into the corner of a coffee table and keep her in my line of sight while, at the same time, concentrating on what the captain was saying.

I've mentioned before the schism between my private, home life and my work life, but there have been few instances where it has been more apparent than this case, from the captain's first words on.

"Mrs. Gibson, I wonder if your offer is still good to fly up here and help us out," Captain Dotson said, almost apologetically, because he knew it had been three months since I'd heard from the Wichita PD.

"Certainly," I said, as Tiffers plopped down onto her diaper-padded butt, giggled, then rolled over to get up again.

"Well, we've been hit very hard by a two-man rapist team. Their favorite thing to do is beat their victims over the head with a claw hammer and their violence is escalating."

Tiffers, our family clown, made a face at her brother, who was trying to watch cartoons, and his laughter rang out over the captain's grim words.

"One of the latest victims," the captain was saying, "was bludgeoned into unconsciousness and her abdomen was slit open..."

Brent was playing peek-a-boo with Tiffers and she shrieked in delight...

"...They pulled out eighteen inches of her intestines and then left her..."

Still giggling, Tiffers waddled toward her brother...

"...But somehow, the victim not only survived, but she got to her feet and walked a quarter of a mile to get help. She was even turned away at one house and kept going to the next one until somebody took pity on her. Just wadded up her guts as she walked along and bundled them into her coat..."

"Tiffy! Move! I can't see Scooby Doo!"

"The media is eating us alive on this one..."

"Stop it, butthead! Get out of the way! Owwwww..."

Shrieks of laughter turned to screams of outrage as Brent shoved his sister and she clamped her teeth onto his arm. Over the squalls of both my children, I listened as the captain asked how soon I could come to Wichita and insisted on meeting me at the airport.

In a daze, shaken by the viciousness of the crime described by the captain, I hung up the phone and numbly separated my two battling children, then sat back onto the carpet, wrapped my arms tightly around my little girl, and buried my face in her tender, sweet-smelling hair.

It soothed us both, but it could not stop the nightmare images in my head of what had happened up in Kansas to some other mother's daughter.

By this time, I had learned how to pack my easel. When folded up, it makes a "T" shape of about four feet in length. A female FBI agent had suggested that the easel could be packed in a double rifle case, where, cushioned in several layers of cardboard, it would just fit with an inch to spare.

Drawing supplies I packed in with my underwear, to keep them from being crushed. The drawing boards and paper acted as a press between clothing I didn't want to get wrinkled.

Since infants could fly free, I didn't want to pass up another opportunity to take Tiffers along for a visit to her grandparents. (Brent was a terrible flyer, acting as if he was being stung by ants the whole way, struggling to be allowed to run up and down the aisles, so he stayed home with his daddy on that trip.) All Tiffers needed was her pacifier and the doting attention of flight attendants and passengers who thought she looked like an angel, so the flight went very smoothly.

I guess Captain Dotson had insisted on picking me up at the airport because of the level of anxiety that this case had provoked. He was waiting for me at the end of the ramp. Classically tall, dark, and handsome, he seemed so relieved to see me that I wondered if he'd worried that I might not show at all.

On the drive to Mama and Daddy's house, he explained that they'd been using one of those Identi-kit sketches but had had very little response and no useful leads with it.

It reminded me of something Lt. Don McWilliams had remarked scornfully to me one time about Identi-kit sketches, "Damn things look like stick figures."

At my parents' modest yellow wood-frame house with brown trim near downtown, we were both greeted like royalty. My plump little mama's permed brown hair just showed a sprinkling of gray at the time, which only made her dark brown eyes shine. Her face alight with joy, she whisked the baby out of my arms. Daddy was then 62, but he looked ten years younger because he was fit and tan from working construction. (I always thought he resembled the actor Sean Connery.)

Pumping the captain's hand like the born salesman he was, Daddy engaged the captain in animated conversation, then took my luggage into the house, leaving us standing outside at the foot of the front porch steps so that we could make our arrangements for the following day.

Captain Dotson informed me that he had several different witnesses lined up. He seemed to worry that I might be overwhelmed, so I assured him that, whatever came, I could handle it. We set up a time and shook on it.

After the captain left, I enjoyed a lovely visit with my folks, who clearly delighted in their granddaughter, and the world of slashed-open women seemed very far away.

The next day, a uniformed officer picked me up for the ride to the police department. It's not that he was disrespectful, but he was clearly doubtful of my ability to be of any help to the detectives. He made a point of letting me know that the first victim had utterly refused to speak with investigators.

"I don't see how you could get anything useful outta her," he insisted. "She's not speakin' to anybody about anything. I don't even know why they called her in."

Unspoken in the remark was the follow-up, *And I damn sure don't know why they called YOU in.*

I was unfazed. By this time, I'd heard it all from cops. Frankly, I was itching to get away from them and be alone with the witness, whoever she was. Thankfully, the drive was short.

However, when investigating officers filled me in on the case of the first victim with whom I would be working, I was dismayed to learn that it was much worse than I had imagined. Not only had she refused to talk to the detectives, but she had *adamantly* refused even to admit that she had been attacked!

The only reason they knew for sure that she had been assaulted was that she'd been forced to call an ambulance and the hospital had notified detectives of what the paramedics had found at the house—an overturned refrigerator, broken lamps, chairs flung about, evidence of vomiting in three separate places—obviously, a violent struggle had taken place in this home. The extent of the woman's injuries had borne that out. Her clothing had been ripped, there was evidence of sexual assault and, even more telling... she'd been hit in the head with a hammer.

Since this assault had taken place following six others with similar crime patterns, the detectives were certain that this woman had been attacked by the same two men who had raped and beaten the other women, even though she steadfastly refused to admit it.

And yet, even though there were other witnesses waiting to see me, the detectives had chosen to give me the hardest one first. Why? Was it some kind of test, to see if I could handle it? Did they hope that a sympathetic woman might get more out of her than they had? Or were they subconsciously hoping that I would fail, so that then they wouldn't have to feel so bad?

To this day, I couldn't say why the investigators sent in this brutally traumatized woman to describe attackers she refused to admit had actually done the attacking. It was the eighties after all. But the captain had called me in and they'd paid for my plane ticket, so I have to assume that they were hopeful that I could be of some help, somehow. Obviously, nothing else had worked.

As resolute as Tiffers learning to walk, I gathered up my easel and supplies and followed the detective into a room they'd set aside for me. He introduced me to the witness, Sarah, and almost immediately, I had a powerful, instinctive urge to be alone with this woman.

It's not that the detective had been in any way unkind to either me or this shattered victim—not at all—but there was something I saw in her hollowed-out eyes.

Something I recognized.

Have you ever flipped through a book on body language? Ever seen the illustration of somebody who does not want to talk? It could have been a photograph of her.

Dressed in blue jeans and a flannel shirt, she stood stiffly, her arms barred across her chest like a shield, her head ducked down, mouth set in a grim frown. Her hair was unkempt, gathered loosely in a rubber band, as if she hadn't even bothered to brush it.

I knew, because I'd been there.

This is all very nice, sir, I found myself thinking. *Now please get out.*

Finally, he went out of the room and shut the door behind him.

I kept my distance from her, the way you do a trapped wild animal that does not want to be approached. I had placed my easel so that I was facing her and she could see only the back of my drawing board. There is a reason for this. For one thing, I don't want witnesses to be distracted by what I'm doing, nor do I want them to be upset by the face that's taking shape in front of them. Also, by sitting opposite them I'm giving them space. As I remember so vividly from my own attack, usually the last thing someone wants after being assaulted is to be crowded or touched. Victims need to be able to breathe. They need to be able to think.

In my lap I put a piece of hard pressed board that makes a sort of desk, and on top of that I arranged my materials: a dark colored towel scrunched up like a nest and, in a pile, small pieces of pastels in shades of raw and burnt umber, black, white and everything in between.

There are some artists in my business who criticize me for using pastels in my forensic sketches, as if I'm somehow outdated, hopelessly behind the times. This is ridiculous. The reason I use pastels rather than pencils or charcoals is because it gives the faces three dimensions rather than that flat quality that makes some sketches I've seen look like all the others.

In as soft a voice as I could manage, I said, "The reason I do this work is that I was attacked in my home by a guy who tried to kill me for fun."

At that, every rigid muscle in her body seemed to droop with relief.

"I don't know exactly how anyone feels," I continued, "but I think I might have an idea how you might feel right now. I'm not a cop. And after I was attacked, I couldn't talk to *anyone* about it for more than six years. In fact, I didn't even admit it to myself."

With that, Sarah's eyes brimmed with tears and she immediately began to tell me what had happened. From what I gathered, her attack had been somewhat different from the others because she had been the only victim attacked in her own home.

"We live in the country," she said softly. "Our house is set back, like, two hundred feet from the road. My husband had left for work and I was alone in the house. The mailbox is located down on the road, and every day I like..."

She hesitated.

I waited.

Clearing her throat, she went on. "I *liked* to walk down to get the mail. The dogs would go with me and we'd have a fine little walk. On the way back to the house, they started barking and ran off. I figured they were chasing a rabbit and didn't think anything of it."

I nodded, but was careful not to interrupt her. She was lancing a wound and it was important that she drain out all the pus before we could ever hope to get a sketch. The words gushed out of her.

"I took the mail into the house and had just laid it down on the kitchen table when I heard, like, an *explosion*. It was..."

Her voice broke.

"When I turned around, I saw these two men who had just broken down my door—that's what the explosion was. One was blonde and one had brown hair. That's all I saw before they hit me with something and I blacked out."

This time, the pause was longer. I knew the worst was yet to come.

"When I came to...um...when I woke up? I was lying spread-eagle on the floor, and one of the men was tearing my jeans off. The other guy went over to the fridge, and he found a..."

She cleared her throat. "A carrot. He found a carrot. And then..."

I stifled a shudder.

"...and then, he took that carrot and he stuck it inside me, all the way to the end. And I screamed and... and he took the carrot out of me and he jammed it down my throat..."

That had been the first time Sarah had vomited, violently.

"I tried to fight them, I really did, but I couldn't move. One of them grabbed a lamp and hit me over the head with it and I blacked out again."

When she came to that time, one of the men was holding her arms to the floor while the other was preparing to rape her. Sarah kicked and struggled, but her efforts were feeble.

"I thought I was going to die," she said quietly, "and if it hadn't been for my dogs..."

Just then, all Sarah could see was a blur of flying fur while the air was filled with the snarls and growls of her beloved pets and the screams of her attackers as they tried to fend off the ferociously protective animals, who were biting the men's faces, arms, anything they could grasp in their sharp teeth.

Both men jumped up and ran out of the house, hotly pursued by the dogs. Battered, bleeding, but alive, Sarah felt as if she'd been dropped onto the floor by a tornado.

And it was so... so quiet.

The detectives were amazed, not just by the quality of the drawings I presented to them, but by the warm hug Sarah and I exchanged as she left. They were certain that these were the same two men they'd been trying to catch all summer. Buoyed by my success with their most difficult witness, they described the line-up of witnesses I would be seeing the rest of the day.

All three were waitresses. One had been run off the road as she drove home from work; two others were attacked as they walked home. All had been hit in the head, most likely with hammers, and one had sustained a skull fracture.

And then there was the incredible lady whose skull was bashed in; when she came to, she discovered that her guts were strewn out on the ground around her, yet still had the presence of mind to gather them close to her bleeding body and stagger down the road for help.

All the girls had been battered about the head so severely that it seemed as if the men were intent on killing them. With each attack, the men seemed to be growing more and more out of control.

I must say that so much suffering being laid at my feet hour after hour began to blur after a while, but one of the witnesses I will never forget.

Betsy was a stunning beauty, one of those natural blondes whose cheeks flush pink, with perfect teeth and skin like a ceramic doll's. She had that kind of soft sweetness about her that makes you want to shelter and protect her.

I couldn't imagine a more vulnerable prey for two such savage predators. They had run her pickup truck off the road, dragged her from the cab and beaten her into unconsciousness. She'd lain in a coma for almost two days.

Her boyfriend brought her to the police department and she seemed stoic enough until the detective finally left us alone. But once the door had closed and I tried to talk to her, she seemed to sink into herself and silent tears began to course down her cheeks while she mewed quietly, like a tiny, injured kitten.

Instantly I set aside my pastels, crossed the room, and touched her shoulders. It's important that not to grab a victim of sexual assault for a hug unless they indicate to you that they want one. Some can't stand to be touched at all, so I've learned to let any touch be gentle. Leaning over, I pressed my forehead against hers and said, "I'm so sorry this happened. I was attacked, too..."

I told her, briefly, what had happened to me, and she said, "I'm so sorry that happened to you!"

Kneeling down, I looked straight into her eyes and smiled. "I'm not!" I said. "I've taken my pain and I've turned it into this job. Now I get to catch hundreds of guys just like the one who attacked me. I'm *over it*, baby,"

I added with a confident nod. "And don't you worry. Some day you will be, too. It just takes time. You'll see."

A timid smile peeped through the tears, but still she wept.

"I bet you were scared to come here," I said, moving back over to my easel, "because you thought it was going to be hard."

She nodded.

"Well, don't you worry a bit. Shoot, I've worked with five-year-olds. This'll be easy. Watch and see."

I keep tissues mixed in with my art supplies, and I handed her some. She dabbed at her eyes and I gave her a few moments to compose herself.

When I knew she was ready to begin, she held herself together pretty well. "Here's a book that will help you remember." I handed her the *FBI Facial Identification Catalogue*. I know of at least one high-profile forensic artist who doesn't like to use the catalogue, thinking it contaminates the witness, but I have found this not to be true at all. Working with it is faster, more successful and—most importantly—much easier on the witness.

Over the years, I've collected half a dozen of the catalogues. When a witness selects, say, a pair of eyebrows, I'll take one of my copies of the catalogue and clip it to the left-hand side of my drawing board. While they search for another facial feature, I'll start sketching the eyebrows they've chosen, using my copy of the book as a guide. Eventually, I'll have catalogue pages clipped up and down both sides of my drawing board so that I can glance at them as I construct the face from a crime victim's fractured memories.

While we worked on the first sketch, Betsy would sometimes cry a little and I'd find a way to make her laugh. I asked her about her boyfriend. He was apparently a great guy who was wonderful to her and it soothed her to talk about him.

I've found through the years that, when dealing with multiple attackers, people often describe first the one who scared them the least. When I turned the drawing board around to show her the first sketch, Betsy broke down and wept, but she was able to calm herself again and we moved on to the second suspect.

We got through the second sketch quickly and I turned the easel around for her comments and changes. I could see that this was extremely difficult for her, almost unbearable, and I worked quickly to incorporate the changes, then hurried to turn the easel back around so that the drawing was no longer in her line of sight.

Suddenly, Betsy's face began to swell with huge purple hives. I'd seen hives before, but I'd never before in my entire career seen a witness react so horribly to seeing the face of the attacker. Soon, her face had swollen so severely that she no longer even looked like herself.

While tears continued to stream down her reddened, bloated face, I tried to hide my alarm and comforted her as gently as I could. Pulling up a chair close—but not too close—to her, I said, "They're going to catch him, I promise. He's gone now and you're safe here. And don't you worry, you don't have to leave until you're ready."

But her face kept growing redder—the most dramatic physical manifestation of terror I have ever seen.

"Listen, you know what's so good about these guys being the most horrible creeps you ever saw?"

"What?" she muttered into her tissue as she tried, in vain, to staunch the flow of tears.

"The more terrible they are and the more often they attack, the more likely they will be caught!"

Snuffling, hiccuping, she regarded me through the slits of eyes swollen nearly shut, and I could see that she had not thought of that before. The more destroyed a victim is, I've found, the more likely they are to believe that their attackers will somehow get away with it, maybe even come back for them.

"Yeah, Betsy, these are some of the sickest guys I've ever heard of and I work in Houston, Texas. We had over five hundred murders last year alone. I'm telling you, these creeps will get caught and you will have the privilege of watching them go down!"

Still, it was another twenty minutes before the hives had subsided to the point that Betsy felt comfortable enough to leave. I went to the door, cracked it open and gestured to her boyfriend, who came right away. After giving me a hug, she threw herself into his strong arms and walked out of the building with her face buried in his coat.

After nine hours of this kind of thing, I dragged myself and my easel through the front door of my parents' house, where Mama met me with a happy hug, followed by a toddling Tiffany, chocolate chip cookie clutched in her fat little fist. Wearily I dropped my gear onto my bed, then went into the living room and sank into the sofa, so drained I could barely hold up my head.

Mama appeared in the doorway, fragrant cooking aromas wafting in the air after her. "So," she asked with a bright smile, "how was your day?"

I stared at her. How innocent was the safe, loving world of my parents' home. How different from the horrors that inhabited my world.

Could I explain it? *Should* I explain it?

If you've ever had a cop in the family and you've wondered why he or she seems unwilling to talk about his or her work, well, now you know why.

Swallowing back the tears, managing a stiff smile, I said, "Great, Mama. Just great."

The next day, I took all the information I had gleaned from all the witnesses and put together a true composite of the images of the two men. My sketches aired on local television news that night and were published in the paper. A local businessman offered a reward of $13,000 for information leading to the arrest and conviction of these two men and the composites and reward were featured on a Crime Stopper's Wanted poster.

One of the local television news crews asked if they could interview me on-air, and with Captain Dotson's permission, I agreed. At the end of the interview, I pleaded with people to please turn these guys in, to call, that they could remain anonymous even after collecting the reward.

When I got back from the TV interview, Mama greeted me with a crazy, funny, high-spirited dance. Slapping her sewing button-tin on her fanny like a tambourine, she was singing, "There's an expert from Texas who does good sketches and now they're puttin' her on the eve-nin' news!"

I couldn't help but laugh.

That night, we watched the broadcast together and Mama and Daddy were so proud of me; they thought I was a hero. Mama even got calls from friends saying they thought I looked like her. She loved it.

But there's one small problem that comes with being good...something that can take a good sketch and turn it into something bad.

Turns out those two monsters were watching, too. They saw themselves on TV. And they knew it was only a matter of time until they got caught.

So they ran.

None of us knew it at the time, of course, but even as the evening news credits were rolling across the screen, two born losers were hitting the road out of town.

They wouldn't stop, either, until they got to Tulsa, Oklahoma. And then the true horrors began.

On the plane home, Tiffany and I were seated up front, close to the first class cabin. She was charming as usual and, as we settled into the flight, the facade I'd worn to please my parents and hide my own distress from them began to fall away like plaster from an old ceiling.

Without warning, I heard myself whisper, "They gotta kill someone."

In a flash, it came to me. These guys wanted to party while they killed someone, and they liked to egg each other on. All of the witnesses had reported that the men had appeared to be drunk, and I was sure they were doing drugs, too.

Most likely they were aware that all of their victims had gone on to survive their attacks, I figured, and they wanted to kill, they *needed* to kill, and they for sure didn't want to leave any witnesses who could provide a handy description to a sketch artist.

All the pent-up grief I'd felt in the presence of so many shattered women, combined with the very real fear I felt for their next, unknown, victim, seemed to hit me at once and tears began to flow down my cheeks the same way they had poor Betsy's.

I tried to sit still, to will the tears to stop, but nothing worked. Using a cloth diaper that I kept in the diaper bag to throw over my shoulder while holding Tiffany, I kept swabbing at my face and pretending that nothing was wrong, but soon the flight attendants spotted me. One of them asked if I was okay and I said the same thing I would have said to Mama, "Sure, I'm fine."

But I wasn't fine. Tiffany seemed to sense my distress, the way babies do, and she responded by squawking and fussing and generally drawing the kind of attention that you *don't* want your child to get on an airplane. I thought she was sleepy and took care of her the best I could, while, the whole time, I continued to sob silently.

After about ten minutes of this, the flight attendant emerged from the first class cabin and said, "Ma'am, why don't you come on up here to first class?"

I was mortified enough in coach class, struggling with a fussy baby with tears streaming down my face. The last thing I wanted to do was foist myself off on more passengers. I turned down her offer with a smile so fake she must have wondered if I was having a nervous breakdown.

Who knows. Maybe I was. And who wouldn't?

She disappeared into the first class compartment, then came right back out. Leaning down close to my ear, she said, "Everyone in first class wants you to come on up. I asked, okay? Now, come on."

Defeated, I gathered up my baby and my stuff and wearily followed her into first class, where I grabbed one of the seats at the rear. Both seats on that side were empty, which gave me ample room to lay my baby down on a soft blanket for a nap, patting her padded behind and trying—*for goodness sake!*—trying to stop crying, myself.

Finally, Tiff fell asleep. I leaned my head on the chair back, closed my eyes and tried to imagine that my brain was like a toy Etch-a-Sketch. All I had to do was turn it upside-down, give it a shake and erase the nightmare images on the screen.

It didn't work, really, but it was the best I could do and still hold on to my tattered sanity.

I guess if I had to use one word to describe Robert Wayne Lambert, twenty-one years old at the time, and Scott Allen Hain, his angel-faced seventeen-year-old partner, it would be *depraved*.

Lambert was an ex-con, just paroled from Alford Correctional Center in Springtown, Kansas, where he had served two years for robbery, when he met Hain, who had escaped from a Sand Springs, Kansas juvenile detention facility while on a three-hour pass.

Lambert had been the lucky recipient of the state's "cap law," meaning that, since his conviction had been for a non-violent offense, when the state's prison population reached 95 percent capacity, he was one of hundreds of inmates set free. Had he not been released, he would not have met Hain.

I'm not saying Hain wouldn't have committed brutal crimes on his own anyway, but there was something about the marriage of these two minds that converged into pure evil.

Court documents show that, as early as 1983, Lambert admitted having a problem with drugs. He confessed to having used marijuana, tranquilizers and even hallucinogens. It is not known whether he was using any of these drugs with Hain during the subsequent attacks, robberies, rapes, and murders they committed, but I think we can assume that Lambert wasn't exactly an upstanding, tax-paying, church-going citizen, either.

Two days after my sketches of the men were circulated throughout Wichita, Kansas, they broke into the home of Charles Stanton and his girlfriend, Terry Martin, near Tulsa, Oklahoma.

"I was asleep in my bed with my girlfriend," Stanton later testified, "when we were awakened by somebody screaming at us." Stanton was horror-struck to see a man—later identified as Hain—standing at the foot of the bed, with a gun pointed at his face. He was ordered to roll over onto his stomach.

"Give us your money and your jewelry," the man demanded.

Terry Martin asked who the man was and he said, "Shut up, bitch, or I'll kill you!"

Stanton then heard "a loud crack." He thought he'd been shot in the back of the head. He found out later that his skull had been smashed with a hammer.

"I took a deep breath and went limp," he said, adding that the last thing he tasted before going unconscious was blood, and the last thing he heard was a terrified Terry, her voice shaking, saying, "Where are you taking me?"

Terry Martin was driven to a remote location near the small town of Sapulpa, Oklahoma, where the men raped her, hit her in the head with a hammer and left her for dead.

When she regained consciousness, she stumbled across a field and crawled through a barbed-wire fence, which punctured her in the neck, before finally getting help.

At the trial, months later, Terry's boyfriend testified, but prosecutors did not call Terry Martin herself.

She was just too traumatized.

But it turns out that Terry Martin and her boyfriend were just a practice run for Lambert and Hain.

A couple of weeks later, they struck again.

At about 2:30 A.M. on October 6, 1987, the two predators were prowling around, looking for someone to rob, when they came across Randy Young, twenty-seven, and Debra Mitchell, twenty-two, sitting in a parked car behind a club.

Both Randy and Debra worked at a Tulsa restaurant. Randy was a bartender and Debra was working her way through Oklahoma State University as a waitress. They were good friends. Sometimes they liked to go to a club after work and unwind, but they were not lovers. They just enjoyed one another's company. Randy's truck was parked nearby and they were sitting in Debra's car, talking.

The two men crawled up onto the car and forced their way inside. Hain slipped into the back seat and pressed a knife to Randy's throat, while Lambert shoved into the front seat and aimed a gun at the petrified couple. They demanded money and both young people immediately complied, turning over all they had to Lambert and Hain.

It amounted to around $400.

To show their appreciation for the couple's cooperation, the men bashed Randy Young in the head with a hammer, then bound his hands and feet with rope and hog-tied him. They stuffed him into the trunk of Debra's car.

Then they brutally raped and sodomized Debra.

After clubbing her over the head with the same bloody hammer, they crammed Debra into the trunk of her car next to her injured friend who, like Debra, was not only still alive, but conscious. She was not tied up.

Robert Lambert had once lived with his sister in Sapulpa, Oklahoma, and that's where he and Hain had taken their last victim, Terry Martin. They returned to this same spot with Debra's car, the two victims still locked in the trunk. Scott Hain drove. Robert Lambert followed behind in Randy Young's red Isuzu pick-up truck.

What happened next differs depending upon whom you believe, but at trial, a jury, mesmerized in horror, watched an eighteen-minute videotaped confession of Robert Lambert, who, in a guttural voice, stated that he and Hain had decided that the young couple needed to die because, "they saw our faces."

Lambert claimed that he took a bolt-cutter and snapped in two the fuel-line to the car, then walked back and said to Hain, "I can't do it."

On the video at this time, Lambert burst into tears and cried, "Scott lit it up! The car blew up."

As the vehicle became engulfed in flames, the couple in the trunk began to scream, kicking and beating on the inside of the trunk, howling for help like banshee ghosts straight from the bowels of hell.

Sobbing, Lambert swore that when he heard the screams, he tried to put out the flames with a blanket, "but I couldn't."

He seemed to recover fairly quickly, however. The two men climbed into Randy's truck and drove off to have a few beers with a buddy.

Whether Lambert or Hain set the fire is still unclear, but medical examiners confirmed one part of his sickening story: the victims died with a great deal of smoke in their lungs, indicating they were still breathing when they burned alive.

Although dogged Tulsa PD investigators closed in on Hain and Lambert within three days of the terrible burning deaths of Randy Young and Debra Mitchell and arrested them, it was a traveling salesman who made the connection between these two suspects and the unsolved rapes up in Wichita, Kansas.

By this time, it had been three weeks since I'd traveled to Kansas and done the composite drawings, but the detectives there had not given up on those victims. My sketches were still being published in the newspapers, on the Crime Stoppers' wanted poster. The $13,000 reward was still being offered and the poster, which described the suspects beneath their composites, ended with the chilling words: **THEY ARE ARMED AND CONSIDERED DANGEROUS**.

Then, a man from Wichita, on a business trip to Tulsa, sat down to a fast-food breakfast and glanced at the morning paper. Pictured on the front page were Scott Hain and Robert Lambert, who had been arrested the day before.

His mouth agape, the man stared at the paper. He was convinced that these were the same two men he'd seen on the Crime Stoppers Wanted poster. He couldn't check right away because his wife had copies of the composite drawings at home, so he just tore out the photographs from the Tulsa paper and took them home with him.

As soon as possible, the couple called Wichita detectives, who came to their home and collected the newspaper photographs the man had brought from Tulsa. Within the week, detectives drove down to Tulsa with three of the four rape victims and a deputy district attorney. With help from Tulsa authorities, they staged separate line-ups for Hain and Lambert.

All three victims positively identified the men as their attackers.

Soon after the announcement, the NBC affiliate in Wichita asked if I would give an interview by what's known as a "live remote," meaning I would be interviewed by Wichita newscasters, but I would be giving the interview from an NBC affiliate in Houston.

I agreed and, once I was settled in front of the camera, the news anchor from Wichita asked if I was glad the serial rapists/murderers had been caught.

"Of course I'm glad they're in jail, for the survivors' sake," I said. "Most of all, I'm glad for the women who helped me. Wichita owes them a debt of gratitude. They cried with me and relived their ordeal and they gave me the images that enabled me to do the sketches that helped police track them down."

At this point, I directed my remarks, not at the absentee newscasters, but toward the victims, the survivors, the women with whom I had cried. I knew they would be watching.

"I know you suffered through it, girls," I said. "But it *worked*! They're in custody now. Tomorrow, you can get up and watch a sunrise and know that those two will never see a sunrise or sunset for the rest of their lives."

My voice broke a little then, but I added, "I'm just thankful to all of you."

Both Robert Wayne Lambert and Scott Allen Hain, who was tried as an adult, were given the death penalty by the state of Oklahoma.

In the formal sentencing on June 6, 1988, Judge Donald Thompson ordered Scott Allen Hain—whose sentencing testimony had revealed him to be the more savage and heinous of the two men—to be sentenced to "...death by lethal injection; if lethal injection is held unconstitutional, death is to be by electrocution; and if electrocution is held unconstitutional, death is to be by firing squad..."

One way or the other, that judge wanted to see those guys *dead*.

As for my part in it all, well, all I had wanted in the beginning was a free plane ticket home, but what I got along with it was a powerful lesson in how bad can turn to evil and how sometimes it can seem as if dying would be almost better than surviving a head-on collision with the devil.

Some of my cop friends have used words like "clairvoyant" and "psychic" to describe how I do my job, but, really, all it takes is a powerful intuition and a strong sensitivity to human nature based, in part, on my own experiences.

Those qualities, combined with a keen ability and willingness to listen, sometimes enable me to "see" things before they happen. Not a vision or anything like that, mind you, but I guess you could call it more like a premonition, which is what happened to me on the plane flight back to Texas.

Through the years, whenever I come across some factual, scientific validation of the kinds of things I've always known instinctively, I find it very gratifying. Like how some bad guys aren't content to be just garden-variety bad. They've got to keep going until they cross the line into pure evil.

As he explains in his landmark book, *Signature Killers: Interpreting the Calling Cards of the Serial Murderer* (Pocket Books, 1997), Dr. Robert Keppel spent more than twenty years investigating and studying the crimes of some of the most infamous serial killers of our time, and interviewed extensively such hall-of-shamers as Ted Bundy and Jeffrey Dahmer. Dr. Keppel described a pattern (in sometimes gruesome detail) of how certain vicious criminals escalate the violence of their crimes, seeming to grow more bloodthirsty with each crime they commit.

An example would be a peeping tom who "graduates" from peering into windows of single women to eventually breaking into their homes and stealing mementos like underwear, to raping his victims, to more serious attacks such as aggravated sexual assault and, finally, committing sexual homicide. If he gets away with his first murder, he will use the "lessons" he learned from that one to commit another and continue as long as he's able to outwit his law enforcement pursuers. The "Green River Killer," for instance, murdered dozens of women over two decades before finally being arrested.

With each crime committed, the serial offender develops a certain pattern or "signature" that can enable the astute investigator to recognize similar signatures in other crimes and thereby narrow the focus of the investigation by linking the crimes and searching for a single suspect or pair of suspects, rather than assuming that the crimes are unrelated. With Hain and Lambert, it was the use of a claw hammer to smash the heads of each of their victims.

Sex crime investigators, especially, learn to look for these signatures, because rapists who are not apprehended seldom commit only one rape. As my friend, Sergeant Rusty Gallier, once pointed out to me, nothing distresses an investigator more than interviewing the second, third or fourth victim of a rapist he or she has not yet been able to catch.

"The way I look at it," he said, "I feel like it's my fault. Like I didn't do my job. If I'd caught the guy after the first attack, he wouldn't have been free to assault anyone else." He related the pressure that can put investigators under, "a stress," he said, "that I didn't even know I had until I transferred to another division."

But if investigators are stressed by the fact that a rapist is continuing to rape and they can't stop him, it's even more devastating when the violence of each sexual assault begins to escalate. They know that, in most cases, if the violence continues to worsen, then they will eventually be dealing with at least one homicide. Unless, of course, they can catch him before it comes to that.

When Captain Dotson called me that fall day in September, Wichita investigators were already seeing this pattern of escalating violence, particularly in the case of the young woman who was gutted.

If killers' first attempts at escalating the violence of their crimes are not as satisfactory as they'd hoped, these sociopaths will use the experience as "practice" and try again. Dr. Keppel calls this a "vicious psychodrama."

Hain and Lambert, who tried assaulting one woman in her home and wound up facing attacking dogs, settled on their routine of following waitresses home from work and attacking them along the way.

Yet what even the fine Wichita detectives couldn't have imagined during those dark days was the fact that some of the more craven signature killers will up the ante of the challenge... meaning they'll go for more than one victim at a time, deriving a kind of sick pleasure from watching the terror of one victim while another is being tortured, something Keppel calls "depraved."

This is, of course, what Hain and Lambert did in Tulsa when they attacked the young couple asleep in their bed.

Once they've experienced success in one kill zone, chances are the killer or killers will return to what Dr. Keppel calls favorite little spots, with which they are not only comfortable and familiar, but where they can also be reasonably certain that they will not be interrupted. This is why the two killers chose to take Randy Young and Debra Mitchell back to Sapulpa, where they had first taken Terry Martin and where Lambert felt comfortable.

You don't really have to be "psychic" to figure out for yourself all the things criminalists have been researching through the years. All it takes is common sense and a deep understanding of what makes up the human psyche, both good and evil.

The Kansas case presented a real challenge for me—coaxing a traumatized witness to recall for me the faces of her attackers when she didn't even want to admit she'd been attacked.

But I would soon find myself embroiled in a case that was far more challenging, because it would have to answer the question: *How do you do a witness sketch from a victim who is blind?*

Chapter Seven:

Blind Justice
or
"Would you please just throw that sketch in the trash?"

Terror can come in many colors.

For poor Betsy up in Kansas, it was the hot pink of hives her face broke into just at the memory of the faces of the men who attacked her. For police officer Paula Franks, it was the misty gray of a drizzle that shorted out the wire she was using to call for back-up when a serial rapist attacked her during a sting operation in Memorial Park. For me, it was the pasty-white complexion of the man who tried to kill me.

For the traumatized family and friends of Maria Santos, terror showed itself in ugly, brassy orange.

But for Maria herself, terror was the same color as the rest of her world: solid black.

I can look back now, through the long lens of time, and see things not just as they were, but as they should have been. I know, now, that Maria's hair is normally lustrous and long, the color of mahogany, and it tumbles down her back and around her plain, honest, sweet face.

But on the first day we met, Maria's hair had been chopped off shaggy and short and dyed to a color not seen in nature—not because some unscrupulous hairdresser had figured the blind woman would never notice, but because her terrified family was trying to protect her from a monster who had threatened to return and hurt her all over again.

Maria—small of stature, gentle and six and one-half months pregnant—had planned to take the bus to a pharmacy to get a prescription filled on August 4, 1988. Maria often used certain methods to navigate her way, such as identifying surrounding aromas and sounds for a given area, counting steps from one place to another and occasionally accepting the kind help of strangers.

When she crossed the busy boulevard that stood between her apartment complex and the bus stop, for instance, one young fellow assisted Maria across the street and while she awaited the bus another man struck up a conversation with her. He said his name was Julio.

While she sat on the bus, Julio continued to talk to her and he offered to help her get to the pharmacy. But when Maria lumbered to the front of the bus and asked the driver if this was Hammerly Boulevard, Julio spoke up and claimed that no, it wasn't. The bus driver yelled out, "It is too Hammerly! What's wrong with you?"

This was her stop, so Maria got off the bus, extended her cane and began tap-tapping her way down the sidewalk. Soon she heard the same man at her elbow and before she could say anything, he had grabbed her arm and said, "The pharmacy's right down here."

Maria felt an instant sense of uneasiness. There was something about this strange man's urgency to "help" her and his firm grasp on her arm was frightening to her. She'd lost count of her steps by this time and didn't like feeling at his mercy.

It'll be all right, she told herself. *Once we get to the drugstore, I can wait until he's gone before I leave.*

But something wasn't right. For one thing, Maria could now smell the aromas given off by restaurants and she knew there weren't any restaurants near the drugstore. Then, she felt the pavement underneath her feet change in texture and she knew something was very wrong.

They weren't going to the pharmacy. In fact, Maria could tell from the sounds that they were walking up to what was most likely an apartment building.

She intended to pull away, to say something, but before she had a chance, the man called "Julio" had opened a door and hurled her into a room that she immediately sensed was vacant.

Grabbing her by the wrists, he dragged her face-down across the floor on her pregnant stomach, but when she tried to scream, he twisted her close to his face, put a knife to her throat and, in Spanish, snarled, "You make one sound or say one word and I will take this knife and plunge it into your stomach. I will kill your baby AND you, understand?"

He ordered her to take off her clothes and when she hesitated, he yanked the cane out of her hand and began slashing her over the head with it. Then he pressed his hand against her stomach and threatened to jump on her abdomen "with both feet" if she did not comply.

Shaking, crying, trying to curl her small body around the baby within, she submitted to a brutal rape. All the while, "Julio" kept sneering to her that, because she could not see his face, he could do whatever he wanted to her and no one would ever be able to catch him.

When the man had finished, he said, "When you're not pregnant any-more...I'll come back."

But before he left, he pulled his belt out of his pants, wrapped it around her throat and choked her into unconsciousness.

I'm sure this vicious, evil man walked away from that empty apartment convinced he had committed the perfect crime on the perfect victim—someone who could not recognize him.

But one big thing he failed to factor into his wicked equation was then-Sergeant (now Lieutenant) Manuel "Manny" Zamora who, at the time, worked sex crimes. Manny Zamora has always been one of my favorite detectives. A tall, handsome Latino man with long, sensitive fingers, Zamora is gentle, with a very soft, bilingual speaking manner. I never knew an investigator who worked harder to find justice for his complainants.

"When I first interviewed Mrs. Santos and heard what had happened to her," Zamora said later, "It sent chills down my spine. I'd never seen anything like this before."

He made up his mind, then and there, that he would not rest until he had caught this creep and put him behind bars. And to do that, he would use every resource he could find. In 1988, for instance, DNA evidence had never been used successfully in a Houston court of law, but Manny Zamora changed that with this case.

He took one more unorthodox step—he called me.

By this time, I had attended the FBI course in forensic art and could claim enough successes with my composites that I was being called upon on an almost full-time basis by law enforcement officers in the entire Harris County area and surrounding counties. So it was not all that unusual that Lt. Zamora would call me; in fact, I had worked with him many times before. What was different—*really* different—about this case was that the victim was blind.

Lt. Zamora was not deterred. After all, many of his victims in sex crimes did not see their assailants. Either they were attacked from behind or they were blindfolded or their attackers wore ski masks, pillowcases or some other disguise. But he didn't give up on those victims and he was surely not about to give up on Maria Santos.

"Conducting an investigation," he said later, "is like working a jigsaw puzzle. Every little bit of evidence is like another piece of the puzzle. You put them all together and soon, a picture emerges."

The first thing he did was go back to the place where it had all started—the bus stop.

"People are creatures of habit," he said. "They're going to do pretty much the same thing every day or, at least, on the same day of each week." He figured he would hang out at the bus stop at pretty much the same time of day Maria had taken the bus and speak to people who, most likely, had also ridden the bus that day, as well as other people who lived and worked in the area.

Most people, he knew, go by what they see. A pregnant blind woman making her way alone was likely to attract at least some attention and he depended upon human nature to be reliable. People would have noticed her and they could tell him what they'd seen.

"They acted as her eyes," he explained. He managed to track down the young Asian man who had helped Maria cross the street. He also found people who had noticed the man called "Julio" talking to Maria.

When Manny interviewed the bus driver, a tall African-American woman, he learned that she had not only noticed this man "Julio" shadowing the blind woman, but that she had overheard their conversation on the bus. Even though the man had only ridden the bus for one-quarter of a mile, there was something about his manner that had disturbed the bus driver. For one thing, he was noticeably intoxicated in the middle of the day. For another, he had told Maria that they weren't stopping on Hammerly Boulevard, when they were. Furthermore, he kept grabbing Maria's arm.

It had bothered the driver enough that she had felt uncomfortable dropping Maria off, even though the man had stayed on the bus for one more block.

"She saw it as her duty, her responsibility," Manny told me later, "to take care of the people who rode on her bus. She was worried about the blind woman."

Unfortunately, Lt. Zamora could not have chosen a more reluctant witness for me. It's not that she didn't want to help, it's just that she insisted, repeatedly, that she had not seen the man.

"You spoke to him," Zamora pointed out. "You *had* to have seen him."

Shaking her head firmly, she said, "Not really. I just got a glimpse of him out of the corner of my eye. That's all."

"That's enough," Zamora said.

Manny knew how powerful the subconscious is, even in witnesses who swear that they didn't see anything. "They don't know until they do it," he pointed out, referring to the composite sketching process. "They really saw more than they think they saw."

It was worth a try, Manny figured. "I don't hesitate to use composites as an investigative tool," he said later. "I figure, hey, if it doesn't look like the guy after all, then we haven't lost anything."

But the truth is that, by this point in the investigation, they just didn't have anything else. On the one hand, they had collected good evidence samples from Maria's rape kit. A "rape kit" contains evidence collected by physicians during an examination following the assault. It can include blood and semen samples, as well as swabs of saliva taken from bite marks, pubic hairs and other identifying markers left behind by the rapist. However, until they had a suspect in hand, they had no basis for comparison.

They had to start someplace.

Over the bus driver's adamant objections, Manny made an appointment with me. I was still not on staff with the HPD at that time, so I didn't have an office and had to bring my gear out to the Artesian building, where Sex Crimes was located. When I passed the waiting room on the second floor, I spotted a blind man with a cane chatting with two detectives and it surprised me. For some reason, it hadn't occurred to me that Maria's husband might also be blind. How helpless he must have felt at that point, though he did not display the rage that victims' husbands and boyfriends so often did. I guess he was more used to dealing with the injustices of life than the rest of us.

As I was setting up my gear, Lt. Zamora came to get me and led me out to meet Maria. Although I would not be working with Maria on the sketch, Manny knew me well. He knew what stoked my fires and gave me my energy and he knew that once I'd met Maria, I wouldn't stop either, until we had caught the thug who had hurt her.

She was sitting demurely on the edge of a chair, her big belly sort of resting on her lap, her white cane threaded around her hand with a strap. The orange hair flamed out from her shy, quiet little face like a sign to me that spelled one word: *FEAR*. Although nobody had told me that her family had cut and dyed her lovely hair in a desperate attempt to foil her attacker should he return, I somehow knew it instinctively, simply because I know only too well what fear can do to a person.

When Manny introduced us, Maria gave me the sweetest smile and I took her small hand in mine. In soft tones, she thanked me for my help, her sightless eyes staring down and to the right as she spoke. The old rage bubbled up inside—just as Manny had known it would—and I exchanged a glance with him that said all we needed to say between us.

I returned to my easel and Manny brought in the bus driver, a statuesque, 6'2" African-American woman with a lean, athletic build and a no-nonsense attitude. To put her at ease, I asked her about her job.

"I'm the first female ever to win the bus rodeo," she boasted proudly and went on to describe this annual competition where drivers compete to show their agility in handling a bus through a driver's obstacle course.

"Congratulations!" I hoped she knew that I was being sincere. "What a terrific idea, to have a competition like that, because I expect it helps to prevent accidents later, since drivers become more proficient at what they do."

She beamed and agreed that yes, it was great.

When I felt that I had broken the ice sufficiently, I began to work, but before I'd put two pastel strokes on the page, she spoke up and in almost-angry tones, said, "Look, I don't know why that detective even brought me here. I did not see that guy, I'm telling you. I didn't see him at all."

"It's all right," I soothed. "Everybody feels that way when we first get started. You'll be surprised at what comes to you as we go along."

Crossing her arms over her chest, she stuck out her chin and said, "No. I didn't see him! I can't tell you anything!"

By this time, I'd faced all kinds of challenging witnesses in this work, but this woman was openly hostile and I had to take care not to lose my temper too.

"Sgt. Zamora said you caught a glimpse of him out of the corner of your eye."

Her shoulders relented ever so slightly and she said, "Well, yeah—just a side view. "I did not see his face!"

"That's great!" I encouraged. "Don't worry about that at all. I've been to the FBI Academy and they taught us how to do a frontal composite of someone's face based just on side views. Anyway, you don't *have* to do well. Even if we come up with a sketch that's not all that great, it will still be okay. We'll do whatever we can and then we'll be out of here. Trust me."

I could see that she was impressed by the term *FBI Academy*—most people are—but she was still defiant. "It was just a quick glance," she insisted. "I had my hands full opening the door." She sighed. "Look, I heard what that guy was saying to the blind lady and it bugged me, but I was watching the road and concentrating on opening the bus door. Passengers were getting off and passengers were getting on. I just didn't get a good look at him. I can't tell you anything."

"Sure you can," I coaxed. "You can tell me if he was black or white or Latino."

"Latino."

"There you go. It's a start!" I smiled, but inside, I was clenching my teeth. It wasn't the witness's uncertainty that was so infuriating—I see that all the time. It was that, clearly, this had become a power struggle to her. She seemed to feel that she was being forced to do something she did not want to do and she was determined to give me nothing that she perceived as an advantage.

Poor little Maria Santos suddenly seemed very far away.

Still, though, I have to interject here—this woman had been asked to shoulder a very great responsibility. She didn't want to give a witness description that could get the wrong man arrested. I guess she didn't realize that Lt. Zamora would employ *many* investigative tools and put together corroborating evidence before he would ever make an arrest. This was just a beginning, the first few pieces of the puzzle.

Looking back, I can understand the bus driver's reluctance and nervousness. Some years after the Maria Santos case, I had the privilege of being interviewed by television journalist Stone Phillips for a piece that appeared on *Dateline, NBC*. One of the things Mr. Phillips asked me to do was set up my easel on the banks of the River Walk in San Antonio, where I had done so many portraits years before. We did a little exercise: Mr. Phillips took a quick Polaroid snapshot of a random tourist, pocketed it and then sat for me as a "witness," describing the tourist from memory for me to do a sketch. As I began to draw, the cameras started to roll.

We hadn't been working very long when I asked Mr. Phillips to describe the tourist's eyebrows. Almost immediately, he began to stammer around, struggling to recall, and I could see that he was embarrassed.

I assured him that he was doing fine and that it was perfectly all right for him to admit that he plain didn't know.

"Okay," he admitted with a charming smile. "I don't know." He went on to say, "I'm not even a crime victim and it's nerve-wracking pressure to sit here and feel like you can't remember."

I try to keep that in mind when I'm working with witnesses—it's a nerve-wracking process for them—even when they are handsome television personalities just playing a game—so the pressure is all that much more intense for a real crime victim or witness.

Still, back when I was trying to pry a description out of this unwilling bus driver, I hadn't yet met Stone Phillips. I do believe that what Lt. Zamora said is true, that the driver did feel a sense of responsibility toward her passengers and especially for Maria Santos. On the other hand, for some reason, once she began to work in a quiet room with me, she became every bit as obstructive as an old buffalo who doesn't want to be penned up.

"Here," I said, handing her an *FBI Facial Identification Catalogue*. "Just look at this catalogue, okay? Let's start with the hair. See...on these pages? They're just pictures of hairlines. Pick out a style that reminds you of the man you saw on the bus. And don't worry about it. It doesn't have to be perfect."

Impossibly, she shook her head. "I keep *telling* you people! *I did not see him that clearly!*" By this time she was nearly shouting.

To diffuse the situation, I tried to distract her with small talk and in a predicament such as this, I was not adverse to a little flat-out flattery.

"You're so tall and beautiful," I said. "I bet when you put on a pair of hoop earrings and high heels—"

"—not *too* high!" she interrupted, laughing.

"I bet you look just fantastic."

She didn't hesitate to nod her head at that assessment.

"Do you have a boyfriend tall enough?" I pressed.

"A couple of them," she said with a grin.

"I don't doubt that...Now, over here. Why don't you see if you can pick out a pair of eyes that resemble the man on the bus?"

"I don't know..."

And so it went. Back and forth. At one weary point I pictured myself bracing one foot against her chest, reaching both arms down her throat and *pulling* the information out of her. It would have been easier, I think.

By the time we made it to the chin in the sketch, I was completely drained—and running very, very late for an appointment to do a composite over in Homicide. Naturally, Homicide was located in another building entirely and I was going to have to pack up my gear and haul it over.

When we were finally finished with the sketching session, my eyes were burning, my neck was stiff and it was all I could do not to start screaming and make a lunge for this maddening woman. Wearily, I turned the easel around and showed the composite to her.

With a quick, dismissive shake of her head, she said in no uncertain terms, "No. I can't really say that's him. Maybe the hair...I don't know. I *told* you. I didn't see the guy."

I was a little distressed that her reaction was so negative and adamant, but over the years, I had learned to trust the process. It would have been nice if at least this witness would trust me, as well.

But apparently, that was too much to ask. Pursing her lips, the woman said, "No. I don't want you to show this to the detective. Would you please just throw that sketch in the trash?"

With a heavy sigh, I did as she demanded. I took the sketch down off the drawing board, walked over and tossed it into the wastepaper basket in the corner of the room. She left with, I must say, almost a triumphant gleam in her eye. She'd won the power struggle, after all.

And Maria Santos had lost.

Trying to hurry, I started packing up my gear (Homicide still waited), dreading having to do another sketch after this nightmare session.

Manny came in. "I've finished interviewing Mrs. Santos," he said. Glancing around, he added, "Where's the sketch?"

Without a word, I crossed over to the trash can and pulled out the sketch.

He took it out of my hand, gave me a funny little grin, shook his head and left. Talk about feeling like a failure—I'd done better work in the fourth grade—and that big tall bus driver had completely worn me out.

It would take a miracle, I thought, for Maria Santos ever to see justice or to even feel as if she could ever grow out her hair again, letting it fall freely down her back.

But it didn't take a miracle, after all. All it took, really, was one dedicated, hard-working detective who really *cared*, not just about this victim, but about doing his job to the best of his abilities.

He started by ignoring the bus driver. Not her witness statement, of course, but her insistence that the drawing could not be accurate. By this time, I'd worked with Manny through a number of cases and he trusted me. He trusted my talent and he trusted the process. He also trusted his instincts, which were superb.

"There are several good reasons to use a composite sketch," he pointed out. "One is that it helps others help us (the detectives) solve a crime. And two—a good sketch warns others that there's somebody out there they need to watch out for. It protects others from being victims of this same guy."

Armed with my sketch, Manny knew just where he wanted to go.

"At the time," he explained, "I had read an article about a study on burglaries done in San Francisco, which concluded that the vast majority of burglaries were committed within two miles from where the criminals lived. I figured that same statistic would most likely apply to this case. So I started right there—in the neighborhood."

Taking my composite in hand, he showed it in some key places around the neighborhood that dovetailed with information he'd been gathering on the case. For instance, one witness claimed to have heard the man say that his car had broken down, so Manny checked out nearby parking lots, repair shops and towed vehicle reports. He'd show my sketch to, say, a mechanic in a repair shop and ask if he'd seen someone who looked similar bring in a vehicle recently.

He showed it to some of the people who'd been waiting at the bus stop and he showed it to the elderly woman who'd been sipping coffee in her front yard the day the suspect, gripping the arm of a blind pregnant woman, had passed by. He showed it around convenience stores and also to a few grocery store managers in the area.

One manager said that the sketch resembled a couple of brothers by the name of Zayas who worked for him, cleaning the store after-hours. From the manager, Manny got a name.

Before a week had passed, Manny had put together enough of the case, with help from my sketch, to stage a line-up. Since the victim was blind, Manny asked some of the witnesses to come in and see if one of the men in the line-up looked like the man they'd seen with the pregnant blind woman that day.

When he'd gotten a positive I.D. from those witnesses, he brought in Maria Santos and he asked each of the men in the line-up to say a few words in Spanish that matched comments Maria had heard from her attacker.

Without hesitation, Maria said, "It's number five. That's him."

When David Alberto Zayas was placed under arrest, he was reported by the officers to have said, "What took you so long? I thought you guys would've caught me sooner."

Interesting comment from a brute who had boasted to his terrified victim that he would never get caught because she'd never be able to identify him.

But an arrest was just the beginning, as far as Manny Zamora was concerned. The use of DNA evidence at that time to positively identify suspects was still in its infancy. Most police departments were still relying on simple blood typing. But Zamora was determined to keep this guy off the

streets. He sent evidence from Maria Santos's rape kit to the FBI labs at
their headquarters in Washington, D.C.

It took some time—at least two months—to get back the results, but
it was well worth it. By the time the case went to court, Manny had done
such a thorough job piecing together his puzzle of an investigation that he
was not even called upon to testify in court. David Alberto Zayas was convicted of aggravated sexual assault on the evidence and sentenced to spend
the rest of his life in prison.

Through the years, I often think about that stubborn witness who
made me throw my sketch in the trash and the dogged investigator who
insisted we use it anyway. They say justice can sometimes be blind, but in
the case of Maria Santos, justice was as unblinking as a detective, bent over
a jigsaw puzzle, snapping each and every zigzagging piece solidly into place,
until the whole picture shines out clean, clear and unforgettable.

Then, a few months later, a gentle, sweet woman, denied the sense of
sight, could still gaze into the face of her healthy newborn child, shake her
long dark hair loose and smile.

Chapter Eight

Portrait of a Serial Killer: "Ha!—Would a madman have been so wise as this?"

"True!—nervous—very, very dreadfully nervous I had been and am; but why *will* you say I am mad? The disease had sharpened my senses—not destroyed—not dulled them. Above all was the sense of hearing acute. I heard all things in the heaven and in the earth. I heard many things in hell. How, then, am I mad?...Now, this is the point. You fancy me mad. Madmen know nothing. But you should have seen *me*... Ha!—Would a madman have been so wise as this?"

When Edgar Allan Poe wrote those words in his macabre short story "The Tell-Tale Heart," he might just as well have been writing about Theodore Goynes.

Throughout Goynes's miserable life, law enforcement couldn't seem to make up its mind whether Goynes was just evil or whether he was a psychopath. I know what his victims would say—at least, the ones who survived. And I know what one prosecutor in one of his numerous trials said, that he was, "the poster-boy for the death penalty."

I'm not sure what Theodore Goynes himself would have said. He might have had to consult the voices he claimed to hear in his head, the ones who urged him to "do bad things."

I do know this: the things he did were very, very bad.

The Goynes case, which spanned almost two decades as well as two different states, focused a powerful magnifying glass on many different aspects of the criminal justice system: the meaning of the term *criminally insane* (and the huge gaps in treatment of those who meet that definition), early good-behavior releases of violent felons, dangerous overcrowding of prisons, concurrent versus consecutive sentencing, the degradation of neighborhoods by the presence of too many halfway houses—and the part that most personally affects me—the uncommon, almost unbelievable courage and will to live demonstrated by crime victims fighting for their lives.

It is this aspect of the Goynes cases that I will never forget. The women whose lives were devastated by Theodore Goynes (at least, those who lived to tell about it) were average, everyday women. And although they each appeared to possess almost unimaginable strength, courage and endurance, I believe it is these qualities *we all* have within us that give us that same incredible power: *the will to live*.

We never know when that power may be called upon, but please rest assured that it lies within each and every one of us. I believe it was put there by God. I know I found it, deep within myself, when the man I've spoken of earlier tried to strangle me to death while raping me. I found out then that I, an innocent girl from Kansas who'd never met a mean person in my life, needed to fight to survive even as he choked the life out of me and somehow I found that will, that strength, that courage.

As I would come to find out, the women who met up with Theodore Goynes would be sorely tested by his depravity.

My experience with Theodore Goynes began on February 15, 1989, but for the victims of Goynes, it goes back—way back—to November, 1973. At that time, out on parole, Goynes had already done five years for burglary in the Illinois Department of Corrections and had done two years at Jacksonville Development Center, an Illinois state psychiatric hospital, where he had been treated for "schizophrenic and auditory hallucinations."

Psychotropic medications seemed to reduce his symptoms, so when Goynes was released from custody, he was urged to keep taking his medication.

He did not keep taking his meds.

A few months later, a twenty-two-year-old woman was sound asleep in her own bed when she was awakened by what sounded like "a scratching" on the back door.

"And now at the dead hour of the night, amid the dreadful silence of that old house, so strange a noise as this excited me to uncontrollable terror," wrote Poe and no more apt description applies to what Goynes's first victim heard on a cold November night.

She got out of bed and crept to the back of the house, to the door where she'd heard the strange noise. Just then, that same door was suddenly smashed open by a man with a sawed-off shotgun and a knife, who forced his way—and her—back into her bedroom. He raped her, then stabbed her multiple times, finally plunging the knife into her throat, where he made a clumsy attempt to sever her carotid artery. He grazed her windpipe instead.

Then he tied her up on the bed and piled clothing on top of her body. By this time, certain she was going to die, the young woman decided to "play dead" in hopes that he would leave.

But Goynes wasn't finished with her yet.

She caught a whiff of a horrifying odor—lighter fluid.

"I could hear the can popping as he squeezed it," she later testified. "As soon as he got through sprinkling it all over the bed, he lit it."

As the bed burst into flames, Goynes left.

With amazing, almost superhuman presence of mind, the woman managed to free her hands from the cord Goynes had used to tie her up. She then pulled the knife out of her own throat and rolled off the bed.

"I prayed to God, 'Don't let me die,'" she said.

Then, naked, bleeding, her hair on fire, she leapt from a second-floor window to the street and stumbled down the block to get help.

A few nights later, Goynes struck again, only this time there was no demure scratching at the back door. A twenty-nine-year-old woman was sound asleep in the house she shared with her four children, when the kitchen window was brutally shattered. When she leapt to her feet and rushed down the hall to investigate, she found Goynes in her kitchen, a sawed-off shotgun in his hands.

As he had done with his first victim, Goynes forced the young mother down the hall and into her bedroom, where he raped her while her children—from five to ten years old—slept in the next room. Something about the bedroom light being on seemed to disturb him, because he dragged her down the hall to the darkened living room and raped her again.

Maybe evil can't stand light. It thrives on darkness.

"I'll be watching the house, bitch," Goynes told his trembling victim, "and if I see any cops anywhere around, I'll come back. I'll kill you and your children."

The mortally fearful woman didn't report the rape for one full day.

The same day he left the terrified mother shaking in her home in the room next to her sleeping babies, Goynes stalked and raped a third woman in the back room of a record store where she worked, made her perform oral sex and stole $50 from her. Like his first victim, she escaped and ran screaming stark naked down the street until she found help.

When Theodore Goynes was finally arrested and brought to trial, his attorney mounted an insanity defense. When he was not taking his medication, Goynes, who admitted suffering "black-outs," forgot such things as his own birthdate, the name of his attorney, the name of the hospital where he was incarcerated or even why he had been arrested in the first place.

"He's crazy," said Goynes's lawyer.

But a psychiatrist who examined Goynes mentioned only that, with an IQ of 70, he "has a bad temper and gets into a lot of fights." The court-appointed shrink declared Goynes "of sound mind" to stand trial.

Goynes pled guilty to a staggering list of felony charges: rape, burglary, assault with intent to commit murder and arson.

In 1974, the Illinois judge sentenced Goynes to forty years for each rape, twenty-five years for assault with intent to commit murder, twenty years for arson and twelve years for burglary.

But the judge set all the sentences to run *concurrently—not consecutively*. Goynes was given one forty-year term.

In prison, Goynes took his medications regularly and his hallucinatory symptoms abated. He adjusted well to the routine of prison life and, because of his model-prisoner behavior, got good-time years deducted from his sentence.

In all, Goynes received something like *three years* of good time taken off for every *one year* of his sentence that he served.

By the time he had served fourteen years in prison, Goynes was adjudged to have served his *full sentence*—only fourteen years out of forty.

Subsequently, he was not even paroled—*he was released*.

On December 18, 1989, Goynes was set free. He was encouraged to take
his medications. Goynes decided he'd had enough of Illinois and wanted to
return to his home state of Texas.

He did not take his meds.

Four months later, on April 18, 1989, in Houston, Goynes was arrested
for burglary. After reviewing his history and the report of a court-appointed
psychiatrist who examined him—and reported that Goynes was a "confused adult" who sometimes acted because he heard voices—the judge
acquitted Goynes on the burglary charges.

Not guilty, by reason of insanity.

Goynes was sent to a mental hospital. He was put back on his medication, which quieted the voices and stopped the hallucinations. This made
him a peaceful patient. After a few months, Goynes was once again set free.
And once again, he was urged to take his medication.

He did not take his meds.

In February of 1989, in Houston, Theodore Goynes—whether from
madness or evil, no one knows—went on a violent rampage.

The late January evening was crisp when forty-one-year-old Jane Carr,
who was driving home from work, stopped off at a market along the way
to pick up a few groceries and a couple of movies for the weekend. As she
was loading her bags into the back of her late-model black car, she felt a
gun pressed into her back.

She turned to see two African-American males standing in front of
her. One of the men ran away, but the other one—short, wiry, with an
angular, angry face and dirty hair, forced her to get into her car. He
made her drive to an abandoned house in Houston's Lake Forest sub-
division.

He seemed to know his way around and, with the gun to her head,
forced her to climb into a kitchen window, where he shoved her to the
floor and raped her. After that, he pushed her down the hall and into
one of the bedrooms, where he raped and sodomized her again.

"You've seen my face," he told Jane, "and so now I'm going to kill you."

He hit her over the head with the gun, then again and again—and then
he picked up something else, maybe a brick, and smashed her skull with it.

While she fought and struggled, he pulled out a knife and stabbed her and stabbed her and stabbed her. After that, he took a cord and tied her hands and feet.

Like an earlier Goynes victim, Jane decided that the only way to escape with her life at this point was to play dead. She let herself go limp.

But Goynes was not to be fooled this time. To make sure she was really dead, he took a tire iron and smashed her in the ribs, breaking eight of them.

She didn't move. She didn't cry out.

Satisfied that he'd finally killed her, Goynes dragged the bloodied and battered woman's inert form over to the closet. Inside the closet was a built-in wooden storage bin, just the right size for a woman's body.

Grunting with the effort, Goynes stuffed Jane Carr into the wooden bin and closed its heavy lid, like a casket.

Jane's skull was fractured in numerous places; she was suffering from multiple stab wounds and her right arm was shattered.

"But I was determined to live," this brave, brave woman told investigators later. "I was not going to die in that house."

In her cramped little coffin, she worked her hands loose, then pushed up the wooden lid, dragged herself out and began a torturous journey, crawling naked and bleeding from house to house until, at last, she found one good Samaritan, a fifty-five-year-old man who wrapped her gently in a sheet and called for an ambulance and the police.

The investigating detective was Deputy Chief Charles McClelland, who was, at the time, a sergeant in Sex Crimes. A tall, broad-shouldered African-American with scholarly glasses and a moustache, McClelland is known for his easy smile and warm laughter

Unlike some of the officers with whom I've worked over the years, especially in the beginning, who refused to take me seriously, Chief McClelland has always treated me with respect. He once told a friend of mine that he thinks of me as what he called an *adjunct detective*.

He said, "I've always used Lois as a valuable resource. Not only is she very talented, she's unique in the way she deals with traumatized victims, the way she convinces them to talk to her. She has incredible patience. After she's done with a sketch, I'll go back and talk to her, ask what type of guy she thinks this is, if she has different ideas about the victim. And usually, she does. She'll have some kind of information that no one else has been able to get."

I was really blown away when I heard that. No forensic sketch artist could ever hope for a finer compliment. I'd worked with Sgt. McClelland before, so I wasn't surprised when his call came through.

"Lois," he said, "I really need your help on this one." He went on to describe the horrific attack on Jane Carr and I could tell that he was determined to catch this guy.

"It's a miracle she's alive," he said. "She should have been dead."

The victim, a petite and lovely African-American woman, was still recovering at home in the care of her devoted husband. Since the attack had been so savage and her injuries so critical, I went to Jane Carr's home to do the sketch.

When I knocked at the door of her ground-floor apartment, juggling easel and art supplies, I was surprised when a 6'8" man answered. Taking some of the heavier items out of my hands, he held the door wide and led me to his wife, who was curled up on the sofa, covered with bandages and casts. After speaking softly and lovingly to her, he settled down in a big easy chair nearby to watch, his long legs stretching halfway across the floor of the small room.

By this time, I had a hard and fast rule against anyone sitting in on sketch sessions. But there was something about this man's demeanor, his quiet concern and the way his wife seemed to take comfort by his mere presence...I just didn't object.

All he said, later, was, "During that whole thing, she never lost consciousness."

He seemed in awe of her courage and I could see that his love for her made him feel helpless. As we neared the end of the session, I asked him what he did for a living.

His eyes took on a fierce cast and in a tone deadly in its quiet, said, "I'm a guard in the prison system."

I stared into those eyes and in one brief moment of silence, we communed, this grieving husband and I, a wordless dialogue. I knew, without asking, how he ached to get his hands on the man who had done this terrible thing to his wife and I also knew that, if it had been me, I would have felt exactly the same way.

Mrs. Carr was obviously in a great deal of pain, so I tried to distract her by asking what she did for a living. With a keening wail, she burst into tears.

"I drove a school bus," she sobbed. "I loved it. It's the only job I have ever loved. Now he took that from me. The bones in my arm are so crushed, the doctors don't think I'll ever be able to drive again!"

As she wept, I crossed the room, touched her shoulders and tried to comfort her as best I could. "Maybe you can compensate, when the time comes," I said softly. "Maybe you can use the other arm more..."

"No!" she cried. "I have to pass a test to drive a school bus again."

She was so inconsolable that I went back to the drawing. Her tall silent husband got to his feet and murmured in her ear, smoothing her hair through the bandages with his big hand, and she slowly got herself back under control.

When I thought she was able to handle it, I turned the drawing board around to see if she wanted me to make any changes.

"That's that *tramp!*" she cried. "That's that tramp!"

She seemed relieved, even jubilant to see the sketch of her assailant. I packed up my gear to go and her husband helped me to carry it out to the car. I noticed he had to duck his head to get through his own door.

As I stowed my gear in the trunk of the car, he thanked me and said, "She never lost consciousness you know, during that whole thing."

My composite sketch was printed up on a Crime Stoppers "City-Wide Alert."

Sergeant McClelland was convinced that the man who clearly meant to murder Jane Carr lived in the same neighborhood where the attack had taken place.

"The scene of the abduction, the scene of the assault and the bayou where police later found the victim's stolen car are all within a half-mile of each other," he pointed out. "That indicates to me that he usually travels on foot." He added, "I'd be willing to bet my badge that he lives there."

McClelland threw himself into the investigation with a vengeance, combing "that whole northeast side" of the city for suspects, chasing leads, hauling men in for line-ups, questioning suspects, checking out alibis.

The viciousness of Jane Carr's attack added another worry. "He's a threat to that area," said McClelland, "and I have no doubt that the next time, he'll make sure his victim is dead."

And although Charles McClelland did everything in his power to keep that from happening, Theodore Goynes slipped through the dragnet once again.

Another woman, though she fought as hard as the others, was not as lucky.

It was the weekend of her birthday and Angelica Jackson had a special lunch date with her husband that Saturday to celebrate. But the children, two boys, aged five and one, wanted a party, so the family was planning a little to-do on Sunday for family and a few friends.

Angelica worked as a clerk at a drug store in a little strip mall on Mesa and after work, she stopped off at the market to pick up the birthday cake her husband had ordered for the next day's party.

The market was just down the street from where Jane Carr had been abducted nine months before. And Angelica drove almost the exact same model and color of car that Jane Carr had driven.

As Angelica leaned over to put the cake in the back seat of the car, a man whom witnesses had seen "loitering" in the parking lot earlier suddenly appeared and tried to force her into the car. Angelica was a tall, athletic beauty and she fought hard with the man—so much so that two women clerks inside the store heard her screams and saw the struggle going on outside. They ran outside to see if they could help.

The horrified witnesses watched as the man pointed a gun at Angelica and shoved her into the car. Determined to do *something*, the two women piled into a car and followed the woman and her abductor as Angelica's car sped out of the parking lot.

Sadly, the suspect was able to elude the two women and they rushed back to the grocery to call police.

From what police were later able to piece together, Theodore Goynes had his routine down-pat and true to form, he forced Angelica to drive to an abandoned apartment complex where, most likely, he intended to do pretty much the same things to her that he had done to his other victims, both eighteen years before in Illinois and more recently in Houston.

But Angelica was a fighter and when he started to push her up the stairs of the empty apartments, she twisted loose from his grip and ran for her life.

He shot her in the back of the head.

When a wrecker reported coming across her abandoned car some hours later, officers responded by searching the nearby empty complex, where they found Angelica Jackson slumped onto an outside stairwell.

Her birthday cake still rested on the backseat of the car.

She died tragically as her birthday dawned, leaving two children motherless, a widowed father shattered and a grieving mother-in-law obsessed with changing the flawed criminal justice system that had turned a monster like Theodore Goynes loose.

As Angelica's devastated mother-in-law later explained, she was "the backbone of the family," caring not just for her own two children and her loving husband, but for her elderly grandmother who was ailing and had no one else to care for her. She was beloved by her entire family and greatly liked by her co-workers. No one could understand how such a terrible thing could happen to such a good person.

No one, that is, except for maybe Theodore Goynes.

But even before Goynes was arrested, Vivien Jackson mounted a protest on behalf of her beloved daughter-in-law. At the time, the state of Texas had some 300,000 people on probation and 70,000 more on parole—more than any other state in the country. The neighborhood where the abduction had taken place was crowded with halfway houses and loitering, ill-supervised parolees—a neighborhood Mrs. Jackson referred to as a "rape nest."

Mrs. Jackson notified media outlets of her outrage and involved everyone from the governor's office to the Houston City Council.

"This is not someone you will forget," she said. "We will not let this story die."

Homicide Sergeant John Silva called me in on a Saturday morning to do a sketch from the grocery-store parking lot witnesses.

Now a full-time employee of the Houston Police Department, I was in my very own office. Sunlight streamed through the windows that looked out on the Houston city-scape of tall, mirrored-glass buildings; but the dark world of hawk-faced, scowling men in dusky parking lots, brandishing guns at terrified young mothers before dragging them off to their deaths, was very much in the room as the two clerks described the killer to me in careful detail.

When I was done, uniformed officers whisked me off to a previous engagement—painting the faces of children at the Heights Festival, a local fall carnival where I had volunteered to help my church raise money.

Having spent the early morning sketching the glowering face of a brutal murderer, I spent the rest of the morning painting Teenage Mutant Ninja Turtles, Bart Simpsons, rainbows, clouds and butterflies on the faces of children who squealed with enchantment whenever I handed them a mirror.

Light and dark. That is my world.

Over the weekend, I'd though a lot about Jane Carr—the woman who'd been stuffed in the box like a corpse. I don't know why, but I felt strongly that her case was somehow linked to Angelica Jackson's. So first thing Monday morning, I followed up on my powerful urge and called Sgt. McClelland.

"Sgt. McClelland...There's something about this Jackson murder that makes me think it's linked to your Jane Carr case."

Of all the reactions I would have come to expect from McClelland, laughter was not one of them, but that's what he did—laughed out loud.

"I can't believe it!" he cried. "I just this minute got off the phone with Homicide!"

Sgt. McClelland had spotted a connection between the two cases, too, but his was based on fact, not the hunches I had: the similar locations of the abductions, the similar automobiles of the victims, the way the abductor got into the *back seat*—not the front—and pressed a gun to the ribcage of both victims and the way they were both taken to abandoned buildings.

Homicide agreed and soon with renewed vigor McClelland was hot on the trail of Jane Carr's abductor.

That same night, officers responding to a "domestic disturbance" call noticed that the man at the apartment resembled my sketch of the man who had abducted and murdered Angelica Jackson.

The officer who recognized the resemblance was an officer whose head was in the game; he was paying close attention; he was taking compositry seriously. And because of his alertness, a case that spanned two states and twenty years and involved untold suffering by numerous victims, was eventually cracked.

The key was a forensic sketch that took less than an hour.

Officers respond to hundreds of domestic calls every year, but the patrolman answering that call was alert to the fact that a composite sketch had been done regarding a particularly vicious unsolved murder and because of that, a very bad man was caught.

A man named Theodore Goynes.

They hauled Goynes in for a line-up and McClelland made sure that, along with the grocery-store clerks who had witnessed Angelica Jackson's abduction, Jane Carr was also there.

A week later, while I was at the Artesian building working another case, I saw Sgt. McClelland coming down the hall.

"Did you do a line-up?" I called out.

He gave a triumphant, "Yes!"

"Was Jane Carr there?"

Again, he yelled jubilantly, "Yes!"

By this time, he'd drawn close to me and I said, "Well, did she pick him out?"

Suddenly, he lunged down onto one knee, pumped a fist in the air and gave a cheerleader shout: *"YES!"*

When he got to his feet, I laughed with happiness and said, "Did she cry?"

With a relaxed grin, he answered, "Ye-e-es."

"And did you hug her?" (I already knew the answer.)

In a satisfied, peaceful tone, he nodded and said, "Of course."

It was over, for us, but for the victims of Theodore Goynes and their families, it would never be over. In Illinois, for example, three women, who had believed the monster who had tried to kill them would be locked up for forty years, now had to come down to Texas to testify, once again, as to the horrors they'd experienced at his hands years before.

After sitting, dumbstruck, through hours of testimony by women who'd been raped, sodomized, bludgeoned, stabbed, tied up and set on fire by Theodore Goynes, the jury two hours later convicted him of capital murder in the death of Angelica Jackson. They sentenced him to death by lethal injection.

Vivien Jackson was there. She praised the homicide detectives who she said "didn't get any sleep at all" during the investigation. She also thanked God and the jury, saying, "The system is still broken, still needs fixing," but stated that the trial had helped her come to terms with her loss and had drawn the family closer.

And she continued the fight. "They've put a lot of Theodore Goyneses out there," she told newspaper reporters, "and every one of them can hurt a lot of people."

She added, "They're just like cockroaches...and one cockroach can lay a thousand eggs."

Eventually, this determined lady testified before both the Texas Senate Committee on Criminal Justice and the Texas Pardons and Paroles Division of the Texas Department of Criminal Justice. Because of her efforts—and those of others like her—reforms were eventually instigated in Texas, such as the "three strikes you're out" law, that locks felons up for life after the third conviction and the "life without possibility of parole" sentencing guidelines which had not been available to Texas juries before then.

Her brave and determined efforts came too late to save her own family from the vicious consequences of Theodore Goynes's crimes, but untold numbers of unsuspecting potential victims of other savage criminals like Theodore Goynes are going about their lives today, thanks to the protections put in place by the reforms Vivien Jackson helped to bring about.

Theodore Goynes was a diagnosed paranoid schizophrenic who experienced auditory hallucinations too—but from the very beginning he stalked his victims, eventually took them to isolated locations he had clearly already checked out, tied them up and made every effort to kill them before leaving them for dead.

The FBI considers violent paranoid schizophrenics to fit a profile they refer to as "disorganized."

How, exactly, is what Theodore Goynes did disorganized?

The problem with such obviously mentally ill criminals is that, no matter whether they are confined in prison or in forensic hospitals, they respond well to the routine and structure and when they are forced to take their medications every day, they blossom. Their symptoms subside, they go about their lives in a visibly "normal" fashion and eventually, it seems as if there is no longer any reason to keep them incarcerated. They are paroled or released or judged "of sound mind" by psychiatric staff and, after being encouraged to continue taking their medications, are released on an unsuspecting society.

Here's where it gets sticky, though. Once he or she is free, someone who is mentally ill can *choose* not to take his or her medication. Now, at some point, they have to know the consequences of *not* taking their meds. And yet some, like Theodore Goynes, steadfastly refuse to continue taking their medication.

When they stop taking their medication many slip back into insanity, they commit more crimes, they are incarcerated or hospitalized, they are medicated, they calm down, they are released, they stop taking their meds... and if they are Theodore Goynes, they start prowling the streets almost immediately, looking for hideaways, looking for victims to kill.

And, just like the fictional character in Poe's "The Tell-Tale Heart," Goynes then took great care to hide his crimes.

The most terrifying aspect of this story is that it happens so many times, in so many places, all over this country, because we as a nation seem incapable of hitting upon a solution for handling the Theodore Goyneses of the world.

In her book, *The Mad, the Bad and the Innocent: the Criminal Mind on Trial—Tales of a Forensic Psychologist* (Little, Brown, 1997), Barbara R. Kirwin, Ph.D., draws upon twenty-five years of experience working with the criminally insane and those who claim to be. She has consulted on more than a hundred homicide cases and often appears on television.

Dr. Kirwin explains the inadequacies of an overworked and underbudgeted system, groaning under the challenges of deciding sanity or insanity on one simple rule, the M'Naghten Rule. The M'Naghten Rule simply states that, if someone knows what he did and knows it is wrong—then no matter how mentally ill he is or what his psychiatric or criminal history— *he is sane.*

Dr. Kirwin makes a compelling case for a new plea, different from the one that has so many prosecutors, defense attorneys, juries and judges hamstrung—the old and outdated *innocent by reason of insanity*.

She urges that more states adopt the more sensible *guilty but insane*.

If a defendant is adjudged "guilty but insane," then he is to be incarcerated for the rest of his life, with no possibility of parole or release—not in
prison—but in a tightly-guarded, high-security forensic hospital. He would
be given the treatment he needs as well as any medication that helps with
his symptoms, but no matter how well he responds to those medications,
no matter how much he promises to keep taking them on the outside...he
is never, ever, ever to be released.

In other words, no court-appointed shrink or panel of psychologists
can conduct a cursory interview and scrawl, "the defendant is of sound
mind," and turn him over to be set free, as with Goynes. No overcrowded
prison can release him because, since the criminal is so well-behaved on his
medication, he has added up many years in "good time," as happened with
Goynes. And no judge can simply turn this kind of savage criminal over to
the sloppy care of a mental hospital on the grounds that he is "innocent by
reason of insanity," thus setting up the very real possibility that, in a few
short months' time, he can be released, as happened, again, with Theodore
Goynes.

On the other hand, convicted felons who are seriously mentally ill
would not then be turned over to the prison system and blended in to the
general prison population, as so many of them are now, where they may or
may not receive adequate psychiatric care. After all, is it really fair for, say, a
two-bit non-violent burglar to be forced to share a cell with someone who
might slit his throat in his sleep simply because the voices told him to?

As a society, we just don't seem to know what to do about or with the
mentally ill. And when it comes to the criminally mentally ill, especially
those as violent as Theodore Goynes, we seem comfortable handling the
problem only one way—with the death penalty.

Don't misunderstand me. I'm not saying Theodore Goynes didn't
deserve to die. He chose to stop taking his medication. He chose to stalk
women, attack them, try to kill them and eventually, hide their bodies. Like
Poe's fictional narrator, on some deep level somewhere in his mind—he
knew what he was doing.

In the final analysis, I believe if any of us should ever find ourselves at
the mercy of another who fully intends to see us die, there is only one thing
we can do and it doesn't have anything to do with courts or mental health
professionals or cops or lawyers or doctors or anybody or anything else.

It has to do with what each and every one of us possesses, deep within our souls: *the will to live.*

That God-given will to live I pray will grant us a supernatural strength or courage, or cunning, or endurance, or wisdom—whatever it takes to survive.

In the end, that's what we all have to have while there are so many Theodore Goyneses out there running around loose in the world, looking for victims.

Live.

Like those three heroic women in Illinois and Jane Carr in Houston...we all just have to do whatever it takes to live.

Chapter Nine:

"Some People Just Need Killin'"

John Wesley Hardin was one of the most notorious outlaws ever to ride the old West of Texas during the mid-nineteenth century. At the age of thirteen, he killed a classmate on the playground and by the time he was seventeen years old, he'd killed a dozen men. While still a teenager, Hardin is even reputed to have backed down the legendary marshal, Wild Bill Hickock. Eventually, he would put more than thirty notches on his gun before finally being shot down himself in 1895 at the age of forty-two.

I knew an old-time west Texas cowboy who was related to John Wesley Hardin, whom the family called "Wes." The old-timer liked to grin with a twinkle in his eye and say, "Uncle Wes never killed nobody that didn't need killin'." Then he added, "Wes used to always say, 'Some people just need killin'."

Well, as a Christian, I can't just come right out and say that I agree with my old friend (who has since passed on), but I will say that if such a thing were true, then there are few people who I think might need killin' more than Donald Eugene Dutton.

When he wasn't thieving or fighting, Dutton liked to wear his favorite plaid shirt, crawl through open windows of women's apartments, threaten them with a knife and brutally rape them. In 1980, he was convicted of aggravated sexual assault and sentenced to twenty years, but he was paroled after serving six and a half years of his sentence.

Almost immediately, Dutton put on his plaid shirt and went back to raping and pillaging. After seven different victims reported similar attacks in the Galleria area, he became known as the "Galleria Rapist." In 1987, before police identified the Galleria Rapist as Dutton, I did a sketch of him from a witness description. A cop who stopped Dutton's car on suspicion of drunk driving thought the driver looked like my sketch and when he looked closer, he saw that Dutton was wearing a plaid shirt.

Dutton was arrested again. When the witness who had sketched his image with me picked him out of a line-up and testified in court, Dutton was convicted of aggravated sexual assault with a deadly weapon and burglary of habitation with intent to commit sexual assault. He was given a forty-year sentence.

On November 15, 1990, after serving seven years of that sentence, Dutton and a buddy, both of whom worked in the prison kitchen, climbed over a fence and escaped from the Ramsey I Unit of the Texas Department of Criminal Justice in Rosharon, in Brazoria County. The other guy was caught by law enforcement within hours, but Dutton stole a pickup truck from a residence and made his getaway in a dense fog, slipping through a police perimeter.

From there, stealing cars and license plates as he went along, Dutton drove to Houston. He lived on stolen credit cards and numerous burglaries of private homes.

On January 5, 1991, Dutton once again donned a plaid shirt and began cruising the general vicinity of Houston's Galleria mall, his old stomping grounds. Located near the busiest freeway in the United States—the West Loop—the mall and its surrounding developments have since become the nation's eighth-largest business district, marked by the kind of soulless gray monotony that characterizes Houston's out-of-control oil-boom growth that soon went bust.

Though I confess I do like shopping there, the Galleria was unfavorably described in a December, 2003 *Texas Monthly* article, "The Accidental City," by Michael Ennis. In the article, a former University of Houston writing professor named Phillip Lopate is quoted as saying, "Managing to combine the twin nightmares of claustrophobic congestion and anemic vacuity, the Galleria is my idea of hell...Houston suffers from this malaise of placelessness and nowhere more so than in the Galleria area."

If the Galleria vicinity is "hell," then surely Donald Eugene Dutton was the devil. On the night of January 4 and the wee hours of the morning on January 5, Dutton kidnapped and attempted to sexually assault a woman near the Galleria mall. Whether he intended to kill her is unclear, but the terrified woman managed to get away from Dutton and ran for her life.

Just a few minutes later, about 2:30 A.M., while Dutton was driving around (no doubt searching for easier prey), he rolled through a stop sign, thus attracting the attention of thirty-four-year-old Patrol Officer Paul A. Deason.

Deason, stocky with a military-style crew cut and built like a wrestler, was a ten-year veteran of the Houston Police Department and known for being tough. When he switched on his cruiser lights and pulled over what looked like a new Buick Electra with spoked wheels, Deason did not notify police dispatchers or radio in the license plate number. This is because the departmental safety and procedure policy had recently undergone a change and officers were no longer required to make such reports.

Getting out of his patrol car on the deserted, dimly-lit street, Officer Deason was completely alone and he had no warning as to just how dangerous the driver of the car he had stopped was.

"In this line of work," he often said, "we don't know who we stop, who we come in contact with, or who we're dealing with."

This is the very reason that law enforcement's number one commandment is, *There is no such thing as a routine traffic stop.*

When Officer Deason approached the vehicle, Donald Dutton climbed out of the car, walked straight toward Deason and shot him with a 9mm handgun point-blank in the face.

The impact of the bullet entering Deason's left cheek spun him around. As he was going down, Dutton shot Deason again in the back. The officer fell to the ground, but that wasn't enough for Dutton.

Calmly, he got back into the car, pulled a U-turn and deliberately drove over the inert form of Paul Deason.

As Deason rolled and tumbled beneath the car, his utility belt, which contained his gun and holster, got caught on the underbelly of the vehicle and Deason was dragged over the pavement for ten, twenty, thirty, forty, fifty...sixty feet.

Unbelievably, the tough cop was not only still alive, but conscious. He reached up and pushed against the undercarriage of the car. One of his hands happened to land on the hot muffler and the skin of the palm of his hand was burned off before his belt broke away and he fell free of the speeding car, which roared off into the distance.

Incredibly, this brave officer staggered to his feet and stumbled all the way back to his patrol car, where he radioed in his own assist call.

Astonished police dispatchers recorded Officer Deason, in a voice amazingly calm and coherent, saying, "I've been shot and run over," before requesting back-up and an ambulance.

Help came screaming up within sixty seconds and officers thronged from squad cars, thunderstruck to see the injured cop still standing, blood pouring from his face and back, uniform hanging in tatters, body bruised and scraped and grease-stained from his ordeal.

In clear, cognizant language, Deason described the vehicle he had stopped, what he saw of its driver and told what happened. Then he added, "I'm not feeling so good and my back hurts."

An ambulance arrived with lightning speed and Paul Deason was raced to the hospital, where things got grim and serious very, very quickly. He was rushed into surgery and operated on for three hours. Then he was put in Intensive Care where after two days he was still in guarded condition.

That's when they called me.

Homicide paged me just as I was emerging from the elevator in the lobby of my doctor's office, where I'd gone for an emergency Monday morning visit. The Friday night before, a freak accident at home had left me with a serious puncture wound in my upper thigh, near the buttocks. Unwilling to brave big-city hospital emergency rooms alongside victims of gunshots, stabbings and car wrecks, I'd waited until my family doctor's office hours began.

By then, the spreading infection in my thigh and buttocks had reached such a ferocious state that the doctor ordered me hospitalized. When I begged off he handed me a bottle full of pills and demanded that I go straight home and stay in bed.

"Don't get up for four days," he commanded. "Don't get up for anything except to go to the bathroom, do you hear me? You mess around with this wound and you are flirting with amputation."

Amputation. Four days. Straight home. Bed. Got it.

And then Homicide called.

I'd been with the police department long enough by this time that these cops were my brothers and sisters. I'd heard on the news about Officer Deason two nights before and had been grief-stricken along with the law enforcement officers who served alongside him. I assumed he might die, but the detective who called me assured me that Paul not only was still alive, but ready to talk with me so I could do a sketch of the vicious criminal who'd assaulted him.

Listening to the officer from Homicide tell me the details I knew I couldn't go home. Not yet. This was *family*.

The emergency sketch would have to be done at the hospital, where Officer Deason, heavily sedated, was drifting in and out of consciousness. Nobody knew who had done this terrible thing to such a fine and good man, but whoever it was, he was still out there and he had to be stopped.

Cop-killers and potential cop-killers engender such passion for justice, such an intense urge to catch them, from other cops because, hey, first it's one of our own. You hurt him or her, you hurt us. And I won't lie to you, that is definitely part of it.

But not all. There's another even more compelling reason.

If a man is willing to shoot a police officer point-blank in the face, run him over in a car and drag him sixty-five feet...then what do you think he would do to a civilian?

Let's say a young mother is in her car waiting for a traffic light to change and this killer wants her car. He wouldn't hesitate to shoot her, yank the car seat with screaming child out of the back seat, throw it over his shoulder and take off in the car. If he wanted a pack of cigarettes, he wouldn't think twice about killing the convenience store operator who was too slow to get them down for him. Cop-killers are known to be the most dangerous criminals out there. When a cop-killer roams the streets, not one of us is safe.

So I'd have to wait to follow my doctor's orders to go home and rest. I limped out to the car, went to retrieve my easel and drawing supplies and drove—sitting sideways avoiding my one throbbing buttock-cheek—to Ben Taub Hospital where Officer Deason lay near death.

Hobbling out of the elevator, wincing with pain, I grappled with my easel and supplies, nodded at the handsome officer guarding Officer Deason's door and entered Paul Deason's room.

All it took was one glance at him and I forgot all about my own dis-
comfort.

There he lay, swathed in so many bandages that he easily could have
passed for a mummy in some Hollywood B-movie, tubes dangling from
every orifice, his strong body draped with sheets like a child.

He was sleeping. I set up my easel and sketchpad as quietly as I could,
blinking back tears the whole time. Seeing his wounds and condition and
having had the details of the attack told to me by Sergeant Boyd Smith
from Homicide, I, like all the rest of the Houston Police Department, marveled that Deason was still alive.

All I could think about was that I knew how it felt to be almost-dead
and my heart broke for him.

Stop it, I scolded myself. *You have to show at least as much courage as he has.*

The space beside his bed was very narrow, but I pulled up a chair as
close to him as I could and balanced my equipment, my pastels, lapboard
and facial identification catalogue in my lap. When I was ready to begin, I
leaned over and put my lips close to his ear.

"Paul, I'm Lois, the sketch artist," I whispered. "I'm going to try to
draw a picture of the guy who did this to you. I'm sorry to put you through
this, but I can sketch very quickly so it won't be so hard for you."

In a soft tone I continued to talk to him until he began to awaken, but
because his sleep was drug-induced, he was very groggy.

His voice slurred, he muttered, "All I saw was the fire coming out of
his gun. I never saw his face."

This is a very common reaction from any victim of a point-blank gunshot. In their conscious mind, all they can remember is the barrel of the
gun; often it assumes exaggerated proportions in their imaginations, black,
ugly, deadly. They can recall the explosion of the gunshot, the deafening
noise, even the smell of gunpowder, but in most cases, they insist that they
did not see the faces of the gunmen.

Still, I knew that there were 5,000 law enforcement officers waiting for
me to produce a likeness of this vicious criminal. I couldn't let them down
and I couldn't let Paul Deason down.

Over the years, I had developed a technique that had proven to be
highly effective in helping witnesses recall the faces of their attackers. I
decided to try it here. With no argument, I dropped the idea that he had

to remember. Instead, I spoke about how good it was that he was alive and safe. I assured Deason that he was going to make it and I teased him gently, saying, "You look cute all wrapped up like that."

He gave a soft, hesitant chuckle at my little joke, so I said, "You are so tough and it's so wonderful that you have survived. I can't believe what a crummy person this guy must be. What kind of person would do this? What kind of expression did he have?"

Then, biting my lip, I fell silent and waited. Inside, I was *praying* that my little ploy had worked.

It did.

After a breathless moment, Deason's voice became strong and clear and he said, "He didn't have any expression. He looked like a shark. Like he didn't care about anything at all."

My mind screamed *YESSSS!* and it was all I could do not to pump my fist in the air. *He had seen the face.*

So maybe...*maybe*...I could get this done.

I asked him standard questions about an attacker any cop is trained to notice: race, height, weight, average build and age. Then I got to the hard part.

Opening the *FBI Facial Identification Catalogue*, I turned to the first page of eyes and said, "Just pick out the eye shape that is as close as possible. I can make any changes you want, no matter how small."

I had to stand up, hold the book horizontally over his face and wait. There were 180 different eye shapes in the catalogue. Paul pointed to the third pair of eyes on the page. Unsure if he was clear about what we were supposed to be doing, I turned a few more pages, but he stuck to his first selection.

While I drew, he began to slip in and out of consciousness. When I was able to show him noses, he pointed to the first nose on the page—again, out of 180 examples.

I was starting to get worried. Was he just trying to get rid of me? Not that I blamed him, but it was so important that we get it right. I asked him about the hair and forehead.

Again, he chose the first example on the page.

Trying not to show my concern, I sketched as quickly as possible.

"He had a moustache," Paul said.

Though it takes me less than a minute to draw moustaches, we were abruptly interrupted by hospital orderlies, who banged into the room, unhooked various IV drips and proceeded to roll Paul's bed right straight out the door!

Yanking up the basics of my gear, I flew out of the room, racing after them, hollering, "Where are you taking him?"

As they disappeared into an elevator, I thought I heard one of them say "CAT scan."

Almost in tears, I ran back to the room, grabbed my purse and took the next elevator.

Scanning directions posted on hospital corridors, I managed to find the room where they'd taken Paul and pushed my way through swinging double doors after him. They were positioning his bed in a long line behind other beds along the side of a large open room. At the head of the line, patients' beds were being rolled through a large machine that I guessed to be a CAT scan.

Resolutely, I headed for Paul's bed.

"You need to get out of here."

Blocking my way was a man in scrubs. I didn't know if he was a doctor or a nurse or a technician or what, but he was stern and unyielding.

"Authorized personnel only!" he barked. "You must leave now."

"I'm a forensic artist with the Houston Police Department," I told him. "How long will Officer Deason have to wait until he gets to the machine?"

The man frowned. He wore glasses and his eyes were haughty behind them. "About half an hour," he said. "At most."

"Look," I said, showing him the sketch. "As you can see, I'm almost finished. All I need is the moustache and mouth. I can do that in two minutes. Literally 120 seconds."

Voice dripping with sarcasm, he said, "Your hearing must be bad. I said, *get out.*" He took a threatening step toward me.

I stood my ground. "I have to do this sketch," I pleaded. "We've got to catch the man who did this to him. You said we had a half-hour before he gets to the CAT scan and I'm telling you, I can finish this sketch in less than two minutes!"

"That's it," he snarled. "I'm calling security and having you thrown out right now!"

Something in me snapped. There was a vicious criminal who was a potential cop-killer on the loose.

A killer.

An entire police department was depending upon me to come up with a likeness that could get this guy caught before he did something even worse than what he'd done to Officer Deason.

Not only that, but my own leg wound was screaming at me by now and I could only imagine what my doctor would have said if he'd seen me tromping all over the hospital when I was supposed to be in bed myself.

I didn't have time to wait. Period.

I didn't have time to put up with this little bureaucratic creep.

And most of all, I didn't have time for social niceties. Not when Paul Deason lay there, fighting for his life with every breath he took.

I smiled at the man in scrubs and, leaning very close to him, I put my lips up to his ear and in my most sweet and seductive tones, said, "I'm trying to catch a mother-fucking potential cop-killer, here. The monster we're trying to catch shot this man twice, ran over him and dragged him sixty-five feet. It's a miracle this officer is even alive. I just told you this sketch could catch the guy!" My voice rising, I cried, "What is the matter with you? Do you want to run into this guy on your way home tonight?"

Stepping back from my scorching words, he blanched, blinked behind his glasses, turned on his heel and pushed his way out of the swinging doors.

I didn't know if Paul had heard my angry exchange or not, but I knew I had no time to waste. Holding the catalogue over his face, I asked him to select lips and a chin.

Each time, he pointed at the first picture on the page.

Oh, Lord.

By this time, I was seriously worried. It was hard for me to imagine that this suspect somehow resembled the first set of features shown on every page of the catalogue. Sadly, I decided that Officer Deason must be too seriously hurt, too drugged, to be able to hold his concentration long enough to be of much help.

"One last question," I said with a sigh. "What kind of shirt did he have on?"

Without hesitation, Officer Deason whispered, "A plaid flannel shirt."

In the back of my mind, I felt a tiny jolt of recognition, but was too busy and rushed at that moment to give it much thought. All I could think of—ask any artist and they'll all tell you—was that a plaid shirt is one of the most difficult items of clothing you can draw. It's not the pattern itself, it's what happens to the lines when draped over the human body and the lines go every which way, especially near buttons and collars.

Here I was standing on a leg throbbing from a massive infection, dodging hostile doctors and congregated cops, working with a half-dead witness...and having to draw a freakin' *plaid shirt.*

Why oh why couldn't that son of a bitch have at least been wearing a *solid shirt?*

But, thanks to all those River Walk portraits I once did (you would not believe how many male Texas tourists wear plaid cowboy shirts), I was able to complete the drawing quickly. I held the sketch over Paul's face and asked him if there were any changes that needed to be made.

Without a word, he slowly lifted his hand and, with his index finger, pointed at the sketch, but didn't speak.

"Honey," I said patiently, "does this look like the guy?"

But Paul didn't answer. He just pointed at the sketch.

I had seen this kind of reaction a couple of times before in my career, both times with hospitalized witnesses dazed from drugs. It was as if they'd exhausted every single reserve of strength they had in their poor broken, injured bodies and traumatized minds. Just getting through the sketching process had left them with not one more ounce of energy simply to say, "Yes, it looks like him," but that's what the reaction meant.

With a soft squeeze of gratitude on Paul's arm, I gathered up my gear and left him as quickly as I could so he could rest. I limped on my throbbing leg back to his room. Sgt. Smith showed up just as I was leaving and it was a good thing, because by this time I was feeling weak and ill from my own infection. I had neglected to bring any fixatif to spray on the drawing, but I handed the sketch to Sgt. Smith, who thanked me profusely in his usual princely manner.

Though I had serious misgivings about the accuracy of the drawing, since Paul had chosen each feature so quickly without hardly looking, I didn't say anything about these doubts to Sgt. Smith.

But as I dragged my painful way down the hall toward the elevator, I suddenly remembered what it was about that plaid shirt that had struck me.

The Galleria Rapist. What was his name? Punching the elevator buttons, I shifted my weight to my good leg and pondered.

Dutton.

Yeah, that was it. Donald...Eugene...Dutton.

A couple of days later, about 7:30 in the evening, Donald Eugene Dutton decided to shoplift a chain saw from a Sears store at Memorial City Mall in Houston.

It made me shudder. Why would a guy like Dutton need a chain saw? It's not like he was planning to cut firewood for the old fireplace, was he?

I thought about his last victim, the one he'd grabbed and tried to rape before Officer Deason pulled him over that fateful night. She had escaped.

I have a theory—and it's just a theory, mind you, not based on any legal documents or anything Dutton is known to have said either to law enforcement or in court—but I strongly suspect that he was planning another kidnapping and sexual assault.

And *this* time, I figure his plan was that his victim would not escape.

And she would not be able to testify against him.

With a chain saw, he could dispose of a body pretty handily, I think.

It's just a theory.

But you have to wonder.

Anyway, he decided to shoplift the chain saw—for whatever diabolical reason—but when he tried to leave the store, a manager spotted him with it and yelled, "Stop him! He's a shoplifter!"

Store security personnel gave chase. Dropping the chain saw, Dutton sprinted out the door and took off across the parking lot. Three bystanders joined in the chase. One of them, an off-duty DEA agent, caught up to Dutton first. Grabbing a handful of shirt and trousers, he tackled Dutton, dragged him indoors and with store security, held him in the manager's office until an HPD officer arrived.

By that time, my sketch had been widely distributed in the media and had been on the evening news of all three local Houston networks, as well as published in the *Houston Chronicle*.

The DEA agent remarked to the HPD officer that this guy sure did seem to resemble the sketch he'd seen on TV of the man who had tried to kill Patrolman Deason.

"Sure does," agreed the cop.

Almost immediately, the HPD arranged a line-up, which they video-taped and showed to Paul Deason in his hospital room.

He picked out Donald Eugene Dutton.

After that, a group of detectives converged on the Sears parking lot and crawled around, shining their powerful flashlights up underneath the cars.

And before very long, they found a vehicle with pieces of Paul Deason's uniform hanging from the undercarriage and a handmark of his skin burned into the muffler.

Paul Deason not only survived his horrendous wounds, but as soon as he was recovered, he went right back out on patrol, where he can still be found today, protecting and serving the citizens of Houston.

At the trial of Donald Eugene Dutton, I was called to testify and as I walked up to the wooden bench outside the courtroom to wait to be called, I spotted a police officer sitting there. He was muscular, clean-shaven and his name tag read *P.A. DEASON.*

With a big smile, I said, "Well, hi, Officer Deason."

With a taciturn, somewhat stern expression, he folded his massive arms over his chest and said, "Can I help you, ma'am?"

He had absolutely no idea who I was.

A little hurt, I responded, "Oh, Paul, I'm the person who did the drawing with you in the hospital. I'm the sketch artist."

He was immediately apologetic. "I'm so sorry!" he cried. "I never did see your face." Then, with a big grin, he said, "All I remember is your sweet voice and that you're the one who cussed out that doctor."

Blushing, I had to laugh. Little did he know that I almost never use that kind of language, but hey, as the saying goes, desperate times call for desperate measures.

Nevertheless, he was laughing with me and it was like we had survived a war together. We were vets.

After we each testified, we were permitted to enter the courtroom to hear closing arguments. And though the defense attorney did his best to persuade the jury that it was only a coincidence that Dutton had in his pocket the keys to the car on which detectives found bits of Paul's uniform and skin—they didn't buy it.

Donald Eugene Dutton was convicted of multiple counts that included attempted capital murder of a police officer and aggravated sexual assault and given a life sentence.

After the trial, Paul Deason came up to me, pulled me close and kissed me on the cheek. It was a wonderful kiss, a brotherly, professional, appreciative kiss and I loved it. From that moment on, our friendship was sealed.

He said, "I really don't remember doing the sketch with you. All I remember was at the end, when I put my finger out to show you it looked like him."

Later, Paul said that he was so amazed at the likeness that we managed to produce of his assailant that it was as if I had been reading his mind that day, even though he could barely talk. He added, "She's clairvoyant."

But as far as I'm concerned, this is yet another example of one brave officer's heroism. Clinging to life with every fiber of his being, fighting against the morphine and the Demerol and whatever else was pumping through his body at the time, struggling to remember a glimpse of a face that held no expression "like a shark," before the flash of the gun that had nearly killed him, he somehow managed to come up with the description that put one twentieth-century Texas outlaw behind bars for the rest of his life.

As far as Deason picking out the first feature he saw in the book I'd shown him, the joke was on me. Turns out that all of Dutton's features *did* resemble the first one or two displayed in the *FBI Facial Identification Catalogue*. Officer Deason, for all his bleary-eyed struggle, had not been trying to get rid of me, after all. He'd been picking out his assailant's correct features.

So thanks to Paul Deason, there won't be any more notches on Dutton's gun.

Or any more cause for him to go looking for chain saws.

Still, my most fervent hope, where Donald Eugene Dutton is concerned, is that he never, ever gets out of jail.

Because the first thing he'd do, I'm sure, is shoplift a nice, new plaid shirt for himself.

Chapter Ten:

Tricky Drawings, Successful Endings

Before long, I was working on over 300 cases a year. It was a juggling act, scheduling rapes and murders and robberies into jam-packed days. However, not only did I finally have my own office, but both of my children were in school, so I didn't have to worry about not being there for them during the day. But life was hectic, all the same.

In the middle of a particularly busy day, I got a call from a young woman with one of those little-girl voices that made her sound like a child. Her name was Christina ("Tina") Shiets. She lived in Cypress, a suburb of Houston.

"Ms. Gibson," she said, "I have called just about everywhere, it feels like, looking for someone to help me. I've written to the producers of *Unsolved Mysteries*—the TV show? And they've turned me down twice. I even called the FBI. In fact, they're the ones who gave me your phone number."

I must admit, she had my attention. "What can I do for you?"

She cleared her throat. "Well, thirty-two years ago, my mother was killed in a car accident."

"Oh, I'm so sorry..." I began, but she cut me off.

"My two brothers and I were left basically orphans."

She paused a moment. Then her voice became clear and positive. "That's okay, I mean, I've accepted that part of my life. But what I need is help finding my two brothers. We were separated not long after Mom's death."

"How old were you?"

"I was four and my brother Chris was two and my baby brother, Chip, was a year old. Anyway, my great aunt and uncle took me to raise and they would have gladly taken my brothers, but they went with their biological father. I had a different dad. Eventually, he found that he couldn't care for them the way he'd thought. Chris and Chip were put into foster care and eventually, they were adopted."

I murmured sounds of sympathy and she went on. "The truth is, we were all just victims of circumstance; nobody had any real choices. But the thing is, nobody ever asked me how I felt about losing my brothers or even if I wanted to keep in touch with them. They just vanished from my life.

"I've always longed for my brothers and wanted to be with them. From the time I was sixteen, I tried to find my brothers. Finally, about six months ago, I managed to track down the foster parents who first took them in and the woman gave me a couple of photographs of them and an old home movie and even the two little baby bow ties they were wearing in the photographs."

Before I could comment, she said, "Finding my brothers' original foster parents, getting this tape and all, well, it's been a tremendous breakthrough. I've been overjoyed. Now I'm bound and determined to find someone who can help me. Ms. Gibson, do you think you could do a drawing of my brothers' faces, the way they would look now?"

So, let me get this straight, I thought, *you want to give me a picture of a one-year-old baby and a two-year-old toddler and want me to do a sketch of how they would look at thirty-one and thirty-two years of age?*

At that point I didn't know any artists who had ever done an age-progression of an infant into an adult in their thirties. The computer programs of that time that were designed to do age-progressions didn't go past the age of seventeen! In fact, one expert in the field had been asked to take an eight-year-old and age-progress her to the age of forty-two and he had refused.

For heaven's sake, where would I even START?

"Ms. Gibson, I don't know who else to ask," said Tina, "All my life, I've felt this big hole in my heart where my brothers belong and I will never be able to rest until I can fill that hole. Even if...even if they're dead or something...I just want to *know*."

Somewhat desperately, I imagined myself sitting in front of my easel, trying to warm up, preparing to take a photograph of a baby and turn him into a full-grown man.

How would I even WARM UP?

Then I remembered something that almost made me laugh out loud. Once I'd seen a comedian on TV, who had this routine where he said, "What about the guy who catches a bullet in his teeth? Where's the warm-up for THAT? I mean, what does the guy do—have the guy who's gonna shoot the gun start by just throwing the bullet in his face so he can catch it? Then, after a few times, he shoots? Where's the warm-up for THAT?"

Somebody else—a foolish woman, surely not me—said, "Sure, Tina. I'll try to help you. I'll do an age progression of your brothers."

Ready...aim...FIRE!

Tina came to my home and carefully laid out the precious photos of her long-lost brothers. To my relief, they weren't fuzzy snapshots, but high-quality studio portraits. Every detail of their baby features was clearly visible. Having transferred the brief, 8mm home movies of the boys onto VHS, Tina handed me the video and we plugged it into the VCR in my living room.

I watched as two happy little boys romped in the ocean, gleefully chasing waves back and forth in the warm sunshine. The next scene depicted one of the boys buried in the sand, his arms and feet and rounded little tummy poking up, the other child patting the sand around him. They were both laughing. Then, briefly, a few shots of the two boys' faces stretched into big grins, approaching a deer in a petting zoo.

That was it.

Tina explained that the video of the boys had originally been an old 8mm home movie and that it had been smoke damaged. She'd had the film repaired and transferred to VHS.

By the end of the brief, happy video, any doubts I might have had about taking this case were gone.

"I've worked with *Unsolved Mysteries* many times," I told her. "And on three different occasions, we've been able to arrange family reunions because of age progressions that I've done for the show."

Looking her straight in the eye, I gave her my word. "Tina," I prom-ised, "I'll help you get on *Unsolved Mysteries* and we'll find your brothers."

We talked over a few other details of the case and Tina left.

And I was alone, staring at a blank piece of paper, wondering what in the world I was going to do next.

Pray.

That's what I did. I prayed. I was in over my head on this one and I knew it. I needed help, H-E-L-P.

I started with the younger brother first.

One thing I knew for sure going in was that there are certain features on the human face that remain identical from infancy to adulthood: the shapes of the nostril holes, the shapes of the eye openings, the shape of the eyebrows, the lip crease (the dark line where the lips meet), the shape of the top of the lip and the bottom lip contour. Also, the top of the ears lines up with the end of the eyes and eyebrows and the bottom of the ears lines up with the bottom of the nose.

There are also features that do change. The iris, for instance, occupies less of the eye opening, which means more white of the eye will be visi-ble; the iris exhibits more of the shape of a circle; the nose will lengthen; the whole face, in fact, will lengthen, from the bottom of the eyes on down. This makes the chin elongate and widen slightly. Eyebrows will take on a slightly darker, thicker-gauge of hair, but amazingly, the number and place-ment of those hairs will be identical to what they were when the subject was a baby. Adolescence tends to darken hair color somewhat—even more so into adulthood.

Since this boy was a blond, I figured his hair was likely to be a light brown by now. He had a "cowlick" on one side of his forehead—this was good. Cowlicks don't change.

Ah-HA! I thought. My cousin had a cowlick just like the one in the photograph. I remembered how he was wearing his hair now, so I used that hairstyle on my adult rendition of baby Chip...

...and I was on my way.

When Tina came to pick up my drawings, she stared at them with awe, even reverence and her eyes clouded a little. For a long time, she kept gazing at them and I felt that, even if we weren't able to find her brothers, this alone was a comfort to her.

But I wanted her to have the real thing.

Next we made good color copies of the drawings, the photographs of the boys, snapshots of the bow ties and I told her to have a good-quality copy made of the video she had shown me.

"Write a letter to *Unsolved Mysteries*," I instructed her, "and explain your situation briefly, including your struggle to find your brothers. Include the name, address and phone number of the boys' former foster mother." Then I told her to open a Federal Express account.

When she had everything ready, I called one of my contacts, a high-ranking official at *Unsolved Mysteries*. I pitched Tina's story as a segment for their "Lost Loved Ones" portion of the show. At the end, I reminded him that they'd had three successes on the program before with my sketches and added that they would be able to interview the former foster mother.

The producer was definitely interested and asked if I could send him some materials on the case. I promised they would be there the next day.

Within the week, Tina called breathlessly to tell me that the producers of *Unsolved Mysteries* would be flying her to Hollywood to tape her story.

The program aired, and before the show had even ended, the first phone call to come into the *Unsolved Mysteries* hotline was from an aunt of the boys. Within minutes, the boys' biological dad was calling. The next day, Tina was talking to her brother, Chip. Through Chip, she was able to contact her other brother, Chris.

Chris later explained, "I knew I had a sister. I couldn't remember her name, but I recalled that I called her 'Sissy' and that she took care of me and my baby brother. But every time I asked my parents, they swore I didn't have a sister. But I knew...I *knew*."

A Christmas reunion was planned at Chip's home in West Virginia and at long last, Tina was once again able to throw her arms around her brothers and know that she was no longer alone. It was the most joyous day of her life.

Within only a few days of their meeting, Chris moved to Houston to be closer to his sister. In no time they figured out that they liked all the same things and to this day, share a close and loving relationship.

Once Chris was settled in Cypress, I decided to pay Tina a visit so that I could collect current photographs of the two brothers to use in comparison to my drawings. I was anxious to see how I'd done and was gratified to find how closely my drawings resembled the two.

However, when we finally met and I saw that Chris had a moustache and long hair, I learned a valuable lesson for use in the future: whenever you do an age progression, it's a good idea to do one drawing clean-shaven and with short hair, then do transparent overlays with a moustache, long hair and/or glasses—or, with women—different hair styles and colors.

Chris was gentle and charming and when I got up to go, he suddenly drew me into a big hug and said, "I thought I would never find my big sister. Thank you so much for helping me find my Sissy!"

Doing age progression can be pretty tricky but on the long drive home I reflected that, were Tina and Chris the only people I was ever going to be able to help in my entire career…then it would all be worth it.

However, my work for Tina turned out to be only the first difficult age progression on which I worked. My next one was also tricky.

The summer of 1964 had been hot and lazy in Houston, Texas. The year before, there had been 120 murders reported and though the assassination of President John F. Kennedy in Dallas a few months before had shaken the country to its core, there was still a soft patina of innocence that overlay American life in general. The Vietnam War was only just beginning to intensify and the race riots and other violent changes that would take place in society throughout the sixties and seventies had not yet reached a fever pitch. Barry Goldwater was poised to take the Republican nomination for president and President Lyndon Johnson was already portraying him as a reckless hawk.

The Beatles had come to town and gone, but the "British Invasion" of rock groups had yet to hit our shores in waves. Music of the day was sedate; crooners like Sam Cooke, Perry Como and Rick Nelson as well as instrumentalists like Al Hirt and Henry Mancini were selling millions of record albums. Cigarette advertisements lit up the air waves and magazine pages. The sporty Ford Mustang was introduced and shouldered its way through the muscle cars of the day like the GTO and Thunderbird. A mouthy unknown boxer by the name of Cassius Clay TKO'd Sonny Liston for the heavyweight championship of the world. Julie Andrews won an Oscar for playing a British nanny in *Mary Poppins* and on TV, Gomer Pyle, USMC made soldiering something to laugh at.

Most people were not yet desensitized to violence; bad things seemed to happen to people who lived somewhere else. People were far more scared of Russian Communists and the atomic bomb than they were of getting murdered. Some contemplated building bomb shelters in their back yards while they never thought to lock their own front doors.

So when Thomas Martinez worked in his small northeast Houston store near 10 P.M. on the night of July 19, 1964, he thought nothing of letting his little boy, Tommy—ten years old at the time—hang out with him. Mr. Martinez, his brother James, an employee and Tommy were all in the store together when a man walked in and bought a soda. Suddenly, fire truck sirens blew past the building and James Martinez and the store employee ran outside to see what was going on.

At that moment, the man pulled out a pistol. Yanking young Tommy in front of him, he held the pistol to Tommy's head and demanded money.

Terrified for his son, Martinez immediately opened the cash register and gave all the cash to the robber. "Please don't hurt my son," pleaded Martinez. "I'll give you anything you want. Just don't hurt him."

The robber shoved Tommy behind the counter and demanded, "Give me more." Martinez pulled out his wallet and handed it over.

Without a word, the robber shot Thomas Martinez in the chest and fled the store.

Sweating and moaning, Martinez slumped onto the chair behind the cash register. "Carla," he whispered (his wife's name), "Carla..."

And as his sobbing child looked on, Thomas Martinez died.

The Martinez murder made the front page of the *Houston Chronicle*. According to reports, investigating officers later realized that the so-called "fire" that had drawn area fire fighters had been a false alarm, called in by the robber to distract the employee and brother of Thomas Martinez. They found the car of a man named Ora David Lott nearby and traced the vehicle's ownership through a pawn ticket, but by the time police got to his home, he'd already left town.

The FBI issued a warrant for Lott's arrest, but four years later, when Lott still had not been found, the warrant was dropped. At the time this was routine procedure for the FBI, but for reasons that have never been explained—most likely a bureaucratic snafu—the murder and robbery charges against Lott were also dropped.

In 1972, Lott was arrested for beating up a girlfriend in Florida. The girlfriend told Florida police that Lott was wanted for murder in Texas. But when investigators contacted the Houston Police Department, they found that the charges had been dropped. Lott slipped through the dragnet once again.

When the mistake was discovered Lott was reindicted, but it was too late.

He was long gone.

A full generation later, violence permeated American culture. The first bombing of the World Trade Center in New York City had occurred. Pop star Michael Jackson had been accused of molesting a twelve-year-old boy. On TV, Beavis and Butthead made delinquent degeneration cool. Clint Eastwood dealt with a psychopathic assassin in *In the Line of Fire* and in the real Washington, D.C., Bill Clinton presided over a scandal-plagued White House.

The Vietnam War was long over, but it seemed as if the war had somehow moved to the streets instead. Gang violence had exploded. Just the year before, Houston had dealt with a staggering *500 murders*. As for me, I was struggling to juggle more than 300 cases a year as my children entered preadolescence, leaving me exhausted and frazzled.

Meanwhile across town, a young man who had never gotten over witnessing the murder of his daddy on a hot July night thirty years before was still grieving, still angry. One day, still upset that the HPD had allowed the killer of his father to go free, he picked up the phone and called the Houston Police Department's homicide division, asking what had become of the investigation into his father's murder.

When Detective C.P. "Abby" Abbondanolo pulled out the yellowed, typewritten report on the Martinez case, he was intrigued. Young and handsome, he'd been only two years old in 1964, but he was moved that the victim's son still yearned for justice and he decided to do what he could to help. The first thing he needed to find out, if possible, was whether Ora Lott was still alive. To that end, he and assisting detectives combed through death records all over the country, but could find no evidence that Lott had died.

That's when he called me.

"Lois," he asked, "If I were to bring you a photo of a man who was thirty-three years old and ask you to make him look sixty-three, could you do it?"

While he was telling me about the case, I became as fascinated as he was and decided to pry apart my stacked-up schedule to see if I could find a slot to do the drawing for Abby.

Abby came over to see me with Tommy Martinez. Forty years old, Tommy had a stocky build and a pleasant smile. As we shook hands and talked, I could see the anxiety in his eyes and I completely understood his drive to find his father's killer.

"Don't worry," I assured him. "I just did an age progression of thirty years for a sister looking for her two brothers who'd been separated from her when they were babies. Believe me, this will be *easy* in comparison!" Peering at Lott's mug shot, I added, "Basically, when you are doing the aging of an adult, you have to demonstrate the effects of gravity through the years on the face. I'm not going to promise that I'll produce a dead-on portrait, but I'll see what I can do, okay?"

Relief etched his face. However, after Tommy Martinez left I stared out my office windows at the glaring summer sunshine and wondered how on earth I was going to fit this project in when I was hard at work on a slew of others: the murder of an east Texas college kid, the shooting of a high-way trooper, the murder of an old woman by a vicious group of bank robbers, a rape survivor who couldn't drive and needed me to do the sketch in her un-airconditioned home—(you can't let sweat drip off your chin onto the pastels because it degrades their tones)—and a horrific murder case in Kansas that I was scheduled to do a drawing for within the week.

As if that wasn't enough scribbled throughout my appointment book,

I had also promised to produce a painting for an upcoming charity auction.

Now I'd claimed that I could do a thirty-year age progression when I knew full well most forensic artists would have turned it down.

"Oh, yeah, you idiot," I muttered to myself. Feigning a singsong voice, I mimicked, "It'll be easy in comparison!"

To get it all done I decided I would have to do everything in bits and pieces, including the charity-auction painting and the age progression for Abby. Crammed in between witness appointments and a trip to Kansas, I'd snatch a half-hour here to work on the painting, fifteen minutes there on the Ora Lott age-progression. At least that was what I told myself.

Since beginning is the hardest part of any age progression, I started by poring over photographs of World War II veterans that I found and juxtaposed next to their military photographs from the war. That gave me a good idea as to how most men age over a generation.

I finally finished the age progression sketch the day before the charity auction. My painting sold for a nice sum to an organization that benefits literacy programs in the area and I got to have a night on the town in a sequined dress and satin shoes.

Meanwhile, Abby worked on the Martinez case. After displaying the sketch on the evening news, Abby requested help from the public. Detectives J.R. Dees and John Bertolini of the Gulf Coast Violent Offenders Task Force were watching the broadcast. They immediately volunteered to help.

Since they knew Lott was a veteran, the detectives checked to see if he had been drawing any veteran's benefits and when they found that he had not been, they figured he had changed his name to evade capture through the years. However, they also knew that Lott had family in the Louisiana area, so they searched veteran's hospital records there. They were able to turn up a man with a name that was almost identical to Lott's and whose social security and date of birth were also very close. From that, they got an address.

With help from the U.S. Marshals and armed with copies of my sketch, the two men knocked on the door of the man they believed to be Ora

David Lott.

An old man, large in size as Lott had been described, answered the door. "And he was a mirror image to your drawing," a jubilant Abby later told me.

"Are you Ora David Lott?" asked Detective Dees.

The man scowled and answered, "No, I am not."

Dees held up my sketch and showed it to the man.

With that, Lott shrugged, stepped back and allowed the law enforcement officers to enter his home. As they slipped on the handcuffs, one of the marshals asked Lott if he knew why he was being arrested.

"I know I did something wrong thirty years ago," he said.

When we talked, Detective Dees said that, even though he had personally been responsible for the arrest of many violent felons pursued by the task force, he had never caught one who had been free for so long.

"It's an indescribable feeling," he said. "Knowing that you have been able not only to catch a violent criminal, but also to help a family that has been living with this unresolved pain for the past thirty years."

Abby was even more excited. "I've been on the force for thirteen years," he said, "and back in 1983, I caught a baby they threw out of a burning window." With a satisfied wink and a nod, he added, "I'd put this one right on up there."

As for Tommy Martinez, he told newspaper reporters, "I'm looking forward to looking my father's murderer in the eyes the way he did mine thirty years ago."

At the trial Ora David Lott pled guilty to murder, but because of his advanced years, the amount of time since the crime had been committed and the fact that there was no record of his having committed any other crimes during the time he was free, the court was lenient. He was given a ten-year sentence, but adjudication was deferred and he was placed in community supervision. After fulfilling his sentencing requirements, Ora Lott was discharged and the case dismissed with no conviction on his record.

I know that Tommy Martinez and his family were disappointed that

Lott's punishment wasn't more harsh, but I am certain that Tommy was still able to find some measure of peace, once he knew that his father's killer had been held accountable for his crime.

As for me, I was thrilled and gratified that my work had helped to solve a thirty-year-old case, but although I didn't know it then, it had been a romp in the park compared to what was waiting for me in Newton, Kansas.

It was one of those cases that would keep me lying awake for many long nights.

Chapter Eleven:

"Look Mommy!
It's a Picture of Daddy!"

There is something my Houston friends don't usually realize about me, and that is that I have what I like to call my "split personality." Although I've chosen to live, work and raise my family in a major metropolitan area, and enjoy many aspects of big-city life down on the Gulf Coast of Texas...the truth is that my heart will always be firmly planted in the flatlands of Kansas. Deep inside, I'll always be a small-town girl, and I'll always have a real and abiding love and respect for people who come from the country.

It's hard to explain to outsiders the love I have for my home state, but you have to understand that there's something hypnotic about the minimalist scenery and the wide-open spaces, the night sky arching overhead, sugar-frosted with stars. It gives you time to *think*, to ponder the unimaginable wonders of the universe and to realize, finally, who and what you really are.

Kansas is populated by some of the most genteel, sensitive, and thoughtful people I've ever known, generous of spirit and kind of heart. Small rural towns in Kansas still possess the essence of innocence personified by the old TV show, *The Andy Griffith Show*—where good-hearted Sheriff Andy Taylor, his fumbling but well-intentioned deputy, Barney Fife, his little boy Opie and that great lady, Aunt Bee—go about their lives in Mayberry, a place where people never lock their doors and the most heart-wrenching crime occurs when Opie shoots a bird with his BB gun.

For these reasons and many more, I always cherish my visits to family back home in Kansas. They all love me, of course, but there is an aspect of my life that they, too, don't fully realize and that is the unstoppable flood of crime that flows through my office day after day after day. The human suffering that I must confront every day at work is something that—thank God—my loved ones never have to see. I wouldn't want them to.

As the summer started I was exhausted from the hundreds of cases I'd done sketches for and really looking forward to our annual Herbert family reunion that had always been held at my Grandma Andrews's house. She lived on 150 acres near Urbana, Missouri. Every year, my husband Sid and the kids and I drove to Wichita, Kansas where my mom, dad and younger brother, Brent, and his family lived. My sister and her family would come in from Wakeeney, Kansas, and we'd all troop together to Grandma's house.

The trips to Kansas were always my sanctuary from the crime horrors of my daily life. It was always good to pick up the newspaper there and read about things like the local stock show or county fair, rather than the latest murders.

However, lounging around at my brother's house the day before our trek to the family reunion, I was shocked when I picked up a copy of the *Wichita Eagle* to read the brutal headline, **Suspect, Break Sought in the Newton Killing**.

Beneath the headline were two very typically unsatisfactory Identi-kit sketches that looked like something that had been put together with a toy Etch-a-Sketch. A paragraph or two below that was a small photograph of a pretty blond lady with a big, beautiful smile, frozen forever at the age of thirty-six.

Newton, Kansas, a small, predominantly Mennonite community, is located about five miles outside of Wichita. Their population now hovers near 17,000, but in 1994 was even lower. The Mennonites are similar in their belief system to the Pennsylvania Amish, only they do make use of modern conveniences. Still, it's a conservative, strict religion. The church emphasizes community, family and strong commitment to social issues and voluntary service. The Mennonites' is a religion of peace, known for conscientious objection to war. Some of the community's members withhold the portion of their income taxes that would go for military purposes.

At that time, Newton was a town of working dads and stay-at-home moms, where life revolved around the churches and schools. People didn't lock their doors and, until May 20, 1994, people weren't savagely murdered there in their own homes.

On that day, lovely Sarah Rinehart brought her six-year-old daughter, Jordan, and her daughter's five-year-old friend, Ashley, home from a kindergarten field trip and settled them down with bowls of chocolate ice cream in front of the television set to watch cartoons.

Suddenly there was a knock at the front door and when Sarah opened it, the quiet world of Newton, Kansas was forevermore exploded.

A man shoved his way into the house, forced Sarah and the girls to the back of the house, where he herded the children into Jordan's room, then dragged Sarah down the hall to her bedroom, threw her onto the bed, hog-tied her by her wrists and ankles, gagged her, and ripped her panties off.

At this point, Jordan, who was frightened, ran back to her mother's room, opened the door and saw her mother bound and gagged on the bed. She could tell that her mother was trying, desperately, to say something to her, maybe something like, *Get out! Run!*

Paralyzed with terror, Jordan stood stock-still, her mother's ravaged face forever burned into her mind.

"Get back in your room!" screamed the man. He yanked Jordan up bodily, then stuffed her and Ashley into a closet.

"Stay here or I'll kill you," he snarled.

Then, while the little girls listened in horror, he bludgeoned Sarah Rinehart to death. The blows were so loud that Jordan thought her mother had been shot.

The girls were rescued, later, by an uncle, but three weeks after that terrible day, when I was visiting my family, the murderer was still at large.

In the tumultuous weeks that had followed the Sarah Rinehart killing, the traumatized community, with help from the Kansas Bureau of Investigation, had raised a $10,000 reward for information leading to the capture of the killer and police had released those pitiful Identi-kit sketches.

Reading the article, my hands started to shake. *This can't happen here!* I thought. *Not HERE.*

I felt a personal sense of violation that this horrific crime had occurred, not in Houston, where I had come to expect violence, but in a rural, peaceful Kansas town.

My obsession to step in, to pull out my drawing board and work the magic that I knew could possibly break this case took hold. The fact that the only witnesses were two little girls did not make me feel the task was daunting. I'd done sketches from witnesses as young as five years old. I could do this.

Only one problem.

I didn't *have* my drawing board or any of my other supplies with me. After all, I was on *vacation*.

Forget it, I told myself. *YOU CAN'T SAVE THE WHOLE WORLD!*
I reached for the telephone...
YOU'RE ON VACATION.

Nevertheless I couldn't stop myself. I grappled with the telephone directory, found a number...

LET IT GO!
I started to dial...
"Newton Police Department."

I heard myself say, "Hello. My name is Lois Gibson, and I'm the forensic sketch artist for the Houston, Texas Police Department..."

They listened to my offer but didn't take me up on it, not then.

"Until one morning in mid-November of 1959," wrote Truman Capote in his landmark true-crime book, *In Cold Blood*, "few Americans— in fact, few Kansans—had ever heard of Holcomb. ...Drama, in the shape of exceptional happenings, had never stopped there."

Detective Sergeant T. Walton was not a typical small-town Kansas cop.

A native of New York, he'd skinny-dipped at Woodstock and, during his student days at Kansas Wesleyan University, he'd sported dark hair that flowed down his back. His speech had the rapid-fire staccato of a machine-gun blast, rather than a Kansas down-home drawl, and he didn't suffer fools gladly.

On the day Sarah Rinehart was bludgeoned to death in her bed, "T.,"

Lois Gibson during her modeling career, shortly before the attack that changed her life.

A sketch of the rapist who attacked her.

Wanted

Wanted for raping a blind and
pregnant woman.

David Alberto Zayas
See chapter 7, "Blind Justice."

Wanted for raping
a ten-year-old girl.

James Daniel Raiford
See chapter 14, "Making the Case
for Forensic Art."

Each Caught by One Sketch

Wanted

Wanted for numerous rapes and
brutal murders.

Scott Hain
See chapter 6, "WANTED:
Dead or Alive."

Wanted for numerous rapes and
brutal murders.

Robert Lambert
See chapter 6, "WANTED:
Dead or Alive."

Each Caught by One Sketch

Wanted

Wanted for rape and murder.

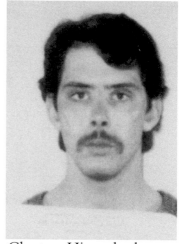

Chester Higganbotham
See chapter 11, "Look Mommy! It's
a Picture of Daddy!"

Officer Paul Deason,
shot twice and run over
by a suspect's car.

Wanted for attempted
murder of a police
officer.

Donald Eugene
Dutton
See chapter 9,
"Some People Just
Need Killin'."

Houston, Texas Police Department

Houston, Texas Police Department

Each Caught by One Sketch

Missing

Christina, a young woman, begged Lois to help reunite her family after three decades apart. The artist began her age progression drawings working only from copies of baby pictures of two-year-old Chris and his one-year-old brother Chip. See chapter 10, "Tricky Drawings, Successful Endings."

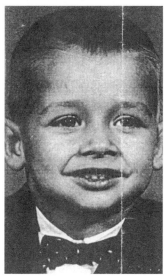 

Baby picture (top left), Lois's sketch (top right) and photograph (bottom left) of Chris. After seeing that Chris had a moustache and longer hair, Lois overlayed these features on a copy of her sketch (bottom right).

Found by One Sketch

Wanted

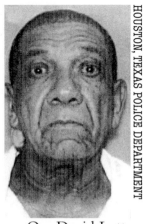

Ora David Lott
in 1964.

Wanted for armed
robbery and murder.
Sketch shown here on
Lois's easel.

Ora David Lott
See chapter 10,
"Tricky Drawings,
Successful Endings."

Wanted for rape,
attempted murder and murder

Theodore Goynes
See chapter 8, "Portrait of a
Serial Killer."

Each Caught by One Sketch

Wanted

average build
5'8" to 6'   25 to 30 yrs.

9.13-02

Composite sketch/photo comparison of Kerry Ashley O'Neal, who liked to call himself, "KAOS." He tried to hire a hit man to kill his fifteen-year-old victim before she could testify against him in court.

Certificate of Appreciation

Presented to

HPD Forensic Sketch Artist
Lois Gibson

In recognition of outstanding service and dedication to duty.
Your assistance in the arrest of two dangerous sexual predators is appreciated.
Your performance sparks enthusiasm and promotes harmony and teamwork.
Congratulations on a job well done!

Given this day, September 20, 2002
by the Harris County Sheriff's Office

Ruben Diaz, Lieutenant
Interpersonal Violence Division

A certificate given to Lois recognizing that her artwork was instrumental in catching O'Neal.

Caught by One Sketch

Wanted

B/m medium build

Gibson
122312494W
HPD
10/27/94

Wanted for the rape of nine-year-old Annie and the murder of Annie's mother.

Jeffrey Lynn Williams See chapter 12, "A Look of Murderous Rage."

Investigator Tom McCorvey and Sergeant J.W. "Billy" Belk bringing in Jeffrey Lynn Williams for the brutal rape and murder.

Caught by One Sketch

as he preferred to be called, was just starting his very first day as a detective with the Newton Police Department.

The original call had come into the police department as a burglary-in-progress. When concerned family members couldn't find Sarah and couldn't get an answer at her door, and when her older daughter, Jackie, came home from school and couldn't get into her own house, they'd called Sarah's brother-in-law, Robby Nachlinger, to go check on her. Robby, who happened to be home from work that day, was married to one of Sarah's sisters and lived close by.

He'd gone over, found Sarah's car in the garage and her purse in the laundry room. Going from bedroom to bedroom, he'd discovered the children holed up in a closet. The hysterical girls told him that "a man" was in the house. As he led them down the hall, past Sarah's closed bedroom door, Robby explained later, he'd had an overwhelming feeling that he should not open the bedroom door—not as long as he had the little girls with him—and decided it best to get them out of the house. He'd dialed 911, reported what he believed to be a burglary and hustled the children out the front door.

The whole time, Sarah's daughter, Jordan, was screaming, "Why did that man kill my mommy?"

Robby always maintained that, since he had the girls with him and he didn't know what he might find behind that closed door, he never looked into Sarah's bedroom.

Police thought otherwise.

While crime scene technicians from the Kansas Bureau of Investigation powdered the Rinehart house with fingerprint dust, sprayed floors, walls, and sinks with Luminol (which causes blood stains to glow in the dark) and pored over the bedroom carpet, picking up stray fibers with sticky-tape, the Newton PD called in Robby Nachlinger for questioning in the death of his sister-in-law.

What was your relationship with Sarah? they wanted to know. *Why were you home from work that day? Why did you call in a burglary when nothing appeared to be missing from the house, including Sarah's handbag?*

But while other investigators clustered around Robby, T. tried to voice his objections.

"This doesn't make sense," he said. "These little girls have grown up in this town and Jordan's aunts and uncles live all around her. She sure as hell ought to know the difference between her own uncle and a stranger."

T. pointed out that the girls had described the man who'd invaded their quiet home that day as having had long, curly dark hair and "yellow teeth." Robby Nachlinger didn't *have* long, curly dark hair or yellow teeth.

But other ranking investigators considered T. a rookie.

"It was pretty much like, 'Go away, kid, ya bother me.'" T. said later.

In the meantime, poor Robby Nachlinger did not help himself. Overwhelmed and nervous from the stressful events, having never been in trouble with the law before and inexperienced about such things, he blurted out to detectives that he'd actually been sexually attracted to his beautiful sister-in-law. That, in fact, he'd even entertained a few sexual fantasies about her.

Nachlinger was a nursing student at the community college in town. Investigators learned that, about the time of the murder, something was missing from the nursing department. It seems that the training dummy used for the instruction of CPR, or cardio-pulmonary resuscitation, normally had sported a dark, curly wig.

And the wig was gone.

"Your pretty sister-in-law wouldn't give you what you wanted, would she?" inquired detectives of the cringing brother-in-law. "So you put on that wig as a disguise, and you forced your way into her house, and you tied her up, and you MURDERED her!"

The harder Robby denied their accusations, the harder they pressed.

At first, the horrified family—Sarah's husband, her parents, and her three surviving sisters—simply could not believe that the Newton Police were seriously considering their relative as a suspect in Sarah's death. They urged Robby to take a polygraph test, so that the detectives would see, once and for all, that he was telling the truth.

And Robby Nachlinger flunked the lie detector test.

At this point, investigators decided, it was time to "take that Houston sketch artist up on her offer."

It was frustrating to me that the Newton Police Department postponed flying me out for the sketch session with Sarah Rinehart's daughter and her friend all the way until the first of August. The crime had occurred the twentieth of May and it had been infuriating enough to me that I'd gone to Kansas in June without any of my equipment and had to come back to do the sketch, but I was surprised that it took until August to set up.

I didn't realize, of course, that the police were so focused on Robby Nachlinger that they didn't think, until they called me, that they needed a sketch. At that time, not only was I asked to do a sketching session with Jordan Rinehart and her friend Ashley, but the police also actually took a photograph of Robby Nachlinger wearing a long, curly dark-haired wig and asked me to do a portrait of him—I guess for comparison purposes.

And so I was, at last, flying back to Kansas, and I was glad that though the purpose in my trip was occasioned by a sad event, I'd get to have a visit with my beloved baby brother, Brent, and his family that did not involve a big family reunion.

I dressed carefully for the sketching session because I knew I would be working with very young children, and I wanted to look more motherly than businesslike. By this time, these little girls had already been questioned so much and had been surrounded by so many law enforcement personnel, that I wanted to stand out in a way that would be entirely non-threatening. I chose a white silk dress that my own little girl at home liked.

I also had the patrol officer pick me up about an hour early, so that I could familiarize myself with the layout of the department and figure out ahead of time where they kept their soda machine. Once I'd set up my easel and drawing board in the room set aside for the session, the nice young officer took me all the way down to one end of the building, down a flight of stairs, and through one room and out into a break room of sorts, where they kept a refrigerator, sink and microwave oven. Beside the fridge was a little cardboard box where you dropped in a quarter and then you selected a soda from the refrigerator.

Everyone just trusted that everyone else would leave their quarters—one of many reasons why I love my home state of Kansas.

But I decided not to get a soda just then. I knew that the time would come when a fidgety little girl would need the distraction of a trip to get a soda, so I returned to the office where my equipment was and waited for Jordan Rinehart.

When they brought her in, I thought Sara Rinehart's daughter was one of the most beautiful little girls I had ever seen. Her hair was platinum blond and her eyes cornflower blue. Once the officers left us alone, she regarded me with serious, solemn eyes and waited to be grilled yet again.

Instead, I said, "What a pretty dress you have on!"

"Thank you." Like most children that age, she was shy.

"Have you been enjoying the summer?"

Surprised at the question, she nodded her head.

"I'll bet you've been going to the swimming pool, haven't you?"

A delighted smile broke across her face and she said, "I love to go swimming!"

"I'll bet you do. My daughter Tiffany just loves to go swimming too; she's like a little duck."

Jordan giggled, and soon, she was relaxing with me, relieved that I wasn't going to poke and prod her about the terrible day her mother died. The fact that I was a mommy seemed to reassure her.

We talked about her school and her favorite teacher, and eventually, I said, "We're going to draw a picture of that yucky man."

She knew immediately who I meant, but I did not dwell on it. Instead, while I got out the *FBI Facial Identification Catalogue* and put my little towel full of pastels in my lap, I asked what her favorite part of Sunday school was and we chatted about other things.

When the time came to begin the sketch, I found that like most children of her age who are asked to give information for a forensic sketch session, she was decisive. They will usually select a feature right away and stick to their choices, whereas an adult will, more than likely, second-guess himself and waffle back and forth. Children also have very vivid memories; they know what they saw.

One thing that must always be remembered when dealing with a child witness is that if he or she is eight or under, they have not yet developed their verbal skills enough to produce a word from the language part of their brain to describe their attacker. The way a small child's brain works is that the visual aid—like the FBI catalogue—sends a message to the visual cortex of the brain. This is the part of the brain that actually *saw* the attacker; therefore, this part of the brain then recognizes the look-alike facial feature.

In one case, a child with whom I worked did not know what the word "moustache" meant. But he could pick out an almost exact likeness from the moustache portion of the FBI catalogue. Of course, this was not the situation with Jordan, but after we had worked for a while, I noticed she was beginning to fidget, which was perfectly normal for a six-year-old. They have short attention spans, but I was ready for it.

"Would you like to go get a Coke?" I asked.

With great enthusiasm, she nodded her head.

"C'mon," I said. "You're gonna like this. It's fun! We have to walk a long way through halls and rooms, but I know where to go."

At that, she hesitated a bit, not sure whether she should leave with me or not. But more curious and intrigued than nervous, she climbed off the chair and took my hand.

I treated it like a grand adventure. We walked down the hall, came to a corner and peeked around like Bugs Bunny, then tippy-toed down the stairs in a silly fashion. She was giggling with me when suddenly, a big tall police officer blocked our way.

"What are you doing here?" he asked, his voice gruff, his brows knitted, as if he just could not figure out what a woman and a kid were doing in his territory.

Keeping my voice happy, like we were departing for Disneyland, I said, "We're going on a trip to get a soda from the refrigerator. We like going down halls and through rooms, because we've never been here before."

He met my eyes. I was absolutely *not* going to lapse into copspeak and say something like, *We're here doing the forensic sketch on the Sara Rinehart bludgeoning murder.*

It was my sincere hope that this guy would figure out that a woman in a white silk dress and a little girl were not there to lay siege to his department.

He glanced down at Jordan, then smiled and let us pass.

Jordan absolutely *loved* it.

She seemed to feel protected by me, the big grown-up lady who acted like she was in charge and didn't let the big scary cop push her around. It was an adventure unlike anything she'd experienced before, and it was fun.

I'd brought quarters, and we carefully dropped in two. Jordan selected one soda and so did I, then we headed back down the labyrinth toward the task that awaited us.

Once we were settled back in the room where I was to do the sketches and sipping our sodas, Jordan was all business. First, from the book I showed her, she picked a hairstyle that was very unruly, curly dark long hair. Then, she told me the guy's eyes were a really light blue and when we were working on the nose, she selected nostrils that were almost perfectly round.

Both of these features are highly unusual. I wondered when she showed me the nostrils if maybe Jordan just *thought* the nostrils were perfectly round because, as a child, she was looking *up* at them. But I found her to be very serious and thoughtful—much more so than any six-year-old witness I'd ever worked with before. She was possessed of a certain earnest intensity unlike what I'd seen in other child witnesses. I could tell that she sincerely wanted to accomplish the task of drawing the face of the man who'd attacked her mother.

When it was time to work with her friend Ashley, the session was quite different. She could not concentrate like Jordan had, and I was unable to get her to focus for very long on the catalogue. But I did notice that, like Jordan, she, too, chose the perfectly round nostrils and the very light blue eyes.

When I showed her the sketch, she said, "That looks like him."

Now it was up to the detectives.

For the family of Sara Rinehart, a nightmarish day in May spilled into a hellish summer, and as the weeks went on and on, they stood by helplessly and watched as the Newton police seemed to focus only on the theory that Robby Nachlinger did it.

"I was really looking forward to having Sarah's murder solved in the first week to ten days," David Guzman, Sarah's father, told a *Newton Kansan* reporter. "I called home every night expecting to hear...but when our son-in-law was accused, it was *guilty until proven innocent*."

And if that accusation, alone, was all there was to it, that would have been painful enough.

But people talked.

Small towns thrive on gossip; it's a form of soap-opera entertainment. People who are born and raised in a community and stay or return after college to raise their own families there, often compete to see who can be first to say, "Did you hear what happened to so-and-so?"

A few, particularly those who are largely housebound or who live extremely insular lives, like to get caught up in the drama, burning up the telephone lines for hours discussing the lives of others. Maybe it makes their own lives seem tame in comparison, or maybe they like the attention, but a scandalous situation like this—violent murder, cops suspect family member—can fuel the fires for months.

Those who knew, loved, and respected the Guzman and Rinehart families never bought into the police theory about Robby Nachlinger. They felt the same heartache and frustration as the family did, burning for justice, wondering if it was ever going to come. Their loving support kept the family going.

But those who didn't know the family or didn't know them well, did wonder about Robby. After all, some thought, the police wouldn't have suspected him if they didn't have good reason. They *must* be onto something.

Perhaps it made them feel safer to go along with the police theory, because then they wouldn't have had to worry about a stranger, a *monster*, invading their own homes some day and snatching away one of their own loved ones.

But the Rinehart and Guzman families worried about it. They worried about it a great deal. They felt that every day, every week, every month the police wasted chasing down the rabbit hole of investigating Robby Nachlinger, someone else was at risk.

For Heidi Guzman, Sarah's little sister, it was unconscionable. Like Sarah, Heidi was a spunky beauty—blonde, blue-eyed, full of energy and outrage. Heidi worked at a mental health facility with troubled, at-risk teenagers, and she had a keen understanding of human psychology.

She also refused to take "no" for an answer. Day and night, Heidi hounded the police. At least two or three times a week, she phoned the department, looking for information.

"There's a halfway house in that neighborhood," she would point out. "Has anybody checked out that halfway house?"

"We're doing everything we can, ma'am," they would say.

"What about the sunglasses you guys found under my sister's bed?" she'd demand. "They don't belong to anybody we know, and they darn sure don't belong to my brother-in-law."

"The KBI (Kansas Bureau of Investigation) is going over everything with a fine-toothed comb," they'd say, in a hurry to get rid of her.

Later, she said, "They were putting all their time and resources and energy into investigating *Opie Taylor!*"

A miserable summer wept into a bleak autumn and Heidi kept begging the police to widen their investigation.

"We're doing all we can," they said.

Autumn creaked into a cold, dead winter, and winter bled into spring and the first anniversary of Sarah Rinehart's death came and went. Newspapers wrote follow-up articles and reprinted copies of my sketch, but nothing came of the articles or my sketch. A $10,000 reward was posted.

Another summer crawled past.

Heidi wanted to scream, tear her hair out, march down to the police department and grab somebody by the lapels, maybe slap him around a little.

Her beloved sister was dead and buried, her family devastated and a killer running around loose...and all along, Heidi felt as if she was trapped in a soundproof room, a room with a big window where, on the other side, she could see police officers laughing and talking, and, even though she screamed and screamed as loud as she could, she felt no one could hear.

No one was listening.

But what Heidi didn't know was that on the other side of that imaginary window, a young cop was sitting over in the corner, watching.

He saw her.

And he decided to listen.

It wasn't just Heidi Guzman that got Detective T. Walton's attention. He'd long been doing some pestering of his own, to the supervisor of investigations and to anyone else who would listen.

"I don't think Robby Nachlinger did it," he insisted. "We've got *witnesses*. Jordan Rinehart is a sensible little girl. She'd sure as hell know the difference between her own uncle and a stranger."

It wasn't proof positive for T. that Nachlinger had incriminated himself with the comments about his sexual fantasies or that he had failed a polygraph.

"The way I saw it," he said later, "to someone who was raised in a strict religious home, well, just the *thought* of being attracted to his own sister-in-law would make him feel guilty. I think the poor guy was just so ashamed of himself for even having those feelings that he just stepped all over his tongue."

T. agreed with what Heidi had so frequently pointed out, that Robby

Nachlinger was so innocent that he *did* spill his guts like a fool to the police.

After all, if he truly was guilty of this horrific crime, wouldn't he at least have been a little bit, well, *cagier*? Wouldn't he have known better than to discuss his sexual problems with the cops during a freakin' *murder investigation*?

"I kept bothering the supervisor about the case so much that, one day, he said to me, 'Fine, T. You think it's not Nachlinger? Then PROVE it's not him.'"

This was all T. needed to hear. It meant he could paw through files and reports and basically, reinvestigate the case.

But it wasn't easy.

"It was like, you're rowin' up a river on a raft, right?" he said later in his rapid-fire way, "and you got one oar and, up on the riverbank, people are throwin' *boulders* at you."

The supervisor of investigations, also weary of hearing from Heidi Guzman, told T., "*You* deal with her."

And so he did.

"That first meeting, she was kind of wary of me," he said later. "By then, she was as suspicious of me for being a cop as the cops were of her brother-in-law. It took a little talkin' for her to accept the fact that I was not only startin' fresh, but that I didn't think Robby did it, either."

From that point on, the blonde activist and the rookie detective became fast friends. It was good that they had each other, too, because the road they were traveling would turn out to be so much more winding, rocky and lengthy than either of them could have imagined.

Laughing, he relayed to me when we spoke how Heidi read books such as FBI profiler John Douglas's *Mindhunter*.

"She called me up, and she said, 'Have you read this book?' And she gave it to me and I read the damn thing." In that particular book, Douglas had commented that killers sometimes visit the gravesites of their victims on the anniversaries of their deaths.

"So there I was," he said, chuckling, "dressed like a landscape maintenance guy, watching her grave on the first anniversary, but nobody showed up except family."

Another summer passed into another autumn. Detective Walton began the weary task of re-interviewing everyone associated with the case, but in

October, he would have to drop everything—at least for the time being—for another case.

In October, the Rinehart/Guzman family's worst fear was realized. There was a second murder.

The victim this time, Jonetta McKown, was not a beautiful, middle-class housewife and mother. She was, in fact, a prostitute.

That did not mean she was not loved.

On the evening of September 16, Jonetta McKown disappeared.

The last person to have seen Jonetta was a friend of hers who watched her being driven away into the night by a man in a maroon Chrysler. For some reason, even though Jonetta often left with johns in cars, her friend was worried about this one. Maybe it was his appearance or the way he acted, but for whatever reason, the friend jotted down the license plate number of the car.

And then Jonetta disappeared.

When a couple of days had gone by without a word from Jonetta, her frantic friend called the Wichita police. They traced the license plate to a man by the name of Matthew Murphy.

Matthew Murphy lived in Newton. This is how the case came across the desk of Detective T. Walton.

Like Jonetta's friend, T. had a bad feeling about this case. For one thing, Matthew Murphy was already on parole. For another, he and the Wichita detectives figured out pretty quick that Matthew Murphy was not the guy's real name.

His real name was Chester Higginbotham.

Murphy's wife was not only dumbstruck by the sudden presence of police at her home, but she was stunned to learn that she was not really married to Matthew Murphy. She'd had no idea that "Matthew Murphy" was a pseudonym.

Deeply disturbed and more than a little distraught, the woman told T. that when her husband hadn't come home one night a few days before, she had gone to look for him.

She found him parked in front of his storage building, sitting in his car, and next to him was a woman who appeared to be slumped over, like she was asleep.

T. and the other detectives exchanged glances. *Storage building?*

They got a search warrant for the storage building.

Among other items in the crowded storage building, searchers came across some black plastic ties, yellow rope, green duct tape with a few stray hairs clinging to it and a white button.

Next, T. served a search warrant on Higginbotham's house and threw Higginbotham in jail on a parole violation—keeping company with prostitutes, which was forbidden under his parole terms.

By this time, T. was convinced that Jonetta McKown was dead. Detectives sent out a search team, looking for what they believed was most likely a body. There was a creek near the storage building. They drained it.

Nothing. Several weeks passed. Still nothing.

Then, on October 11, 1995, a county road worker was cutting the grass alongside a county road outside Walton, Kansas—about twenty-five miles from Newton.

And he found Jonetta McKown.

"I drove out," said T., "and as soon as I saw the body, I knew she had been killed by the same person who'd killed Sarah Rinehart."

Jonetta McKown was gagged. Green duct tape covered both her mouth and nose.

And her ankles and wrists were tied together. Hog-tied, just like Sarah Rinehart.

Further investigation confirmed that the button found in the storage building belonging to Chester Higginbotham, a.k.a. Matthew Murphy, matched the buttons on Jonetta's blouse. The blouse happened to be missing a button.

By this time, Higginbotham had bailed out of jail. T. got hold of the bondsman, who also happened to be a private investigator, and told her that he was certain that Chester Higginbotham had murdered Sara Rinehart. He asked her to withdraw her bond so that they could get Higginbotham back to jail.

While that was taking place, T. started taking a serious look at Chester Higginbotham.

He learned that Higginbotham had worked as an assistant manager at a local restaurant where Sarah's Christian women's group regularly met for luncheon. Sarah had been the group's treasurer, and when Higginbotham tried to charge her more than the agreed-upon price, they had argued. The confrontation had occurred *two days* before Sarah's murder.

And Chester Higginbotham had lived in the halfway house just down the block from Sarah's at the time of the Rinehart murder.

Detective Walton questioned Higginbotham, and he interviewed the manager of the halfway house where Higginbotham had been a regular. But the manager showed T. a sign-out sheet that, he insisted, proved that Chester Higginbotham had been in the house at the time of the murder.

Still, Detective Walton thought Higginbotham was a much better suspect than Sarah Rinehart's long-suffering brother-in-law; Walton just wasn't sure how to prove it.

He decided to have a second, more serious conversation with Chester's bewildered and frightened young wife. T. called her and asked that she come to the Newton Police Department for questioning. He met her in the lobby. She was holding the hand of her six-year-old son.

As Walton led the woman and child down the corridor to his office, they passed a bulletin board plastered with wanted posters.

Pinned to the board was a large photocopy of my composite sketch, the one I'd made with little Jordan Rinehart and her friend Ashley after Jordan's mother, Sarah, had been murdered almost a year and a half before.

And as they walked past the bulletin board, the little boy tugged excitedly at his mother's hand and cried, "Look, Mommy! It's a picture of Daddy!"

Although Chester Higginbotham was convicted of murdering Jonetta McKown and sentenced to what, in Kansas, is called a *hard forty*—meaning, forty years without a possibility of parole, Detective T. Walton had a much harder time tying him to Sarah Rinehart's murder.

Even though the Rinehart/Guzman family had released a statement to the press almost as soon as Higginbotham had been arrested for Jonetta McKown's murder, saying that he looked almost exactly like the forensic sketch I had done with Sarah's daughter and even though, by the time of Higginbotham's conviction, T. was wading in circumstantial evidence tying Chester Higginbotham to the Rinehart murder, the police *still* didn't have any hard physical evidence that put Higginbotham in the Rinehart house that terrible day. Higginbotham cleaned up, left no fingerprints and he hadn't raped Sarah, so there was no DNA analysis of semen, no hairs, *nothing*.

They did have an extra pair of sunglasses, turned over by Higginbotham's soon-to-be ex-wife, that looked just like the sunglasses they'd found under Sarah Rinehart's bed.

Meanwhile, not only did T. prove that it was entirely possible for the halfway house residents to sneak out undetected even when they were signed in, but he found a dumpster in a nearby alley where, he was convinced, Higginbotham would have had no problem dumping the bloody clothes he'd been wearing that day as well as the murder weapon.

But other Newton detectives *still* clung stubbornly to their belief that Robby Nachlinger was a viable suspect.

T. traced Higginbotham's miserable life all the way back to the age of five, when he'd first been put into a juvenile facility.

"I knew him better than *he* knew him," T. said. "He had the big three," he added, referring to warning signs of sociopathic behavior in youth, "setting fires, killing pets, and bed-wetting."

At the tender age of eight, Chester Higginbotham, known then as "Chip," had even tried to kill himself.

T. felt badly about the guy's childhood, but he didn't believe that should in any way mitigate what he had done as an adult. There comes a time, he figured, when you have to be responsible for yourself. You make choices. You choose to be good or you choose to be evil.

During those long dark months, T. and Heidi continued to stay in touch. "Whenever I was down," he said, "she pushed me up, and whenever she was down, I pushed her up."

The deeper Detective Walton dug into the nasty pit of Chester Higginbotham's life, the more convinced he became that there were even more victims out there. For instance, Higginbotham had once lived in Arizona "and there were similar, unsolved crimes, out there."

The more Walton learned, the more he was committed to solving Sarah Rinehart's case. It wasn't enough just to *know* that Chester Higginbotham did it. T. wanted to arrest him for the crime. So what if Higginbotham was already in prison for another woman's murder? So what if he wasn't ever getting out? T. wanted to walk into that prison and serve Chester Higginbotham with an arrest warrant for the death of Sarah

Rinehart. He yearned to take Higginbotham to trial, get a conviction, and to walk up to the Rineharts and Guzmans and Heidi and say, *We did it.*

But the months slowly melted into years.

And then, almost three years after Sarah's death, Detective T. Walton attended a forensic seminar on DNA evidence.

By then the collection and analysis of DNA evidence had grown by leaps and bounds. What would not have been possible back in 1994 was suddenly very possible in 1998.

T. learned, he could now get a viable match off a pair of sunglasses.

It didn't happen overnight.

For one thing, poor old Robby Nachlinger had hired a high-priced defense attorney who guarded his beleaguered client like an attack dog. He refused to allow Detective Walton to take a blood sample from Nachlinger for comparison with the DNA sample that the KBI's lab had taken from the nosepiece and earpieces of the sunglasses found beneath Sarah Rinehart's bed, and had sent on to the Sedgwick County Crime Laboratory in Wichita for analysis.

Even when T. got a court order, the lawyer threatened to sue any hospital that cooperated. *It's the dangdest thing,* T. thought in exquisite frustration, *here I am trying to EXONERATE the guy, and they act like I'm strappin' him into the electric chair!*

Still, after all Robby Nachlinger had been through, T. understood that the poor man's attorney was trying to protect him.

But a court order is a court order, and eventually, T. got his blood sample.

It was no sweat, so to speak, to get one from Chester Higginbotham.

Robby Nachlinger was excluded as a DNA match.

According to accepted DNA analysis at the time, a defendant's DNA profile was unique, based on a comparison of eight different strands of his DNA to statistical calculations provided by the manufacturer of the testing kit.

The laboratory director herself made the comparison.

She found that the possibility that anyone other than Chester Higginbotham would match the DNA marker as well as he did...was *one in 5.5 billion.*

And in August of 1998, when I went home for my thirtieth high school reunion, as I walked into the hotel lobby, I heard the homecoming queen shriek my name and come running over in a throng of people to throw her arms around my neck.

I found this, as Alice in Wonderland would say, curiouser and curiouser, because the homecoming queen never had two words for me back when I was in high school. In fact, I don't believe she ever spoke to me once back then, and now we were great friends, it seemed.

"You caught Sarah's killer!" she cried. "You did the sketch! I'm friends with Heidi Guzman and she told me what you did! You're a hero!"

She wanted to pose for pictures with me and everything.

Well, of course, I knew it wasn't *just* my sketch that caught the killer, but a committed police sergeant and the dedication of a loving sister.

Detective Sergeant T. Walton got his moment—he got lots of moments, in fact, from the day he served Chester Higginbotham his arrest warrant in prison for the murder of Sarah Rinehart, to the day he testified against him in court, to the day (November 24, 1999) that Higginbotham was convicted, to the day he got a *second* "hard forty" sentence—almost five years after Sarah's murder.

Of course, I flew up to testify in Higginbotham's trial, and I got to meet the whole incredible Rinehart/Guzman clan. A handsomer family you never saw in your life. We bonded instantly, and to this day, I count Heidi Guzman a dear friend.

Higginbotham's sentence, Harvey district court Judge John Weckel ordered, was to be served *consecutively* to the one Higginbotham was already serving for the murder of Jonetta McKown.

Chester Higginbotham would never know freedom again.

After the trial, there were big hugs for T. from the Rinehart and Guzman families.

"T's motives were absolutely pure," said Heidi Guzman years later. "He really cared."

During all those years that things hung in limbo on the Rinehart case,

I worked away down in Houston, knee-deep in crime every day, wondering if anything had ever come of my sketch in Kansas.

After the conviction, when the dust had settled and the celebrations were all over, T. got a letter in the mail. It came from Heidi Guzman, and from the little girls, Jordan Rinehart and her friend, Ashley, who were now ten and eleven years old.

Dear T., it began...

And then...one word: **THANK YOU**...written over and over and over, maybe 250 times.

"It's the best thing I ever got," T. told me recently, his voice uncharacteristically soft. "I got it framed and it's hanging on the wall."

Sarah Rinehart's daughters, now teenagers, are, as Heidi put it, "soldiering on." She says she can really see her sister's spirit illuminated in them. "They're gifted, artistic, athletic and smart," she says, "but they're also compassionate, thoughtful, and sensitive."

If anything good could have come out of such a terrible tragedy, I guess that would be it. Surviving such an awful thing at a very young age can make you stronger and more caring toward others who may also be suffering.

About her driven obsession to find justice for her sister, Heidi told me, "I guess it's like a lioness going after her prey. You're going to hone in until you catch him."

Once the case was settled for her family, Heidi took her natural activism and channeled it into the organization, Parents of Murdered Children and Homicide Survivors, Inc. Working side-by-side with T., she often presents programs about her sister's case, what it did to their family, and how they survived the devastation to go on and pick up the pieces of their shattered lives, and try to make something positive from it.

Heidi urges anyone who has suffered a similar tragedy to contact POMC. With more than 100,000 members nationwide, POMC has chapters and Contact Persons in almost every city of any size. (Their website is: *www.pomc*.org. You can e-mail them at: *natlpomc@aol*.com. You can contact them at 100 East Eighth Street, B-41, Cincinnati, Ohio, 45202, or call them at 513-721-5683.) Along with chapter support groups, POMC puts out newsletters and reading lists, and offers other resources to help families cope with the grief that is specific to losing a loved one to violent crime, and to help them navigate the criminal justice system.

"Unless you've been through something like this," Heidi explains, "you can't understand what it's like," and adds, "and I wouldn't want you to, because the only way to understand it is to experience it."

One well-meaning comment that Heidi found particularly prickly after her sister's murder was that, after the trial, she and her family might find "closure."

"There's no such thing as *closure*," she insists. "You don't ever really accept a loved one's murder. You just learn to cope with it and adjust to it. You live with it as best you can."

T. said the same thing. "I don't think it ever really leaves you. It's always there."

Following the conviction of Sarah Rinehart's killer, the editor of the *Newton Kansan*, Doug Anstaett (now the executive director of the Kansas Press Association), wrote an editorial in which he said, "A *Wichita Eagle* story on Monday about the Sarah Rinehart murder concluded that, 'although the homemaker's brutal beating death still haunts the community, some of its drama likely has dissipated with time.'

"That's what happens when a big city newspaper comes into a small town and tries to 'analyze' the effect of what is usually a big city crime.

"In Wichita, murders are forgotten every day. They're often replaced by another murder, another victim.

"But not in Newton.

"We don't forget. And we never will."

And they never have.

Chapter Twelve

A Look of Murderous Rage

No one really knows what was going through her mind during the hour that nine-year-old Annie Tyson spent with her mother's body before finally running to her grandma's nearby apartment for help. Some horrors are simply too unspeakable to probe into.

Newspaper accounts the next day detailed what officers found upon arriving at the scene some time after midnight. Cynthia Tyson, a thirty-one-year-old teacher's aide and single mother, was lying naked on the living room floor with her feet tied together; she had been beaten, strangled, and her killer had attempted to set her on fire. There were also signs of sexual assault.

Detectives later learned that Annie had also been raped.

But newspaper articles are a compilation of facts. They don't tell the whole story. That's up to the detectives, who patiently piece together characters, setting, plot, and theme by paying close attention to what they have learned from the dead—and what their survivors have to say.

The Houston Police Department's homicide division is separated into three shifts. The day shift comprises the largest part of the division, followed by a smaller evening shift. The late-night shift is made up of a skeleton crew who handles calls.

After midnight, day shift investigators who are on call are notified. This is how Sergeant J.W. "Billy" Belk and his partner, Investigator Tom McCorvey got yanked out of bed.

Both Belk and McCorvey were experienced homicide investigators; young, handsome, and physically fit. Once they saw the crime scene, it was obvious to them that this was not a "typical" case, like a barroom brawl or a domestic dispute gone bad. For one thing, Annie was a sweet, beautiful, intelligent African-American child who had a way of making people fall in love with her from the moment they met her.

"When you come on a crime scene," Sgt. Belk explained later, "you learn to take on a professional stance so that you can investigate the scene in a way that's not emotional. What's different is when you're dealing with a case that involves a child, whether it's a child victim or a child witness. And in this case, we had a child who was both the victim *and* the witness."

Although Sgt. Belk was the supervisor on the scene, he and McCorvey usually split responsibilities. McCorvey stayed at the scene with the crime scene unit, documenting and photographing evidence that would then be applied to the investigation. Belk handled interviewing witnesses and canvassing the neighborhood.

There are *details* in every crime scene that detectives are trained to notice, and in a setting like the one they stepped into that night, they may take in details that might not register right away with the casual observer— things one might take for granted that, to an experienced investigator, tell a story.

Like the salt and pepper shakers on the stove-top. They were matching, decorative shakers, arranged neatly, balanced with other trinkets, *just so*, on the spotless stove-top. The same stove-top where one electric coil glowed red like the eyes of Satan, still littered with burnt-out wisps of paper towels that had come from the empty dispenser that sat on the clean cabinet next to the stove.

Officers know, for instance, that in a house in which there is extensive drug use, there is chaos, disarray, clutter and filth; the people who live in such degradation just don't care anymore. Clearly, that wasn't the case here. Cynthia Tyson didn't have a lot of money and she lived modestly, but she'd made a nice home for her little girl, with what luxuries she could afford arranged neatly in clean surroundings. In Cynthia's bedroom, the curtains matched the comforter. Her apartment may have been modest, but it was *homey*. There were family snapshots of a lovely young woman hugging her happy child, both smiling for the camera.

The only chaos in that apartment had been made by the killer himself.

From questioning heartbroken family and neighbors, the detectives learned that Cynthia had called her sister at about 10 P.M. to say that all was well and that she was turning in for the night.

At some point after that, the killer apparently forced his way into the apartment when she'd answered a knock at the door. He fought with her in the living room—crashing over a glass candy dish and other items in the struggle, then choked her and, after yanking a phone cord out of the wall, bound her hand and foot, raped her, then attempted to set her on fire by burning up all the paper towels from the kitchen dispenser. He also burned holes in the skin of his victim's arms, breasts and thighs with a cigarette.

Then he turned his attention to the terrified child.

One of the first things Sgt. Belk learned at the scene (and something he never mentioned to newspaper reporters), was that Annie had witnessed what happened to her mother. I know he tried not to think about that, at least not then. Not while there was so much work to be done.

Homicide detectives investigate every case to the fullest extent of the law, but there are some cases that grab them by the gut in ways that others don't. The best way to explain it is to compare these horrific crimes to a bar fight in which two drunkards go at one another with knives and one ends up dead. It's not that the person deserved to die—I don't mean to imply that at all. But in a case like that, the victim made certain choices that put him in a situation that risked his life.

But in the Cynthia Tyson case, there was a cozy, loving family going about their lives—and suddenly, through no fault of their own, through no choice made by them—they were savagely attacked and their lives destroyed, leaving a child violated and motherless.

That's a gut-grabber, and it's one that the investigators will go above and beyond the call of duty to bring to justice.

As Sgt. Belk examined Cynthia Tyson's burnt and bruised body, he told me later he knew right away that we were dealing with a juvenile or adolescent offender. When he squatted down to examine Annie's mother, he noticed that the killer had tried to set fire to her fingernails and had set fire to some paper towels he'd placed on her abdomen.

"What young people don't usually realize," he told me later, "is that the human body is composed of something like 85 percent water—so it doesn't erupt into flames like that. You have scorching instead. If an adult wanted to destroy evidence by setting a body on fire, what he'd do is pour gasoline or something like that on the body and the area surrounding it, and torch it."

After looking over the crime scene, Sgt. Belk turned his attention to Annie. She was sitting in a squad car with a police officer. "I thought the child would be so terribly traumatized that she wouldn't talk," he said later.

He spoke gently to her for a while and suggested that they go to his office where it would be more private. Making every effort to put her at ease, Belk explained to the little girl that he really needed her help.

Later, he said how amazed he had been by this child. "She turned out to be a big surprise—the exact opposite of what I had expected," he said. "I'd thought she wouldn't talk at all, or would cry and turn away. I found her to be articulate, intelligent, and precocious. She was willing to dig through her memory in order to provide details we needed."

To his amazement, Annie even had the calm good sense to point out things the killer had touched in the apartment so that the crime scene unit could take fingerprints. "For instance, she mentioned that he had parted the blinds to look out. We got a good set of prints from those blinds."

Sgt. Belk said later that little Annie "ranked in what I would consider the top 10 percent of most witnesses and I'm talking about adults." Thanks to this child, Belk was hopeful that the case could be solved quickly.

At that time, the homicide division was located in a two-story, gray stone substation on Mykawa Road in southeast Houston. My old friend, Assistant Chief Charles McClelland—then a lieutenant in homicide— oversaw the case. Later, we talked about how his own little girl was the same age as Annie, and he described how he felt when he first met Annie Tyson.

"It just broke my spirit," he said. "She was so sweet and innocent, such a well-behaved little girl." McClelland kept a bag of teddy bears in his office to comfort traumatized children, and he gave one to Annie, "so she would have something to hold on to, and to help restore her faith that the whole world wasn't bad."

Like Sgt. Belk, Chief McClelland noticed how composed Annie was, "for someone—especially a child—who had been so hurt and experienced such trauma." During the interview, Annie gave the investigators a detailed description of the suspect. They both marveled at her presence of mind. "She kept comparing him to a family friend," said Belk. "She'd say, 'He had this type or that type of feature, like my friend—but it wasn't my friend who did it.'"

At that point, Chief McClelland explained later, "I knew we needed to get you in right away, and I didn't hesitate to call, even though it was 3:30 in the morning."

When the telephone jars me awake in the dark depths of night the way it did then, it's not like it is for most people, whose hearts beat rapidly from fear that something must have happened to someone they love. I automatically assume it's work, but I also know something else—it's bad.

Over the course of a given year I work dozens of murders, sometimes as many as five in one week, mixed in with all my other cases from sex crimes or robbery, but the witnesses or victims all come to my office by appointment. When investigators call me in the middle of the night, I know right away that this is going to be something horrible, something heinous, something that will shock the readers of the morning papers.

As soon as I heard Lieutenant McClelland's voice, I struggled awake and gave him my full attention. I'd felt close to McClelland ever since we'd worked the horrific Theodore Goynes case (when, thanks to valiant serial rape survivors and McClelland's dedication, Goynes had been stopped after murdering one of his victims).

On this night, Lt. McClelland's voice was so soft, so soothing, as he relayed to me the horrific details of what had happened to Annie. Of course, my motherly heart constricted. Like McClelland, I too had a nine-year-old little girl of my own, sleeping peacefully in the next bedroom, dreaming of unicorns and rainbows and all the things sweet young girls should have in their hearts.

Although I had a sore throat and was feeling ill I said, "Consider me en route." This is a phrase I always use when awakened in the night, to ease the detective's mind that I'm going to get there as quickly as I can.

He, like other detectives, asked, "What is your ETA?"

Chief McClelland says that he'll never forget that night, how I said, "Now, I'm a woman. It takes me longer to get ready than a man, but I'm on my way." He chuckles when he tells that story. I told him I'd be there in about half an hour.

Sid and I had been married at that point for fourteen years, and our older son, Brent, was thirteen. We'd long since worked out a routine, where I would sleep in after working late-night cases and Sid would get the kids up and off to school. To this day, Sid has a tender heart that makes him a wonderful daddy, but he can't bear to hear the details of the kinds of cases that drag me out of bed in the night, so I don't talk to him about them. Sometimes that can be lonely, but I think of my husband and children as my roots. They hold me firmly to the ground, like a tree, and give me the strength to withstand the storms of my job.

I slid out of the warm womb of my bed, leaving Sid snoring peacefully, and padded silently over to the closet in the dark, where I pulled out soft black knit jersey pants and a top that I kept for just this sort of case. It was comfortable and the embroidered shock of wheat on the front, in shades of gold and yellow thread, looked like a cheerful sunburst—less threatening, I reasoned, than a severe business suit, especially to a child.

Whenever I work with a child, I want to appear more like a mommy to them than a cop.

As I dressed, brushed my teeth and combed my hair, I thought about Annie Tyson. At this point, the little girl had been up all night and along with the emotional and physical trauma, she would most likely be falling asleep while I sketched. So I would have to work fast and I would have to wake her up and force her to live through it over and over again. I dreaded that part.

From the kitchen I snatched up a couple of apples, one for me to eat on the way and one for Annie, and took a little juice box from the refrigerator, the kind kids like. I knew instinctively that this little girl was going to need a lot of nurturing.

There are some in my profession who believe that the forensic sketch artist should be as detached as the police investigators, that we're there to do a job and move on to the next case. They think our responsibilities are more technical than psychological. We render the face of the bad guy and the cops go get him.

I couldn't disagree more. As sketch artists, we're asking a crime victim to relive the worst thing that's ever happened to him or her. They're shattered and shaken and they think they can't remember any of the details we'll need to do a sketch. Some victims, like Betsy in "Wanted: Dead or Alive," tremble and sob—or even break out in hives. Like the bus driver in "Blind Justice," some shout at you. Some don't even want to talk. Some get sick.

Although I keep a full array of paper, pastels and other artist's instruments in my office, by far the most important tool I have at my disposal is

my empathy. My own rape and near-murder years ago has sharpened my
ability to stand in a victim's shoes and understand how they must be feeling.

As I've mentioned before and will do again as long as there's breath in
my body—if I can touch a mutual, responsive chord somewhere deep
inside a crime victim and in so doing, coax the person to remember the
things he or she has tried so hard to stamp out of his or her memory, I'm
not just increasing the trauma. No. What I'm doing is *empowering* the victim.

But it does take an emotional toll. Every time I sit with someone who's
been through hell, it's like reliving my own ordeal all over again. It often
leaves me drained and exhausted.

However, for every moment that I feel worn out by this process, there
are thousands more when I feel not just *energized* but *exhilarated*. I've helped
someone else find justice! It is absolutely the very best therapy I could have
ever had to enable me to triumph over my own attack. It's downright
addictive.

But even though I've done it thousands of times, every time I sit down
with a victim of violent crime, especially a very young child, I'm entering
the unknown—creating substance from thin air. Will I be able to pull it off?
Will my sketch look like the criminal? Will the officers be able to use my
drawing successfully? I always get hammered with self-doubts and I always
have to motivate myself by remembering how many successful cases we've
had before this.

As I drove through the mostly deserted streets of Houston in the
humid early-morning hours that autumn night, I gave myself a pep talk,
reminding myself of the criminals I'd helped to catch, so that I could
approach the job with confidence, but even so I knew—as with other difficult cases—every time I sit down with a witness, it's like the very first
time.

The ride down Mykawa took me past row upon row of massive warehouse parks on the right, with several railroad tracks on the left, separated
by a wide, water-filled ditch. This late at night, it was spooky and lonesome.
Before the police substation had been built, I used to read in the paper
about dead bodies being dumped on Mykawa road—a gruesome reminder
that this world—the police world I inhabit by day—is far removed from

the world I just left, where fifty-foot pecan trees form a cathedral ceiling over my street and people in their safe homes don't usually think about things like little girls being raped and beaten after watching their mamas being tortured and murdered.

By then I'd grown used to that light/dark aspect of my life. In fact, whenever I was invited to a party, I always thought up some funny stories to tell about my work, so that when people made polite inquiries, I didn't scare them.

I parked my car behind the substation next to one other lonely car, got out and walked to the building, balancing the juice and apples I'd brought. I punched in the keypad code so the door would click open and I could get in.

I had worked hard to make my office as welcoming and inviting as I could. I wanted my witnesses to feel like they had entered a special place that did not have the institutional feel of a police department, so it could help them relax.

Painted a soft pale gray with deep green carpeting, the office is small but cozy. Since I do most of my work at my easel, my gray metal desk is usually neat. The focal point of the room is a big, extra-wide reclining easy chair that is covered in navy blue fabric. This is for the witnesses, to make them as comfortable as possible, and is the first thing I asked the department for when they created my full-time position. Within reach of the easy chair is a box of tissues, should one be needed.

In one corner of the room I keep a cheerful red basket full of toys, plastic dinosaurs and fuzzy bears, because so many of my witnesses are children. I also keep candies in a little dish; this helps to make people feel at ease but also aids people whose mouths have gone so dry they can barely speak.

On the walls of my office hang various serene paintings I've made— landscapes, sunsets and a peculiar form where I paint a tree or a segment of countryside and suspend it in the clouds, like a dream. These are designed to ease tensions in the witnesses and give them something lovely to look at during a time when all they can see in their mind's-eye is horror.

I also have a couple of portraits I did of my husband and children. Those are for me, I guess, to ease *my* tensions.

With the smell of fresh coffee percolating down the hall wafting through my door, I called Sgt. Belk and asked him to please send the witness so that I could start the sketch right away. By this time, it was close to 4:30 in the morning, and I knew that child had to be practically numb. Billy was kind enough to send Annie to me even though he hadn't yet concluded his own interview with her.

Sherrie Anderson, a nine-year veteran of juvenile sex crimes, a pretty woman in her early thirties with waist-length hair the color of honey, now an investigator in robbery, brought Annie to me.

Seeing Annie for the first time, I thought how tiny she was, even for a nine-year-old. She was pretty, dressed in neat, clean jeans and a bright-colored blouse. Her hair was tied back in a smooth ponytail.

Something most people don't realize about children who've been through terrible trauma is that they are nearly always remarkably calm—almost relaxed. Of course, they are experiencing deep shock and that's part of it, but it's more than that. It's also an attitude that they've just lived through the worst thing that could have ever happened to them and that now, people are here to take care of them.

Annie was like that, but as Sherrie picked her up and put her into the big blue chair, she seemed somehow royal to me, diplomatic, like an emissary from a country that's been ravaged by war and now has found peace amidst great sadness.

"Annie," I said in as soft and non-threatening a voice as I could, "I am so glad you came down to see me this morning. Your blouse is so pretty."

"Thank you," she said shyly.

"Now, I want you to understand that we are going to draw a picture of the bad man who hurt you but it's going to be very easy. Do you know why?"

Wide-eyed, she shook her head.

"Because little girls like you see and remember things so much better than grown-ups do."

She smiled and nodded.

"I just need a few ideas from you so I can get started," I said, "and then, when I get my rough sketch finished, I'll turn it around and show it to you. Then I'll change anything you want in any way you want so the sketch will look as much like him as possible. After that we'll be done."

I was acting as if this whole thing would be effortless, but in my mind I was telling myself, *Draw as fast as you can!* I knew exhaustion would soon take over and we would not be able to keep Annie awake for long.

Although investigators almost never sit in on sketch sessions, Sherrie pulled up an extra chair and sat down next to me. Since she had already bonded with Annie, I was glad to have her there. I asked Annie if the man was fat, skinny or average.

"Average," she said, in her small, even voice. "But I didn't see his face well enough, so I don't think I can draw him."

This did not bother me. By this time I'd learned that with just the right kind of coaxing, even the most reluctant and doubt-filled witness can give remarkable descriptions.

I reassured Annie that she wouldn't have to draw, that I would do all the work and I casually tossed in a question about his hair. "What kind of hair did he have?"

"Real short."

I started drawing furiously, without letting on that I was rushing.

"Here's a book that will help you remember." I handed Annie the *FBI Facial Identification Catalogue*. I set her to work selecting a pair of eyes from the catalogue. "Try to find the eyes that are as close to his as possible," I explained, "It won't be perfect, but try to get as close as you can."

In less than thirty seconds, Annie pointed to a set of eyes and said, "That looks like his eyebrows and his hair too." This was typical of most children, who tend to pick out features from the catalogue five or ten times faster than adults. Adults always second-guess themselves. Children usually don't.

I guess Investigator Anderson—Sherrie—didn't realize this fact about children, because she reacted as most adults would, by turning page after page even after Annie had made her selection, saying, "Are you sure?"

I knew Sherrie meant well, but the truth is that during a sketch session, you should never disturb the witness or question their choices. I wanted to tell Sherrie that we needed to let Annie tell us what she'd seen alone, but I kept quiet. The mood in the room was peaceful and I didn't want to introduce any negativity.

The little juice box I'd brought from home was sweating with cold condensation. I picked it up and offered it to Annie, who gladly took the box and made a lot of noise sucking the juice down while I continued to sketch as fast as possible. This early in the morning, I noticed that I was definitely not warmed up.

I offered Annie an apple. Shaking her head, she showed me her little bottom biter tooth. The killer had hit her so hard he'd knocked it loose. For a moment, rage at the man who had destroyed this family and shredded this child's innocence boiled up inside me so dark it clouded my vision and I had to sit for a second or two and collect myself.

These are the moments when it's really hard.

After Annie had selected a nose and a pair of lips, she fell asleep in her chair. I let her sleep as long as possible, maybe twenty minutes, until I was almost done. Then, Sherrie and I gently woke her.

"Just one more question, Annie. What kind of shirt did he have on?"

Blinking, she answered, "No shirt. He was naked-chested."

Three years of drawing nude models at the University of Texas in Austin meant this would be very easy to draw—easier, even, than if I'd had to reproduce a shirt. By laying the pastels on their sides, I shaded the areas of light and dark in quick movements, and was done in less than two minutes.

Turning the easel around, I showed Annie the sketch.

Without hesitating, she said, "He had shorter hair."

The paper I use contains a high cotton rag content that is made in France. I use the color "felt gray," so that I'm able to take an identical color pastel and cover over mistakes or make changes without having to erase. It's quick and easy.

I corrected the sketch, showed it to her and she nodded. "That's good."

Sherrie asked Annie if the eyebrows and eyes and nose were right and Annie paused for a moment.

I bit my lip in frustration. I never ask those things. I want the witness to be the complete source of any comments. Otherwise, you're skating perilously close to "leading the witness."

I know that, especially with young witnesses, if something doesn't look right, they'll blurt it out immediately. There was no need to ask.

The seconds ticked by and I began to relax.

Then Annie crossed her arms over her chest and said, her voice firm, "He looks too much like a girl!"

My mind scrambled in all directions. Then I realized what was going on.

When a crime victim is being attacked or they are witnessing some horrible act, the bad guy doesn't carry the same bland expression on his face that you're likely to see in a mug shot or a forensic sketch. During the attack, his face will be twisted, his eyes terrifying.

That look of murderous rage just can't be duplicated.

What Annie was remembering was that she'd drifted off to sleep in her peaceful bed in the house with the matching salt and pepper shakers, and was wrenched awake to watch in horror the monstrous, contorted face of a murderer who tortured her mother and then came for her. The face I was presenting to Annie stared out at her from the drawing board with a calm, steady, somewhat handsome gaze. That was not the face she thought she remembered.

Still, I asked her if all the shapes were correct, my way of checking to make sure the bone structure I'd drawn was right. She said yes but still insisted, "He looks like a girl."

By this time, I knew that even with the most reluctant witnesses, I could tell by the way they had selected the features or the way a face took shape, when we were on the right track and when we weren't.

The way I think of it is simply to *trust the gift*. For whatever reason, I've been given this talent, and I know when to trust it.

And in this case, I knew that my sketch was as close as we were likely to get, so I turned the easel around and said gently, "We've done as good as we can. The sketch isn't perfect, but we're done."

In her eyes I saw the pain I knew so well and I knew it didn't have anything to do with the sketch. "Honey," I said, "You are still beautiful. What that awful man did can't change that." I leaned forward. "When I was a young girl, the same thing happened to me and as you can see, you can still go on and lead a wonderful life."

Her eyes glistened, and she turned her little face to me and said, "Did they kill your mommy, too?"

My heart stopped. It was all I could do not to cry. I got up, leaned over and pressed my forehead against hers. "No, that didn't happen to me," I whispered. "But you should know that there are so many people who love you and want to take care of you."

With a somber nod she said, "Yeah, my aunties love me a lot."

I sat down again. "I'll bet you have cousins you can play with, too."

She grinned and nodded. On that note, Sherrie took Annie back to homicide.

After they left I felt like I couldn't stand Annie's pain. I had to make sure for myself that this precious child would be all right. I went to homicide, to the large waiting area with a glass wall two stories high through which the sunrise was just beginning to peep beneath dark Gulf clouds. I saw a handsome, well-dressed family, who were sitting on one of the heavy wooden church pews placed there for such agonizing vigils.

A bit timid as I approached them, I said quietly, "Are you Annie's kin?"

They gave me their instant attention and all spoke at once, saying, "Yes, yes."

I said, "I'm the sketch artist, and we got a good sketch of the criminal from her."

They had all gotten to their feet by then, and smiling kindly at me, said, "That's wonderful."

I blurted out, "Will she be taken care of?" I couldn't help it. I was feeling weepy and tired now. I'd done my job, and I just had to know that that sweet child was going to be all right.

Women I assumed were Annie's aunts said, "Oh Lord yes! We're fighting over her right now. She won't lack for a thing."

Uncles, aunts, and cousins all introduced themselves, and I took each of their hands in my own.

We were all warmed by the meeting and I went back to my office, sprayed fixatif on the sketch and turned my attention to the obligatory paper work: date of offense, time (in military hours), witness(es) name, address of offense, case or "incident" number, forensic sketch number highlighted in yellow, the beat and district, the detective assigned to the case and the date he gives it, race and gender of the person sketched and so on. After that I made a good copy of the sketch and put the picture in its own folder to keep on file, as I always do.

I hand-delivered the sketch to Billy Belk in homicide. Billy eventually went on to get his law school degree and pass the bar exam while continuing to work full-time as a homicide investigator. But on this exhausting morning, his wavy brown hair was a bit mussed and there were dark circles under his large brown eyes. He motioned me over to a desk, where he had arranged a group of photographs and asked if the man I had sketched resembled any of the men in the photos.

They were snapshots that had been taken at a party. Annie's murdered mother was smiling, happy and surrounded by a large group of smiling, happy friends. Some of the photos had more than a dozen faces. Staring at the pictures, I realized for the first time just how worn out I was. I could barely comprehend what I was looking at.

"I can't tell," I said. "All these people are grinning."

Billy looked at me, his face drawn and unsmiling. "Lois, I have to tell you..." He glanced away. "I don't know if I'm going to use the sketch. I asked Annie about it and she said the sketch wasn't any good. She said it looked too much like a girl."

I felt my face flush hot and the breath whoosh out of me.

How could I explain what I knew, that from the way Annie had chosen the features for the sketch, *she knew* how to pick the right ones. We had the right facial structure.

I couldn't find words to describe what I knew witnesses couldn't explain: that look of murderous rage; it wasn't going to be captured, not in any forensic sketch.

Not anywhere.

That did not mean that the drawing did not look like the killer.

Finally, I found my voice. "Billy, use the sketch," I insisted. "It's as good as I've done." Then, my tone sharp with frustration and fatigue, I said, "*Trust me.*"

Then I wearily left. It was past eight in the morning by then and the sore throat I'd started with at 3:30 when I first got the call was now so inflamed I could barely talk. I was sick and tired.

Yeah, I was sick and tired all right—sick and tired of detectives questioning my value or showing reluctance to trust the work I'd been doing year in and year out. After more than a dozen years, I was *still* having to prove myself.

Muttering under my breath, I drove home, where Sid had already gotten the kids up, fed and off to school. The house was empty and I made myself a cup of tea with honey and lemon, then dragged off to bed. For a while, all the images I'd forced from my mind while working with Annie bubbled to the surface of my fevered brain, how she'd described the burners on the electric stove turned up so high they glowed red-hot while the man tried to burn her mama...how she'd stood over her mama's tortured body...how she'd fought the man when he climbed on top of her, fought so hard that he punched her to make her stop, loosening her little tooth...

The face of evil, I feel, really looks like someone you might pass on the street without a second thought, like someone you might marry, like someone you might befriend. Sometimes it's twisted and monstrous and sometimes it's so handsome that it looks like a girl.

As I drifted off into a daytime dream-tossed fluish sleep, Billy Belk and Tom McCorvey were still working the streets. Unknown to me at the time, Billy had decided to trust me, after all. He started using the sketch right away.

Chief McClelland told me later that the sketch turned out to be so good that, "we began to get an immediate response, people offering names of who it was."

When the sketch was shown on television news programs, the police department was flooded with calls—people who'd seen him hanging around Cynthia Tyson's apartment complex, people who'd seen the killer (and this is unbelievable to me) pull up to his girlfriend's apartment in Cynthia Tyson's stolen car, unload items stolen from her apartment and take them into his own. When Belk and McCorvey showed my sketch to the security guard at the man's apartment, he said, "Oh yeah. That looks like Jeff Williams."

He pointed out the correct apartment and when Belk and McCorvey knocked on the door, a man answered—at least, a guy who looked just like my sketch. They asked his name and he said, "Jeff Williams."

Jeff Williams. He might have had a pretty face, but he was no sweetheart. At twenty-two years of age, he'd already been arrested by the Houston police six times and convicted four out of five times for charges ranging from auto theft to aggravated assault. His most recent arrest had been only a few months earlier, in June, when a warrant was issued to revoke his parole. He'd spent a month in jail and was ordered by the state Board of Pardons and Paroles to wear an electronic monitor.

He never received that monitor. Had he been wearing it, an alarm would have notified authorities that he was not where he was supposed to be after 10 P.M. when he broke into Cynthia Tyson's apartment on that terrible night.

Twenty-four hours after I handed my sketch to Billy, he and McCorvey had obtained an arrest and search warrant for the apartment of Williams's girlfriend, where they found items stolen from Cynthia during her murder. They arrested Williams on the spot.

Later that day, I'm told, Billy showed Annie a photo lineup which included Williams and she immediately picked him out. "That's him," she said. "That's the man who killed my mama."

I'd roused myself from a restless sleep while all this was going on and shuffled into the kitchen. I was eating a bowl of soup and watching the evening news when I saw my sketch followed by film footage of Billy and Tom escorting a young baby-faced man in handcuffs into the police department.

With a rousing cheer, I yelled, "How do you like it?" as if the killer could somehow hear me and the triumph in my voice that we got him.

We won.

And then, I put my face in my hands and burst into tears.

There are plenty of times that I do my best work in a sketch and we still don't catch the guy. I don't have the time or the luxury—and neither do the investigators—to obsess over the cases we don't solve. We all push past it and move on to the next case.

But this time...this time I saw in my mind a terrified little girl fighting for her life with a man who'd just set her mother on fire. In large part because of her courage, we'd caught the guy, he would never hurt anyone else and I could let the emotions wash over me that I'd pushed aside in my office when she'd asked me, "Did they kill your mommy too?"

I am convinced that these fine investigators would have eventually caught Jeff Williams without my sketch. I don't pretend to be superwoman to the rescue. I regard myself as one of several instruments used by detectives in any investigation. But I do believe that they were able to catch this monster much faster *because* they had my sketch and I was able to do the job I did because I had the bravest little person as a witness.

Three days later I got a memo from Billy Belk in homicide:

"Attached is a copy of your composite drawing, as well as a mug photograph of the suspect charged with the capital murder. It looks pretty good to me. To steal a phrase from Rush Limbaugh, sometimes your stuff is like 'talent on loan from God!' Once again, thanks for coming in at 4:30 A.M. and for the insight to go with your instincts. Remember even the nine-year-old victim said after completing your work that the drawing did not really look 'exactly' like him, but looked 'too girlish.' Now I see why you said, 'Trust me.' Thanks again. Billy."

I couldn't ask for any greater reward than that.

Except for maybe one.

Almost a year later, in District Judge George Godwin's court at Williams's trial for the murder of Cynthia Tyson and the assault on Annie, newspaper accounts would relate, it was brought out that when Williams was serving time in prison in 1989, he was removed from a slaughterhouse detail, in which his job had been to kill and butcher hogs. It appeared he enjoyed it too much.

Nobody knows what brought Williams to Cynthia's door that night. He lived in an adjoining apartment complex, and neighbors think he'd seen her around. He had apparently gone to her door about ten that night supposedly to ask for directions. He came back at 10:30, shoved his way in, and attacked her.

Prosecutor Jim Mount took an unprecedented step for his office: he put Annie on the stand. He told me later that the courtroom sat spellbound when Annie reached out her thin arm and pointed out Jeff Williams as the man who had killed her mother, and told jurors how she struggled with Williams and got punched in the head, how she tried to talk to her dead mother, how she ran for help.

Since Sgt. Belk was a witness in the case, he wasn't permitted in the courtroom before he testified, but he says that Annie's amazing composure astonished everyone who was there.

The next day, Jeff Williams was convicted. It took the jury only twenty-three minutes to sentence him to death.

After the trial Annie Tyson went to live with a maternal aunt in Houston, who saw to it that Annie had extensive counseling to help her cope with the ordeal she'd been through. She has been surrounded by love and never wanted for a thing.

Except for her mother. And her innocence. Those were lost forever.

On June 26, 2002, after all his appeals had been exhausted, when Annie Tyson was sixteen years old, Jeffrey Lynn Williams was executed by lethal injection. To his dying day he refused to admit that he had committed a crime, maintaining that he'd had consensual sex with Cynthia Tyson.

He never mentioned Annie.

"There are some cases that stand out in your memory," Billy Belk told me recently, "that you never forget." He paused. "Let's see...how can I say this and be politically correct? In some cases you have what I call *true victims*. Cases where justice just has to be served. In this case, not only was Jeff Williams an animal and a murderer, but he assaulted a little girl. That fact alone makes it much more likely that we will go beyond the call of duty. We'll go the extra mile."

And then he said the words I'll never forget: "We'll see to it that justice has been served."

Justice.

I guess if there was one word driving my life and my career, it would be *justice.*

People often ask me how can I do my job, day in and day out, how can I sit there and listen to people pour out the horrid details of the worst moments of their lives, how can I stand the misery, heartache and gore?

Well, it's not really about the crime and sadness. It's about the heroism of the courageous survivors and their families; it's about the determination and dedication of hardworking law enforcement officers who never give up...and it's about justice.

Because for every person who goes on to find justice due, in part, to my talents and gifts and labors...then there's that much more justice for me.

And there's just nothing in the world sweeter than that.

Chapter Thirteen:

Catching KAOS: "They Can't Hide Their Faces with Me Around"

September 11, 2002.

A whole year had passed since the massive tragedy that changed our nation, and the smaller—but no less meaningful—tragedy of the Angel Doe case.

Angel Doe had been identified and given a Christian burial, while her evil parents had been arrested, charged, sentenced and jailed and their three other children had been put in foster care.

In New York, the memorial service for the last firefighter identified as having been killed at the World Trade Center had been held on September 9 and the city, as well as Washington, D.C., was preparing for the memorials for all who had been lost that terrible day that had come to be known the world over simply as "9-11."

The slow, shaky business of healing was going on. However, as Heidi Guzman, who lost a loved one to violence, so eloquently put it, there is no such thing as *closure*, no real sense of "acceptance."

But you adjust, you adapt, you go on with your daily life as best you can.

For me, that meant continuing to work with victims of violent crime and its witnesses, doing my part to help the cops chase down the bad guys.

As Hemingway said, there is no hunting like the hunting of men.

A couple of days later, I was working a particularly sad homicide. A video store robber, on the run from police, had broken into a home nearby and, after surprising the retired homeowner who was taking a nap, had beaten the man to death in his bed and stolen his pickup. In a sketch session with some teenagers who worked at the video store, I got a call from K.O. Thomas, a detective in the Harris County Sheriff's Office sex crimes division, about a case that had occurred on the morning of September 11.

Detective Thomas, a tall, well-built African-American man, looked twenty years younger than he was. Years before, he'd attended college on a music scholarship and played trombone while getting his degree in history. Clean-cut, with glasses and a gentle demeanor, he seemed more like a scholar than a cop, but when it came to a case, especially the one he telephoned me about, he was all business.

Emily, a fifteen-year-old high school sophomore, had been waiting at her school bus stop for the bus. It was fairly cold that morning for Houston. Some time past 6 A.M., a maroon Dodge Ram pickup truck with two men in it screeched to a halt in front of where Emily stood watching for the bus. One man jumped out and, brandishing a knife, forced Emily into the truck.

They took her to a wooded area of northeast Harris County where they raped and sodomized the young girl. After that violation, they then robbed her of her meager possessions.

Then they warned her, "Don't look back," and shoved her out of the pickup truck stark naked except for her socks.

Sobbing, shivering, holding her arms across her exposed breasts and private parts, Emily stumbled down the road, filled with morning traffic. She was rescued by a schoolteacher who happened to be driving past.

Detective Thomas asked if I could make a "house call" to the county headquarters of the sheriff's department and I assured him, "I'll be there as soon as I can."

The detective bureau for the Harris County Sheriff's Department is located in a massive brick building, a former warehouse that has recently been converted into the investigative offices of the sheriff's department. (The main office for the HCSD is located downtown.) The detective bureau is only a five- or ten-minute drive away from my office at HPD headquarters downtown.

On the drive over, my own rape, so many years before came rushing back to my mind—that crystallizing moment when I'd realized that I was not going to die—followed in the aftermath by the crippling rage, fear and isolation I'd felt as I struggled to get on with my life. I felt so badly for the young girl I was going to see, who had just experienced a similar attack, that I almost wept, but I reassured myself that I would be there soon to help her.

By this time, I'd helped to put away more than two hundred rapists with my composite drawings. The odds were good that I'd be able to do the same thing in this case.

After finding an empty space, I parked my car and gathered my gear together. Then I walked to the building and headed up to the third floor, where the homicide division was located. There the deputies introduced me to Emily, a lovely girl with long dark hair, soft smooth skin and big brown eyes. Her anxious mother hovered nearby. I noticed Emily was working hard at keeping no expression on her face—probably to keep her mother from worrying even more—but she didn't fool me. I knew the pain she must have been feeling.

Catching Emily's glance, I said, "I'm so glad you're here," gave her and her mother a warm, welcoming smile. Then I walked past them into the room I always use at the sheriff's department when I'm doing an afternoon sketch. I started setting up my easel. Hesitating outside the door, Emily moved slowly, reluctantly, into the room.

This is absolutely normal behavior for victims of violent crimes. The truth is that they don't want to be there, because they know they're going to have to relive the worst thing that ever happened to them. Consequently, they almost never barge into my office. In nearly every case, the victims or witnesses sit or stand reluctantly outside the door of wherever I'm doing the sketch and often have to be coaxed inside.

Behind the desk was a big, brown leather chair. I pointed at it.

"You can sit there," I said in a soft, non-threatening voice.

Whenever there is a "power chair" in a room where I'm sketching, I always have the witness sit in it. With that great big desk in front of her for psychological "protection," and me sitting on the other side almost like a supplicant, my hope is that the witness will feel more in control.

For young Emily, this may very well have been the first time in the more than forty-eight hours since those two savage men had dragged her from the school bus stop and torn her life apart that she had been able to feel this sense of comfort.

As I told her what I tell everyone, that this is going to be easy and go quickly, I studied her. Though she was obviously shaken, her back was straight, her head was up and she struck me as someone who was determined not to let this experience destroy her life, but to find some way, somehow, to be happy in spite of it.

Remembering how, after my own attack years before, I had cowered and cringed in my apartment, I was already in awe of her.

"Who would you like to describe first?" I asked. (Again, letting her be in control.) She chose the driver and I wrote the word *DRIVER* across the top of the sketch in black marker as a reference for the detective to use when comparing her statement with the sketch.

I usually start my sketch with the perpetrator's hair and this composite was no exception, but I'd scarcely even begun the drawing when Emily blurted out, "Tonight, my drill team is going to perform during half-time at the homecoming football game." Her face seemed to light up. "It's my first time to perform."

"Oh, how wonderful!" I cried. "What does your costume look like?"

Excitedly, she dug her wallet out of her purse and produced a photograph of herself, smiling and waving her pom-poms in her sparkling blue and silver costume. Watching her, it occurred to me that it wasn't that she was *denying* the terrible thing that had happened to her; it was more like she had made a *choice* not to let it dominate her life.

This was her way of beginning the healing process, by focusing on this happy, momentous upcoming event rather than obsessing over the tragic one that occurred in the past. I took that cue from her and decided to do the same thing.

Over more than twenty years of doing these sketches, I'd learned that one of the best ways to improve a witness's memory is to use mood enhancement. Recent studies have borne me out. The better a witness feels, the better the sketch. And the real bonus comes when the witness (especially a victim of sexual assault) leaves the session feeling better than she did when she first came in.

"How long will this take?" asked Emily, a shadow of anxiety crossing her face. "I have to be at the football stadium by 6:15."

This presented a problem. In order for Emily to be at the stadium by 6:15, we would have time to do only one sketch. And I knew the detectives were depending upon me to get sketches of both of Emily's assailants. It had already been two days since her attack and they were anxious to crack this case.

While I debated what to do, I reflected once again on my own actions and feelings after I had been raped. Starving myself, staying in my apartment for days rather than going out, afraid, alone, spiraling downward...and here was this young girl, who stood ready to grab life again and charge full-speed ahead in her shining blue and silver uniform, prancing in the lights with her friends at her side...well, who was I to hold her back?

"No problem," I assured her. "We'll do just this one today, then you can go on and make the game. We'll do that other creep tomorrow or whenever you can."

She beamed with joy.

"I'm so proud of you, Emily," I said and I meant it. "You're doing great. The most important thing in the world right now is for you to go on to the game and have the time of your life. These two perverts can't take that from you. *No one* can ever take that from you!"

She gave me a shy smile.

"Don't you worry," I added, my voice firm with self-assurance, "They can't hide their faces with me around." She looked very happy.

Quickly I handed her the *FBI Facial Identification Catalogue*. While she selected facial features and I began the drawing, I told her about having been a high school majorette, performing at half-time. Then I asked her what songs the drill team would be using for the performance, how she liked the instructor and who were her closest friends on the team.

As we moved past the nose to the lips and chin, I said, "Tonight, you'll be the best you've ever been. You won't be afraid because, after all, you almost got killed and you lived." I winked at her. "And, really, nobody ever got killed over a drill routine."

She laughed at that.

I told her I'd been attacked, too. "Going through it caused me to throw myself into my art more and to enjoy music more."

She agreed. "I've been practicing at home and I've really been enjoy-ing the music more than I ever did before," she said, "and I just lose myself in the routine."

When I was finished drawing, I told her I could make any changes she requested and turned the sketch around to show her.

Emily gasped and shrank back into the chair, her careful composure lost for the moment. But this remarkable young lady soon recovered and ordered me to make the chin and one of the ears bigger, which I quickly did.

"It looks like him, for sure," she said. Then she grew thoughtful and said, "You know, you really must have a gift from God to do this."

I hear this a lot from witnesses and it always means a great deal to me. "Thank you," I said.

It is a gift, I thought and *that makes what I do my mission in life.*

Giving her a light little hug, I walked her to the door and then went with her and her mother to the stairs. "I know you have to be somewhere soon, so we're done," I said to her relieved mother.

Returning to the sergeant's office, I sprayed fixatif on the drawing and wasted some time while I dreaded the detective's return.

A few minutes later Detective Thomas came into the room and spied my drawing. Glancing around, he said, "Where's the other sketch?"

Four other burly detectives now crowded into the room and they all had pretty much the same reaction he had.

I swallowed, but I have a policy of never lying. "She had to dance with her drill team tonight," I said. "It's homecoming and it's her first time."
Dead silence.

Finally, betraying no emotion whatsoever, one of them deadpanned, "She has to dance with her drill team at half-time at a football game?"

We all knew that time is always of the essence in any criminal investi-gation and the more time a culprit has "on the ground," or at large, the more likely he will flee the jurisdiction altogether and never be caught.

Without dropping my gaze, I said firmly, "That's right."
They stared at me.

"We can do the other one tomorrow, any time you say," I assured them. "Call me and I'll come right over."

Unspoken in that room was what we all knew: that although I'd do anything in the world for those guys, I was a victim's advocate, first and foremost. They also knew about my own attack and that I had very powerful instincts when it came to working with victims of violent crime.

Detective Thomas glanced at my sketch again and commented that the man looked Hispanic, even though Emily had said in her statement that he was white. I told him not to worry about it, that plenty of white males have dark complexions. The witness had said this looked like the guy and that was good enough for me.

Finally, with a half-hearted smile, Detective Thomas said, "Okay. Thanks."

They all turned, walked slowly out and dribbled back to their offices.

I left shortly afterward. As I loaded my gear back into my car, I had a moment or two where I wondered if maybe I'd screwed up. What if they never caught those guys, simply because of a judgment call I had made? What if—heaven forbid—those monsters hurt someone else? I tried not to obsess about this possibility.

When I drove into my garage, I glanced at the clock and felt better. Right about this time, Emily would be lining up with all the other girls in her dazzling costume, kicking up her heels to the jazzy music, smiling for the cheering fans...and I whispered, "You go, girl."

Movies and television detective programs usually show one lone, misunderstood detective or a crime-fighting, wise-cracking duo, working to solve a case in solitude. And indeed, this does happen occasionally, as in the Sarah Rinehart homicide case in Newton, Kansas, which was closed almost single-handedly by Detective Sergeant T. Walton, who had to fight so hard to follow his theory on the case.

But most of the time, cases are closed by a team of investigators from various disciplines and sometimes, different departments. And in all my years of working with law enforcement officers from all over the country, I don't believe I've ever seen a better example of teamwork solving a crime than when the Harris County Sheriff's Department brought their joint efforts to work on the brutal sexual assault of "Emily," the high school drill-team girl.

All cases are important to investigating officers, but as Sgt. Clarence Douglas of the Houston Police Department's homicide division said about the Angel Doe case, "Some cases grab you by the gut and just won't let you go." And for the Harris County Sheriff's Department, one of the cases that really motivated detectives to find the criminal who did it was this one.

A sweet young girl had been standing at her school bus stop early one fall morning, like thousands of sweet young girls all over the country, like my daughter or your daughter. She wasn't doing a single thing to put herself at risk, just waiting to get on the bus to go to school. She was probably thinking about her drill team routine or maybe a boy she liked, or perhaps worrying about an exam scheduled for that day.

And then she was yanked off the street by a couple of vicious losers. The horrible things that were done to Emily and the incredible, amazing courage she displayed in the aftermath of her attack, spurred every law enforcement officer in the county. They would not slow down, they would not stop, they would not rest until the scumbags were caught, locked up and put away so that no other young girls need fear for their lives while waiting for school buses.

And the detectives were right to hunt them down quickly. Kerry Ashley O'Neal was one mean s.o.b. Twenty-three, dark-complected with short black hair, his brown eyes were set deep in his skull. Thick black brows shelved over the eyes gave them a shadowy, sinister appearance and a three-day beard did little to hide his weak chin.

Though he had a common-law wife and a twenty-two-month-old son, this had not prevented him from murdering his wife's mother.

O'Neal was abusive to his wife. One night, while he was out carousing, she ran out of gas. Stranded, she called her mother to come and get her. It was so late by the time they got back to her mother's house that she went on to work and left the baby with her mother.

When O'Neal came by later that morning, his mother-in-law scolded him for having left her daughter stranded. Enraged at the (true) accusation, O'Neal raped and then strangled the woman with a telephone cord.

Then he went on to work, leaving his infant son alone in the house with the body of his dead grandmother.

A few hours later, he called police and reported that his mother-in-law had "committed suicide."

Under questioning, O'Neal claimed that he'd been having an affair with the woman and that she'd threatened to tell her daughter.

None of it was true. And even though the newspapers reported O'Neal's lies as fact, the detectives weren't fooled.

HCSD homicide detective Russell Coleman arrested O'Neal and he was charged with the murder.

A native of the dry and dusty west Texas panhandle, Russell Coleman looked deceptively young, with golden hair, brows and clear skin, but his intelligent eyes didn't miss a thing and he cared deeply for the victimized and those he'd seen in his work who had been hurt by psychopaths like Kerry O'Neal.

According to Detective Coleman, O'Neal wasn't just *mean*, he was *evil*.

"He signed his name KAOS," Coleman said. "Because his initials were K.A.O. and since he'd named his son after himself, that made him Kerry Ashley O'Neal, Sr., so that's how he signed his name: KAOS. It's how he thought of himself. He thought of himself as chaos and he was proud of it."

But on the one-year anniversary of 9-11, O'Neal was out on bail for the slaying of his mother-in-law. Somehow, even though he had a criminal history going back six years or more, he'd managed to raise the 10 percent of the $100,000 bond that was necessary, a fact which "agitated" Russell Coleman no end.

Since O'Neal's wife had left him after her mother's murder, he'd moved in with his grandmother. Most likely, his grandmother had put up her house as collateral for O'Neal's bail.

It would not be the last favor the old lady would do for her grandson.

On the morning of September 11, O'Neal was driving his Dodge Ram pickup with his buddy, Douglas Neil Tickner, another twenty-three-year-old thug. Who knows what those two were thinking when they drove up to the school bus stop in northeast Harris County that day.

All anyone knows for certain is that Tickner jumped out of the pickup with a knife and forced Emily into the truck.

Then Kerry O'Neal drove her straight into hell.

When I left the HCSD on Friday evening and Emily departed for the football stadium, Detective K.O. Thomas had only my one sketch, which he immediately released to the media and to CrimeStoppers.

"Remember, it was a weekend," he said later. "We brought the complainant in that Saturday morning for another interview and I wanted her to take another look at the sketch."

Homicide Detective Coleman had already heard about the sexual assault of "Emily," and, "It just made me sick," he said. In one of those amazing serendipitous moments that sometimes happens in an investigation, Coleman went over to the sex crimes division to have a copy made of an audiotape.

"And as I was walking through the offices," he said, "I saw the composite drawing of Emily's assailant."

What he saw startled Detective Coleman. "Not only did the drawing resemble Kerry O'Neal, but the attack had taken place on the north side, where I knew O'Neal lived."

He approached Detective Thomas and said, "That sketch looks kind of like one of my guys."

The two investigators discussed the case of Kerry O'Neal, who was out on bail for the murder of his mother-in-law. "He lives in that same general area," said Detective Coleman. "And he does resemble that sketch."

Without hesitation, he added, "Kerry O'Neal could have had something to do with this, absolutely. He's an evil, evil man."

Returning to his office, Detective Coleman printed up a copy of Kerry O'Neal's mug shot. He took it over to Thomas and the two men decided that "it wouldn't hurt" to present Emily with a photo line-up and to include Kerry O'Neal's picture in with the group.

Detective Thomas says she picked out Kerry O'Neal immediately.

At the same time, a caller from the CrimeStoppers hotline also mentioned Kerry O'Neal as looking like the man in my sketch.

"When K.O. called me and told me this was our man," said Detective Coleman later, "I actually started shaking. I wanted to get him *right now*."

Coleman wasn't the only law enforcement officer who felt that way. By Monday, Department of Public Safety troopers had also joined in the investigation, driving around the northeast Harris county area, looking for O'Neal's pickup truck.

During their surveillance, detectives from sex crimes, with assistance from Texas Ranger Sergeant Alolpus Pressley of the Special Crimes Service, put together a comprehensive list of possible locations and known associates of O'Neal's.

By Wednesday, they had an arrest warrant prepared for Kerry O'Neal for the aggravated sexual assault of Emily.

At that point, officers from the Gulf Coast Violent Offenders Task Force were deployed to assist in the apprehension of a man who was considered to be armed and dangerous. Later, in a letter of commendation sent out to everyone involved in the case—(including the sketch artist, me)—Harris County Sheriff Tommy Thomas described how the officers "created a net around the area where O'Neal was believed to reside."

Kerry O'Neal attempted to flee when he saw the cops gathering round. He ran out the back door and jumped a fence—right into the waiting hands of a Task Force member.

Later, while being questioned by investigators, O'Neal confessed to the crime and gave the name of Douglas Tickner as his accomplice. Once Tickner was arrested, he gave a statement as well.

Both men accused the other of masterminding the attack.

It had taken less than one week to track down Emily's attackers and put them behind bars.

As for me, I was just so profoundly grateful that, if we had to choose one guy to do a composite of—and I had left it up to Emily—she had chosen the right one for me to draw.

Sometimes, the only tool any of us has to use is our intuition. I used mine and Emily used hers. Together, we got it right.

Along with all the investigating officers who worked this case and their support team, I was honored to receive a certificate of appreciation from Sheriff Thomas, "...in recognition of outstanding service and dedication to duty...in the arrest of two dangerous sexual predators..."

But the ink was hardly dry on the sheriff's letter of commendation before Kerry O'Neal reached out from his jail cell again—not to a lawyer, as you might expect or an investigator or even a clergyman.

But to a hit man.

Although to me most law enforcement officers have a touch of the heroic about them, there are thousands of law enforcement officers like

Gary Johnson who go about their work quietly, unsung, unnoticed and unheralded.

And I know Gary wouldn't have it any other way.

Guys like Gary don't wear uniforms or drive squad cars. They don't flip out I.D. badges and say things like, "Gary Johnson, homicide." And when the big cases are solved, you won't find the Gary Johnsons of the world lined up behind the brass in front of television cameras.

Gary's still going about his job of protecting and serving the citizens of Harris County. Gary is an investigator for the Major Offenders division of the Harris County District Attorney's office, one of only a few who work undercover. Gary handles first-degree felony cases such as "solicitation," or attempting to hire someone to do something for you...like kill another person.

To better understand the scope of Gary's job, it is necessary to understand that Houston covers some 619 square miles. The *Houston Chronicle* recently published a diagram of the city that had been provided by the City of Houston Planning and Development Department. The city was divided into nine puzzle pieces and each piece of the puzzle represented a major city in the United States.

According to that diagram, the following cities would all fit into the geographical boundaries of the city of Houston at the same time: Cleveland, Miami, St. Louis, Pittsburgh, San Francisco, Baltimore, Boston, Denver and Washington, D.C.

Consequently, the Harris County District Attorney's office in Houston employs some fifty investigators, who assist prosecutors handling cases of all kinds, from misdemeanors to domestic violence to juvenile courts to consumer fraud to organized crime to narcotics to...well, you get the idea.

So when an inmate at the Harris County jail told his defense attorney that he had some information concerning another inmate who was looking for a hit man and wanted to know if he could trade that information for some consideration in his own case, the defense attorney contacted the District Court Chief, who then called Gary Johnson.

"I met with the inmate and his lawyer," said Gary later, "and he said that he'd heard Kerry Ashley O'Neal say that he should have killed that little girl he raped and that they were going to seat a jury on his trial on July 22. He wanted her dead before then."

Gary explained to the inmate that he couldn't offer the guy a "deal," but that he would be glad to testify at his trial, "as to the fact that he had come forth with information that had saved a young lady's life," that it might help in the sentencing phase.

The inmate agreed to this and Gary sent him back to jail. "Don't approach O'Neal directly," he instructed the inmate. "Just let him know that you're willing to listen if he wants to talk about it. If he does, then tell him that you know a guy who might do it. Say you don't know him very well, but that you have a phone number." Gary handed the inmate a telephone number and went on about his business.

Within a few days, Gary got a call from Kerry O'Neal. "I should have killed that girl in the first place," he said, "or I might not be in this mess. I need her killed before July 22."

He gave Gary "Emily's" home address and her physical description.

"I told him I'd kill her," said Gary, "and we agreed on a price of $5,000, with half to be paid upfront."

"My grandmother's going to get the money from my mother," said O'Neal. "She'll make the money drop for you." He gave Gary his grandmother's phone number and address, adding, "but if my grandfather answers the phone? Don't mention this to him, because he doesn't know anything about it."

They arranged a time and place of payment.

"I really appreciate what you're doing for me," said O'Neal.

Over the next few phone calls (and no, the Harris County jail does not record inmate telephone conversations), Kerry O'Neal discussed various details of the hit with Johnson.

"He always showed deep respect for me," said Johnson later. "He was always very courteous and grateful."

Which, Johnson added, "is typical psychopathic behavior."

Then Johnson contacted the grandmother. At one point in their conversation the sly old lady seemed to sense that Gary was not a real hit man and suddenly, she wanted him to meet with Gary's mother instead of her.

"She set up the meeting," said Gary, "but I believe she used the mother as a cut-out."

Meanwhile, poor Kerry O'Neal was having money problems. He was having trouble raising the $5,000. He asked Gary Johnson if he would settle for a $1,000 down payment on the murder of the high school drill team girl.

Johnson said yes, he'd take a thousand.

I'm sure Kerry O'Neal rejoiced when he heard of his sudden luck, that he would only have to pay a thousand bucks down to get "Emily" murdered.

I confess that sometimes things from my job get to me. As I've said before, I don't cry for the cases we can't solve and Lord knows that if I cried for every case we did, I'd be crying all the time.

But when I think of that valiant, brave girl with her beautiful soul, going out two days after her horrifying attack at the hands of "KAOS" and his buddy, to perform with her drill team at the homecoming football game... while all along, that miserable psychopath was plotting her death... well, I cry.

"I met with O'Neal's mother in a parking lot outside a hardware store on Highway 59," Gary Johnson explained later. "There were other surveillance officers there and, like all the talks with O'Neal, I recorded our conversation.

"She gave me the money and I said, "So, this is the down payment for the killing of Emily So-and-So?"

At that point, the hapless mother of the devil's spawn "went berserk."

Screaming, "What are you talking about? This is money to hire Kerry a new lawyer! Kill somebody? No! No! It's not to kill ANYBODY!" she jumped out of the car, into her own and peeled rubber out of the parking lot.

Gary Johnson believed the woman. Clearly, she'd been manipulated. She was not put under arrest.

Kerry O'Neal was another matter.

I asked Gary if he at least had the satisfaction of placing "*KAOS*" under arrest for trying to have Emily killed and he said, with no trace of bitterness or frustration, "No, I don't get that satisfaction. The detectives who handle the case make the arrests."

He might have liked to have testified against Kerry O'Neal in court, but when presented with the irrefutable evidence that he'd tried to have somebody murdered from his jail cell, O'Neal chose, instead, to work out a plea bargain with the district attorney's office.

For the murder of his mother-in-law, the aggravated sexual assault of

Emily, the drill-team star and the murder-for-hire scheme to have her killed, Kerry Ashley O'Neal was sentenced to fifty years in prison. (Johnson explained that the sentence was actually more harsh than it seemed, since it was O'Neal's first felony conviction.) His partner in the sexual assault, Douglas Tickner, was given thirty-five years for that crime.

Homicide Detective Russell Coleman, who first identified O'Neal from the sketch I'd done with Emily, was disgusted at what he considered far too light a term, but explained that, according to recent changes in Texas law, O'Neal will have to serve at least three-quarters of his sentence.

"As mean as he is," Coleman said, "I fully expect that he'll have to serve his entire sentence. Kerry O'Neal will be in his seventies by the time he gets out." He added, "and he'll be every bit as evil then as he is now."

Investigator Gary Johnson had a similar opinion of the man who liked to call himself KAOS.

"Oh yeah," he said, "That guy's walking, talking pain and suffering."

But if Kerry O'Neal is "walking, talking pain and suffering," then Emily is walking, talking courage and heart.

Two years after her brutal attack, Emily agreed to go on-camera and give an interview on my behalf to *CBS This Morning*, which was doing a piece on me. Holding her head high and flashing that beautiful smile, she talked about how comfortable she had felt with me that afternoon we did the sketch and said, "If it wasn't for that sketch, they (O'Neal and Tickner) probably wouldn't have been caught."

But if I could, I would tell Emily that the sketch didn't catch these two creeps—she did.

My crime scene is victims' memories and the bravery they have in recounting traumas and helping me to recreate the faces of evil they've been forced—against their wills—to confront on the most terrible day of their lives, inspires me every day.

Remember when I said people ask me if I have nightmares? And they don't just ask me that.

They also ask me how I can go on and do what I do, year after year.

After all, my days are filled with tales of misery and horror, of people brutalized at the hands of destructive predators like Theodore Goynes, Chester Higginbotham, Jeffrey Williams, Donald Eugene Dutton and Kerry Ashley O'Neal—and thousands more like them.

But if I could just let those people who ask this question spend some time with survivors like Emily and Annie Tyson and Maria Santos and so many, many more, who display almost unimaginable courage and tenacity and strength of soul when they climb back up out of the pits of hell...

If I could just introduce them to some incredible friends of mine, like T. Walton, Clarence Douglas, Manny Zamora, Paul Deason and so many more valiant men and women out there every day of their lives, fighting the good fight to find justice and to give peace to those survivors...

If I could put them in touch with other heroic souls who have crossed my path through the years who, in one way or the other, have also made their marks, through compassion, forgiveness and sheer strength of will; people like Heidi Guzman, Tina Shiets and one little boy who grew up and spent thirty years in search of his father's killer...

If they could truly see what I see every day, they would know why I do what I do and why I am so grateful to have the opportunity.

It's been a long time since a terrified girl named Lois Herbert cowered in her apartment after a violent attack waiting for the blood to drain out of her eyes...and it's people like Emily, the high school drill team member who refused to give in to pain and fear and went on to perform only days after being raped, who teach me each and every day...just how far we have all come.

Part Two:

My Mission

Making the Case for Forensic Art: A Dozen Bodacious Myths That Keep Some Cops Away

On the morning of June 5, 2002, while getting ready for work, I and many others turned on our television sets to the horrible news that yet another beautiful, innocent young girl had been wrenched from her safe warm bed in the dark of night by a stranger and abducted.

Over the course of the next year, people the world over anguished over the loss of Elizabeth Ann Smart, a beloved fourteen-year-old girl with five brothers and sisters from Salt Lake City, Utah. We learned she played the harp and dreamed of attending Julliard. The media displayed images of her shy smile, her wholesome, blond-haired, blue-eyed looks—an appearance that was mirrored in the traumatized face of her little nine-year-old sister, Mary Katherine, who had lain in bed next to Elizabeth on the night Elizabeth was kidnapped.

Elizabeth's devastated parents, Ed and Lois Smart, and Elizabeth's large extended family, worked tirelessly to keep those images at the forefront of the people's minds in the progressively less promising hope that someone, somewhere, would know *something* that would bring Elizabeth home. With the eager assistance of John Walsh and the staff at *America's Most Wanted*, Elizabeth's case was featured repeatedly on their popular television broadcast, even after the police investigating the case had told Ed Smart that his daughter was most likely dead and that the man they believed to have taken her had died too, taking the secret of what had happened to Elizabeth with him to his grave.

The ups and downs of this long road are described in their book, *Bringing Elizabeth Home: A Journey of Faith and Hope*, written by the Smarts with Laura Morton (Doubleday, 2003).

Like the rest of the country, I too was spellbound watching Elizabeth's story unfold and like everyone else, I also shouted and wept tears of joy when she was actually found alive and returned—at long last—to her family.

But when high-profile cases like this garner public attention, it hits me differently than most, because of that old nagging burn, that drive that propels me forward in my life, that overwhelming urge to *do something* to help. Naturally, the first thing I would have wanted to do after hearing about Elizabeth's abduction was sit down with Mary Katherine as soon as possible and do a sketch of Elizabeth's abductor.

Unfortunately, not every law enforcement agency in this country is as sold on the use of compositry as is the Houston Police Department and the Harris County Sheriff's Department. And as I've related, it took me quite a while to break down the barriers even at my home department and, in all fairness to them, it took me some time to get as good at compositry as I am now.

For instance, I can now do a complete composite sketch in an hour or less in most cases, but when I first started out, it sometimes took me as long as three hours. Like any other skill, compositry takes practice and I can only suggest to departments who are taking their first tentative stabs at the use of forensic sketches—the more an artist does it, the better and faster he or she will become.

It's not my intention to criticize other police investigators around the country for mistakes they may or may not have made in handling their own high-profile cases, but I do think it imperative to use what cases I think serve as illustrations of what I consider to be various myths about the use of compositry that stubbornly persist within the law enforcement community to this day.

Remember the Sarah Rinehart case in Newton, Kansas? How little Jordan Rinehart and her friend told police repeatedly that it was *not* Jordan's uncle who had murdered her mother? And yet the police kept doggedly pursuing the uncle as a prime suspect not just for months, but for *years*—even excluding leads that clearly pointed to a stranger who still lived within their jurisdiction.

But when Chester Higginbotham was finally fingered as a hard suspect by Detective Sergeant T. Walton—he looked almost identical to the forensic sketch I had done using the descriptions provided by two little girls, ages five and six. If police had only listened to the children and paid attention to my sketch, it is possible that Higginbotham could have been taken into custody *years* before he was, which would have not only spared the Rineharts and Guzmans much pain and suffering, but very well may have saved the life of another victim, Jonetta McKown.

Police departments routinely dismiss the statements provided by young children, even when their stories remain constant. Yet I am proud to point out that the Houston Police Department took very seriously the testimony of little Annie Tyson as to the murderer of *her* mother, Cynthia, calling me up in the middle of the night to come and do a sketch with this nine-year-old. Consequently, Jeffrey Lynn Williams was arrested within twenty-four hours of my doing the sketch with Annie.

Sadly, this was not to be the case with the Salt Lake City Police Department. Just as the Newton, Kansas authorities had done before them, they refused to pay attention to Mary Katherine, who steadfastly insisted that it had not been a family member who had taken her sister. They wasted many valuable weeks chasing their belief that either Elizabeth's father or her uncle had faked the kidnapping.

Instead, once they finally accepted that a stranger had indeed kidnapped Elizabeth, they then concentrated on a man who had frequented her harp concerts—even though, once again, Mary Katherine insisted that this man, who was a complete stranger to the whole family—did not resemble the man who had taken Elizabeth.

It should be mentioned here that the police actually used a sketch artist to get the likeness of the harp-concert man, but they did not listen to Mary Katherine or anybody else in the family, when the guy was not recognized. Eventually, the man was tracked down and completely cleared by police.

After wasting more weeks.

When the name of Richard Ricci surfaced as an ex-con who had done work on the Smart home and owned a vehicle that had once belonged to the Smarts, some Salt Lake investigators became obsessed with the notion that Ricci had kidnapped and probably killed Elizabeth, even though he had no history of sex abuse in his past and even though Mary Katherine—yet *again*—insisted that she remembered Richard Ricci, she knew Richard Ricci and it had not been Richard Ricci who had taken Elizabeth.

Five months after Elizabeth was kidnapped, Mary Katherine suddenly remembered the name of a handyman who had been at the house for three hours one afternoon, months before and had worked on the Smart's roof with Ed Smart.

He called himself *Immanuel.*

In all fairness to the Salt Lake authorities, they did do a computer check on Immanuel, but unfortunately, they used only one spelling of the name in the computer database: *Emmanuel*, which turned up no hits. So they quit there.

According to his account in *Bringing Elizabeth Home*, when a sketch artist named Dalene Nielson walked into the Salt Lake Police Department and offered her services, Ed Smart not only had to beg for a sketching session with Dalene for more than a month, but when the sketch was finished, the police *refused to release it to the media!*

Smart claims that the investigators explained that Immanuel was "one of fifty" homeless handymen who had worked on the Smart home during that time and that to have released the sketch to the media would have brought in too many leads that would have only confused the investigation. Instead, they quietly showed it around to homeless shelters in the Salt Lake area, with no result.

But as I demonstrated in the drill team girl rape case and in the murder of Cynthia Tyson and in many, many other cases—what usually happens is that one name will pop up repeatedly in the leads that come in following the media release of a forensic sketch, thus giving detectives a powerful weapon to use in their investigation, helping them narrow down their efforts considerably and bring the investigation into sharp focus.

Yet after Dalene did the sketch of Immanuel for Ed Smart, months passed while the investigation languished.

Months.

It wasn't until John Walsh released the sketch on his television program, *America's Most Wanted*, that a lead came in from "Immanuel's" sister. She identified the man sketched as Brian David Mitchell, who had a history of sexual abuse of children and of abusing his ex-wife.

Still, investigators did not take the leads seriously. They seemed fixated on their own pet theories rather than a lead generated by a sketch. The police did not put out an all points bulletin on Mitchell, who happened to be in custody in California at the time. Had they done so, he might have been caught at that time. (Salt Lake authorities interviewed the ex-wife and decided that her claims of sexual abuse of the children were only those of a bitter divorce. Had they checked, they'd have found medical records that would have provided evidence.)

Instead, *more* months passed, months while that poor child was being starved, raped and brutalized by Mitchell and his wife, Wanda Barzee.

John Walsh ran a repeat segment and this time, Mitchell's *sons* called in and ID'ed the sketch. The Smart family also uncovered evidence that revealed that Brian David Mitchell often hiked and camped in the mountains right behind their house.

And *still*, police did not follow up.

It wasn't until a *third* broadcast of the sketch and repeat offerings of reward money were publicized on John Walsh's *America's Most Wanted*, that enough tips came in from viewers of the broadcast which finally led to Mitchell's arrest.

By a different police department, though. John David Mitchell and his wife Wanda Barzee were arrested by the Sandy, Utah police department and Elizabeth Smart was finally rescued—*nine months* after her ordeal had begun.

Although it's very tempting for me to maintain, at this point, that if I'd done a sketch with Mary Katherine that first day, they would have found Elizabeth sooner...I just can't make a claim like that, nor would I want to. Any number of sketch artists could have worked with Mary Katherine. Perhaps there would not have been a good result at that time. It might have taken a few months for her memories to work their way past the trauma.

But I do think that had investigators considered her a solid eye-witness from the beginning, discounting family members and individuals she had never seen—or at the very least—if they had released Dalene's sketch that she'd done with Ed Smart to the nationwide media and put out an all-points bulletin on Mitchell when the sketch generated his name as a suspect... then yes, I believe Elizabeth Smart would have been brought home maybe as much as *four months* before she actually was.

She could have been home for Christmas with her family.

I'm not trying to beat up on the Salt Lake City police, believe me. I consider myself part of the brotherhood of law enforcement officers and I see for myself, every day, what investigators go through and how hard they work, under unimaginable pressure, especially in high-profile cases like this one.

All I want to do here is expose those myths that I think trip up many cops and keep them from making use of one of the most effective methods of investigation that exists today.

It's not about me.

It's about finding *justice* for as many crime victims as we possibly can.

There is only one reason I do what I do and that is to catch criminals.

The reason I wrote this book, the reason I teach courses in forensic art, the reason I give interviews to television and radio programs, newspaper and magazine reporters, the reason I get up each and every morning of my life is simple:

I want to catch bad guys.

But I'm only one person, one forensic artist with a full-time job at one police department in one city in the United States.

Over the years, I've kept count of the number of others out there who are like me: working full-time at a major metropolitan police department—that is, whose duties are totally forensic art—and so far, I've only been able to come up with *nineteen*.

According to the *National Directory of Law Enforcement Administrators*, which is put out by the National Public Safety Information Bureau, there are more than 39,320 law enforcement agencies in the United States.

That is, city and county *only*.

That doesn't include state or federal law enforcement agencies.

Nor does it take into account security providers or campus police agencies or any number of places in this country that employ people to enforce the law.

Out of almost 40,000 law enforcement agencies, (not counting the feds, remember), I have been able to track down less than *twenty* full-time forensic artists available—that is, not just called in a few times a year—to do composite drawings that will help to enable law enforcement officers to track down criminals.

In my career many cops have told me they would most likely not have been able to solve their cases without forensic sketches. Multiply that by all the law enforcement agencies who do not have a forensic artist available and a conservative estimate would be... *thousands* of unsolved cases.

Which means, thousands of bad guys who can then go on to do more bad things before they are eventually caught, usually after having committed multiple crimes, crimes that often grow progressively more serious.

Most classes that teach forensic art—including the one provided by the F.B.I.—were not even begun until 1985. If you combine all the legitimate classes that are now available, including my own (at the Northwestern University Center for Public Safety) and you add up all the graduates of those classes over the years, there are at least 2,000 trained forensic sketch artists in the United States today.

So it's not that there aren't enough people out there trained to do what I do. It's that, even after all these years, there are still too many law enforcement officers and their agencies who *continue* to cling to their stubborn beliefs that the use of compositry isn't useful. I hope to bust such myths open once and for all in these pages.

Because the way I see it, for every cop who calls an artist anywhere in the country to do a sketch that helps to catch a bad guy—that's one less criminal out there on the streets.

One less guy like the monster who raped and tried to kill me.

So the more artists we get out there doing what I do and the more crooks who get caught, the better our entire society will be.

And the safer we all will be.

I beg all of you reading this book to make it available to any law enforcement officers you may know. Urge them to read it or at least, to flip through its pages and read this chapter.

Because if, as a result of this book, just *one* cop decides to reach out to *one* artist somewhere and have him or her provide a sketch that could help crack a case and catch a criminal... then, to me, it will be worth my efforts.

MYTH #1: *There is no need to use forensic artists because we've got computer software these days that's just as good.*

This myth is the most pervasive. There is a good reason. Computer software companies can count, as I have, how many law enforcement agencies exist in this country today (and that doesn't include the international market). If they can price their forensic sketching software so that they can make a profit of, say, fifty dollars a unit and if—through high-profile advertising in law enforcement journals and at law enforcement seminars and schools and conferences—they can convince big-city departments to purchase several programs and smaller departments that they need at least one...then the companies stand to make millions.

Before you decide that I'm an artistic purist who fails to appreciate the finer points of computer-use, let me say that I sit on the board of directors for a company called *Faceprint Global Solutions*, which is trying to design a viable forensic sketching software. At my office at the Houston Police Department, I've got a computer on my desk. If I could find a program that worked as well at compositry as a human artist, I'd use it!

But although I've tried all of the programs out there, I've never been able to discover one that worked as well as a good forensic artist.

Unfortunately, thousands of law enforcement agencies have purchased composite sketching software, buying into the illusion that the present technology will allow any cop to sit down and *voila!*—create a composite sketch any time, anywhere.

And when agencies find that the software doesn't work, they often buy *upgraded* software, still searching for that magic-potion program that can create a forensic sketch from computer bytes.

However, any computer program is only as good as the person who is operating it. So first, there has to be a person skilled at interviewing traumatized victims to be able to pull from those victims a viable description of their attackers.

Remember the case of the serial rapists in Kansas, Robert Lambert and Scott Hain, who, at the end of their rampage went to Oklahoma, where they burned their last victims alive? By the time I was summoned to Kansas to work with the surviving victims, one woman was steadfastly refusing even to admit that she had been attacked, much less willing to describe her attackers.

This woman had been questioned repeatedly by all kinds of detectives and even by paramedics and doctors and she still refused to talk. And yet I was able to get from her not only a complete description of what had happened, but a highly usable sketch.

This is not because I am some kind of magician. In fact, in the next chapter we'll discuss my interviewing techniques—what I do can be learned—but as I said earlier, not every cop who sits down in front of a computer can get a victim to give them a good description.

Secondly, just because you are computer-savvy does not mean you know how to draw. With computer compositry, you are still drawing—it's just that you are drawing with a computer. Drawing is a skill not everyone can do.

In Chicago, Joy Mann, a very talented forensic artist, once was called on to do a composite for a high-profile home invasion case in Warrenville, Illinois. The police had already been circulating a computer sketch with no luck. With Joy's outstanding hand-drawn sketch, they were able to nab the criminal within *hours*.

To the chagrin of the investigators, they found the suspect to be an almost identical likeness to Joy's sketch—but to bear no resemblance at all to the computer composite, which is what the victim had been saying all along.

Another problem with the computer software available for forensic sketching today is that it is cumbersome, time-consuming and user-unfriendly. It takes a tremendous amount of patience to work with these programs and it can still take hours to get a usable drawing. Overworked, underpaid detectives simply don't have the training—much less the time—to deal with it. Consequently, the expensive programs are seldom used.

So far, there have been more than 50,000 software programs purchased by law enforcement agencies in this country for use in forensic sketching. If only 1 percent of those programs had produced viable sketches that had resulted in the capture of hard suspects, 500 suspects would have been identified!

But so far, there has been no such recorded success rate by computer compositry programs. So I think we can safely assume that computer software compositry can't even claim to have solved 1 percent of its cases.

That's why not only I, but other forensic artists all over the United States are called in to do composite sketches in cases where the computer has already been used, to no avail.

And our success rate is much higher, not only vastly more than computer compositry, but in another area of criminal identification that just might surprise you:

Fingerprints.

MYTH #2: *Fingerprint identification is more accurate than compositry.*

Everyone who has watched a crime program or movie or read a newsmagazine "true-crime" story has seen crime scene technicians painstakingly go over every surface with their soft brushes and their graphite powder, then carefully lift the fingerprints for identification.

There are so many untrue assumptions about fingerprint identification that have been perpetrated by fiction that I hardly know where to begin to lay them to rest. First, all fingerprints have to be used in *comparison* to other fingerprints that may be catalogued in the federal Automated Fingerprint Identification System—AFIS—or may be compared with a known suspect's prints. However, only individuals who have been charged with a crime and fingerprinted are kept in the database, as well as federal employees or military personnel who have to pass security checks.

So it's not as easy to find a match as it may seem on some popular TV shows in which the investigator-computer whiz taps into a federal database and *bibbity-bobbity-boo!*—they've got a match! In truth, the search can go on for hours, if not days, and turn up nothing. That's if investigators check. You'd be surprised how many cases are simply not checked through AFIS.

Secondly, it's surprisingly difficult to get a good fingerprint from someone. Officers have to be trained how to do it when booking a person who has been arrested and even then, it's tricky. With crime scenes, few fingerprints show up with clearly-demarcated ridges and planes that make up the loops for comparison identification. Most of them are partial prints or are too smudged to identify.

If the fingerprints are gotten from a crime scene.

More and more criminals are wearing gloves of some kind to hide their fingerprints. In addition, some cold climates yield few usable prints anyway, because the sweat glands are not as active in cold weather. Furthermore, fingerprints fade over time, sometimes as quickly as a few days. And finally, though crime scene techs may lift hundreds of prints from a crime scene, most of them can usually be eliminated as having been left by people who either lived there or had good reason to be there, including the victim.

And I'm not even going to get in to the whole debate about how many points of comparison make a match.

I have talked with fingerprint technicians from all over the country and I can say that they are relieved that I'm finally shedding some light on this subject, because they're sick of hearing defense attorneys claim in court that, because there were no good prints from the defendant left at the scene, then it proves the defendant wasn't there.

It's simply not true. A person can be at a crime scene and not leave a usable print, for a variety of reasons.

So what is the success rate for fingerprint identification of viable suspects from crime scenes nationwide?

Not as good as you might think.

The most generous estimate I've been able to find, quoted in professional forensic journals, is barely 10 percent.

That's the generous estimate.

Break it down by city and the statistics actually drop. The percentage of scenes with usable fingerprint identifications can go as low as 2.2 percent. Other percentages hover at around 5 percent.

The statistical average comes from the fact that smaller departments often have higher success rates with fingerprints, but overall, about the best you can hope for with fingerprint identification is 10 percent.

Now, take that statistic in mind and couple it with the fact that since the nineteenth century, fingerprints have been the universally acknowledged method of criminal identification. Every large department has its own fingerprint division.

And now...(drumroll please)...let me give the statistics for identification of viable suspects from the use of forensic composite sketches: *30 percent.*

According to a study done by Terry Westbrook in 1987, the success rate of forensic sketches in identifying suspects can run as high as 80 percent.

This means in cases in which composite sketches are used to aid in identification of criminals, at least one out of three perpetrators can be identified through the use of a forensic sketch. The sketch leads to photo or live line-up and the suspect is nabbed.

And that's the bottom-line average. In the year 2000, I was given a commendation by the Houston Police Department's chief of police for having cleared more than *43 percent* of my cases. For those cases I've worked in Kansas, so far, I have achieved 100 percent. I've also had 100 percent success rate in cases in which an infant has been kidnapped by a stranger, 100 percent in cop-killer and cop-assaulted cases and 100 percent success rate in the small towns in which I have helped out.

I estimate that full-time forensic artists tend to divide their time evenly between homicides, robberies and rapes.

My research adds up this way: every police department in this country considers fingerprint evidence to be dependable and reliable, when only—at best—10 percent of cases are actually cleared due to fingerprint evidence. And yet, the clearance rate from compositry is greater than 30 percent. And there are at least 2,000 trained forensic sketch artists in this country and many more who want to learn. Yet, out of almost 40,000 departments (not including federal or state agencies), there are *less than twenty* full-time forensic sketch artists working today.

So the crucial question becomes, why aren't more law enforcement agencies using compositry?

At the very least, why can't compositry be used *along with* fingerprint evidence for maximum effectiveness in fighting crime?

What's the hold-up?

MYTH #3: *There's no money in the budget to hire a forensic artist.*

This is what I heard from my own department for seven straight years while I toiled to prove myself and get a job there as a forensic artist. No money. Budget cuts. We're broke.

It's usually just not true.

Even the most cash-strapped departments can google-search online and find a plethora of law enforcement-related state and federal grants that are available for everything from a high-tech crime-scene camera to bullet-proof vests to other things needed in law enforcement.

You may recall, when I first started, detectives paid for my services from their coffee-fund jar. Later, the Houston city hall provided a "line of funds" to pay me and that line of funds was a state-related grant that had been made available to the city of Houston. When I was hired full-time, the chief of police at the time paid for my salary out of a grant with which he also hired a lieutenant, a sergeant and several detectives, along with several thousand dollars' worth of audio-visual equipment.

That's right. He signed me up with the VCRs.

The money's out there. It's just a matter of finding it.

It's not just money, keeping police departments from employing forensic artists, though. In some cases, that's just the excuse. Police departments are slow to embrace change. The Houston Police Department did not use photographs of known criminals in their files until thirty-five years after the method was in use in other departments.

But once a method has proven to be worthy, departments can come on board with breathtaking swiftness. In 1989, Joseph Wambaugh wrote a book called, *The Blooding* (William Morrow), in which he described the very first ever mass use of DNA blood evidence to eliminate suspects and close in on a serial sexual killer. Since that time, DNA evidence has come to be relied on almost as universally as fingerprint evidence. What I'm trying to say is that, once a method is proven to law enforcement agencies as being effective in criminal investigation...the money for it will be found.

It would behoove aspiring forensic artists who are having trouble finding work—especially if they're being told there's no money in the budget—to track down their own sources of grant money that they can then use to approach law enforcement agencies.

There are ways to pay for forensic artists. For a thirty percent success rate, isn't it worth it to at least try?

MYTH #4: *Every single police department has to employ a forensic artist in order to have them available to help solve crimes.*

This is not true. For instance, the Harris County Sheriff's Department does not have a forensic sketch artist on staff, but they call me to help them with cases.

It's the same way with my friend Joy Mann in Chicago. Although Chicago is the third-largest city in the country, they do not have a full-time forensic artist, but Joy freelances for them as well as for other departments. She drives to many places and does sketches in suburban Chicago as well as for the metropolitan Chicago police force.

Some states, such as South Carolina and New Jersey, have two artists who work the entire state. I'm not setting up this situation as a model, because I want as many artists working in this field as we can get, but what I'm saying is that one artist can easily work multiple jurisdictions.

In Texas, Shirley Timmons, a very fine artist, works for the Texas Rangers. They fly her all over the state in a helicopter and plane to do forensic sketches. One of Shirley's sketches identified one of this nation's worst serial killers. The victim was a twelve-year-old girl whose throat had been cut so badly that she couldn't talk. (Her best friend had been killed in front of her eyes.)

Shirley Timmons managed to pull a sketch from that child that was immediately recognized by her friend's father, which led to the arrest of Terry Lynn Sells. Sells confessed that he'd murdered so many people he couldn't even remember them all.

In Georgia, Marla Lawson, another talented artist, works for the Georgia Bureau of Investigations.

In Klamath Falls, Oregon, I knew a gifted artist, Yvonne Schmid, who has never had one hour of formal training, just numerous telephone conversations with me. The third case of her career, on September 1, 2002, she helped identify Maximillano Cilero Esparza, a psychopath who had brutally raped and strangled two nuns, killing one—Sister Helen Chaska. Within hours of her sketch, the perpetrator was in custody.

So far, Yvonne's earliest sketches have produced a 33 percent success rate. She could easily sketch for the Medford, Merrill, Grant's Pass and Bonanza, Oregon area (maybe even half the state) and she could clear three times more cases for law enforcement there than fingerprint evidence.

The states of New York, Florida and California each have three full-time forensic artists. These are the most populous states in the union, home to cities with some of the nation's highest crime rates. How many more artists should be working in them, sharing the load, catching more bad guys?

MYTH #5: *We can't trust "outsiders" (like artists) with sensitive information on open, ongoing cases still under investigation.*

In major metropolitan areas, there are literally *dozens* of "outsiders" who help investigators piece together cases, from laboratory technicians to medical examiners to DNA analysts to psychologists to doctors to people from the district attorney's office and sometimes, investigators from the Federal Bureau of Investigation.

That's not counting crime reporters from newspapers and television personalities who are sometimes used to "leak" information for various motives.

I believe a good investigator will not hesitate to use *any* resource available to solve a case and put a brutal criminal in jail or on death row.

Remember, sometimes a sensitive artist who has been trained in forensic interviewing techniques can draw information from a traumatized victim or witness that the person either did not or would not tell detectives. That's what my friend, Deputy Chief Charles McClelland of the HPD meant when he referred to me as an "adjunct detective." Whenever we worked cases together, he always came in after the sketching session was complete and talked to me about my impressions and what the witness had said. Together, we often came up with just the key piece of information needed to crack the case.

I don't mean to imply that I consider myself a cop. I've tried very hard to demonstrate that I consider myself part of an investigative *team*—another tool that an astute detective can pull out of his or her toolbox.

It's not about my ego or the detective's career or anything else.

As I've said before, it's about getting justice.

MYTH #6: *All forensic artists need to BE "outsiders."*

A few years ago, I was approached by Adrian White, a very fine HPD officer. Adrian confessed that, in his spare time, he was an artist, too and that he had always longed to learn how to do composite sketches.

I was thrilled. This was good news for me, because it meant that I would no longer be the only forensic artist in the area. It meant I could go on vacation, for instance, without fretting about cases I would not be working in my absence.

So I started working with Adrian. He took my class and the *very first case* he worked, he helped bring down a serial killer!

Whenever his initial sketch aired on television programs, the killer's wife later told reporters, her husband would get very nervous. I made a video recording of the news broadcast in which she said this and gave it to Adrian for encouragement.

Sadly, in many places there are talented artists who also happen to be cops and who would love nothing better than to be allowed to do compositry full-time for their departments. Instead, they're forced to fill mundane paperwork jobs or perform other tasks that hundreds of other officers—who are *not* uniquely talented artists—could do.

As I said before, money can be found to create full-time forensic art positions for these cop-artists and with a 30 percent success rate (at least), there is justification for the expense. Partnered with fingerprint identification, DNA analysis and other investigative tools, many more cases could be successfully closed each year. Isn't that law enforcement's true goal?

MYTH #7: *Witness descriptions are often too sketchy or otherwise poor to enable an artist to get a workable sketch.*

By this time, having read about the cases in this book, you will know that almost all crime victims and/or witnesses believe that they did not see the perpetrator well enough to provide good descriptions. The bus driver in "Blind Justice" swore she'd only caught a glimpse of the bad guy out of the corner of her eye while she was busy with passengers. She was so sure of it that she actually wanted me to throw my sketch in the trash. But the detective, Manny Zamora, ignored her protests and trusted me; consequently, he caught a monster who had raped a blind pregnant woman.

Nine-year-old Annie Tyson thought my sketch looked "too much like a girl," but the investigator, Billy Belk, trusted me anyway and they caught her mother's killer within twenty-four hours.

One witness, an elderly man who wore thick glasses, had only caught a glimpse of a cop-killer as the man drove past the witness in his car going forty miles per hour, at night—yet the sketch was instrumental in bringing down the murderer of a young sheriff's deputy.

I've done sketches with witnesses who couldn't talk, because their throats were cut or who were drugged-up in hospitals, witnesses who were very young children, witnesses who swore they only saw the suspect from the side, witnesses who had been victimized weeks, months, sometimes even *years* before I was asked to sketch the perpetrator. None of them believed that working with a sketch artist would do any good.

If police detectives take the word of crime witnesses and victims who swear they did not get very good looks at perpetrators, then detectives would never call in forensic sketch artists.

But the truth is that reasonably talented, fairly well-trained forensic artists will be able, in most cases, to elicit witness descriptions and to produce composite sketches that have at least a one-in-three chance of being effective.

What most people don't realize is that the most important aspect of compositry is not the artwork—it's the interview. In the next chapter, I will outline proven interviewing techniques I've developed through the years, that can enable an aspiring forensic artist to get a head start in obtaining an excellent likeness from even the most reluctant witness.

Bottom line: Cops—please just trust your artist. No matter what the witness says about not adequately seeing the criminal, give the artist a chance.

Perhaps the sketch will not help to solve the case.

But more likely...one more criminal creep can be stopped before he or she hurts anyone else.

MYTH #8: *If the sketch does not look exactly like the perpetrator, it will have been a waste of time and money.*

This mind-set equates compositry to a math problem: it's either wrong or it's right.

However, the aim of forensic compositry can not be evaluated in simplistic terms. No forensic artist is ever going to get a rendition from a witness description that is going to be a photographic likeness—although we can sometimes come pretty darn close.

What is needed for the purposes of identification is a resemblance between the sketch and the suspect. A *likeness*. Not a *sameness*.

I can't emphasize enough that I have done and I have seen others do some really poor likenesses that have led, directly, *immediately* to the identification of suspects. Remember my first "hit?" The case where the witness made me spend three hours trying to recreate the evil snarl he'd seen on the suspect's face? It was only the third composite I had ever done and I was so convinced I had failed that I decided, then and there, that I was through with forensic art.

But as soon as the sketch was aired on TV, the suspect's roommate called Detective Osterberg, who was handling the case, and told him that although the sketch looked just like *him,* the culprit was his roommate, to whom he bore a resemblance.

I look back now at my early, primitive effort and I am stunned that we got a hit on that composite at all. I was just starting out; I had no training as a forensic artist; I knew nothing about interviewing techniques. And yet the composite I did broke the case, literally, overnight.

When I did the facial reconstruction in the Angel Doe case, the recreation turned out not to look exactly like LaShondra did, but I recreated enough of her smile, using what I knew of the dental placement of teeth, that her grandmother spotted her instantly while channel-surfing TV one evening months after LaShondra had disappeared. The grandmother said that the portrait was not an exact likeness of LaShondra, but it was *close enough* to prompt her to call Sgt. Douglas and to insist on meeting with him that very night.

Usually, poorly-done sketches have been made by artists who have been under-utilized by police—they simply have not had enough practice. When I first started out, most of my sketches were clumsy. I didn't start getting really good until I was allowed to do at least three sketches in a week.

However, even those early, poor sketches successfully identified about one out of every three criminals sought.

As I said, compositry is a tool for investigators to use. It can be the most valuable tool in the box or it can turn out to be not as necessary as DNA analysis or a confession, depending upon the case.

The way I see it, every carpenter has a toolbox he takes everywhere with him. He never leaves out the hammer or the screwdriver because he thinks they may not be as useful as the saw. He keeps his tools together, because he never knows when one of them might be the right one to use.

As Lt. Zamora said, there is nothing to lose and everything to gain by using compositry to catch elusive criminals.

MYTH #9: *If the composite isn't done right after the crime occurred, it will be too late to get a workable sketch from the witness.*

Remember, for instance, the Sara Rinehart case, in which investigators didn't even call me until months after her murder? Or for that matter, the Elizabeth Smart case, in which her father worked with Dalene Nielson five months after Elizabeth was taken—remembering the face of a homeless man with whom he had worked for less than an afternoon *a year before.*

I can say this from the experience of being attacked. You don't ever forget a face like that.

And to prove it, I have done a composite sketch of the man who raped and tried to kill me years ago. We're including it in this book. Who knows? We might get a hit.

MYTH #10: *It's impossible to get good composite sketches from witnesses under the age of twelve.*

Again, I hope I've laid that myth to its final rest in this book. Three of the cases covered here involved my getting incredible likenesses from young children. I could have included hundreds more. In fact, today, I work at least twenty-five cases a year from the juvenile sex crimes division of the HPD.

Some investigators worry that it might be too traumatic to ask a child witness to provide a description for a composite, but I have found just the opposite to be true. They've not only suffered through the assault, but they have also already been questioned by a variety of law enforcement, social services and medical personnel, not to mention parents or other well-meaning adults.

At no time, during all this questioning, have they been able to feel as if they can do something to help. But time and again, when children are offered the opportunity to contribute to investigations, they are eager to do so. Remember nine-year-old Annie Tyson who thought to tell investigators that the man who had raped and murdered her mother and set fire to her body, then raped Annie—had parted the blinds to look outside? Investigators were able to get an excellent set of fingerprints from those blinds.

I have worked with many victims of sexual assault who were young children and have gotten such good composites from them that one perpetrator, James Daniel Raiford, actually called the police and turned himself in, quote, "because I saw myself on TV."

I've had kindergartners who were so excited by the likeness of the composite that they ran outside and grabbed their mothers' hands, wanting to show them the pictures.

Just like Mary Katherine Smart and Jordan Rinehart, children know what they saw.

It's appalling to me when I think of the forensic art talent out there that is being wasted in this most powerful and important area.

In the eleven years my friend Joy Mann has been sketching for the Chicago area, she has been asked to do a composite sketch for a juvenile sex crimes victim only five times. Two of her five sketches helped solve those crimes. In a city that size, as many as 5,000 stranger-on-stranger child rapes have been worked by police since Joy started freelancing there.

And yet, a talented forensic sketch artist who is readily available to police in that area has only done five composites—two of which led to solving the case.

When I think of how many cases she could have helped to break and how many child sexual predators out there could have been stopped because of her work—and others like her—because law enforcement still clings to this antiquated myth about working with children...it makes me sick.

MYTH #11: *Releasing a composite sketch to the media will bring in too many leads for stretched-too-thin investigators to track down.*

Just as in the Elizabeth Smart case, many, many pessimistic investigators all over this country don't call in composite artists or don't release composite sketches to the media from fear that dozens of leads will pour in, forcing them to dedicate hundreds of man-hours chasing them all down.

What they are unable—or unwilling—to realize is that, in many cases, the leads that come in will mostly point to one perpetrator.

Once I worked a particularly horrible case in which two little girls, ages seven and eight, had been raped. The damage done to their small bodies was so severe that I had to do the drawing at their hospital bedsides. HPD detectives released the sketch without delay.

Almost immediately, the investigators began getting calls saying things like, "That's Al, who works at Thompson's," or, "That guy looks like Al Darden," or, "He sure looks like a guy I work with by the name of Al."

One detective had been up two nights in a row, working this case, and when the calls started to come in, he made little hash marks on the side of his notepad. After a dozen or so hash marks, he said, "I guess the guy's name is Al. I'm going to Thompson's."

He walked into the store, holding a copy of my sketch in front of him, and the night manager said, "What are you doing with a picture of Al?"

The detective not only got his man, but he got an iron-clad confession as well and Houston now has one less predator pervert out there on the streets as a result.

I like the way one of my detective buddies put it. He said, "Hell, give me a lead. I'll take *any* lead—I don't care if there are too many!"

MYTH #12: *Only the police have the authority to order a forensic sketch and to release it to the media.*

This is a dirty little secret and one I wish I did not have to reveal here, but as I've stated before, I am—first and foremost—a victim's advocate.

After twenty-three years working with and for the Houston Police Department and outlying departments in Harris County, as well as other departments in Kansas and other states and the FBI, I can state without hesitation that I love my law enforcement friends like brothers and sisters. I am so proud to be considered a part of them and the work they do.

Over the years, I believe the cops I work with, by and large, have come to love me too and I know that many of them trust me and my gifts unhesitatingly. Each and every day of my life, I thank God for them.

But as I mentioned at the beginning of this chapter, not all law enforcement investigators have the same kind of respect for forensic art as my colleagues do. As we have seen, detectives will often either not use compositry at all in the investigation of a case or they will order a composite drawing, but refuse to release the sketch to the media.

Sometimes as we saw John Walsh and *America's Most Wanted* do in the Elizabeth Smart case, it becomes necessary to step right over the heads of stubborn detectives and release the sketch yourself.

If police refuse to make the sketch available to a family, then all the family has to do is hire one of 2,000 trained forensic artists in America who might be willing to do it freelance and in some cases, for no charge or for only the most modest of fees. (In fact, I would be highly suspicious of forensic artists who may command fees in the thousands. Hire someone you can afford or someone willing to do it for free in order to draw attention to their abilities through the resulting publicity.) In fact, in the case of Elizabeth Smart, the composite drawing which actually led to the arrest of Brian David Mitchell and the release of Elizabeth Smart was done for free by Dalene Nielson, who just wanted to prove to the Salt Lake authorities that her work could help find the perpetrator.

Sometimes, even when authorities agree to use a forensic artist, they refuse to budge when new details come in. I know of one artist who would rather I not use his name (he doesn't want to anger the police he's trying to convince to hire him more often). But this fine artist did a good composite of the infamous Angel Resendiz serial killer. Resendiz was known as the "railroad killer," for his habit of riding rail cars from state to state, then jumping off whenever he came across homes close to the tracks and brutally, horribly murdering its occupants. Then he'd just leap back onto the train and disappear into the night.

The first sketch done by my talented friend was completed in a hospital; the witness was so badly injured that she could not talk and the resulting sketch was rough. Later, when the witness had recovered a bit, she contacted my friend and told him that the killer had worn a pair of glasses, the frames of which were tinted a peculiar light color. She absolutely insisted upon doing the drawing again, this time in color, and my friend faithfully recreated the light-framed glasses.

But the investigators handling the woman's case had already printed up posters using the original sketch and they stuck with their posters. When

America's Most Wanted profiled the case, my friend's second sketch was not released.

Angel Resendiz went on to slaughter nine more people.

Turns out Resendiz had relatives living in the area where my friend had done the sketch. Had the sketch been released to the media, Resendiz could have been identified years before he finally was. (I can say this with assurance, because newspaper photos of Resendiz look almost identical to my friend's color sketch.)

So although I would love more than anything to be a cheerleader for everything law enforcement investigators do, I am only too painfully aware that, like everyone else, detectives are human too. They make mistakes just like the rest of us.

If you are victimized and the police department in your area does not have a forensic artist, hire your own artist, get your own sketch and release it yourself to the media.

You just might find yourself becoming your own hero.

It is my passionate hope that if the cases you've read about in this book have not laid to rest these persistent myths about compositry, then at least this chapter will do so.

If you are a law enforcement officer who has hesitated to use the skills of a forensic artist because of one or all of the myths I've discussed, I hope with all my heart that, at the very least, you might consider trying this technique.

In fact, I hope you give it a try not just once, but three times.

I guarantee that at least one of those times you'll succeed in identifying a criminal who might — without the sketch — be allowed to roam free.

Chapter Fifteen

What You Need to Know to Become a Forensic Artist

I not only believe, but sincerely hope, that at this point more than a few people reading this book are thinking, *You know, I've always wanted to be a forensic artist, but I have no idea how to go about breaking into the field.*

There are more than a few discouragements and obstacles preventing talented people from making forays into becoming forensic artists, but I don't believe it has to be that way.

My mission in writing this book has been, from the beginning, to *get more forensic artists out there* and to convince, wherever possible, more law enforcement agencies and the public of the need to hire forensic artists.

If I could accomplish these goals, I would be thrilled and if, in the process, we all catch more savage criminals and, in so doing, empower more crime survivors, then I would truly feel fulfilled.

After I spent more than twenty years working as a forensic artist, in their 2004 and 2005 volumes, the *Guinness Book of World Records* chose to feature me as the forensic artist whose work had helped to solve more crimes than any other forensic artist in the world.

I'd love to have more of you join me. This chapter is me, speaking to you, the aspiring forensic artist, telling you just what you need to know to make your dream come true and to help us all solve more crimes.

The first most important thing you need to know.

This one might come as a surprise, but when you get right down to the basics, forensic art *is not about art.*

Though, of course, you need some artistic talent and an ability to draw faces well and quickly, this job is not about being an artist or about producing fine works of art for all to admire and hang on their walls. (Although, like me, you might do that in your spare time.)

Forensic art is about law enforcement.

Before an artist can sit down with a crime victim or witness, he or she needs to be a special kind of person, a person who can talk at length with someone who has just experienced quite possibly the worst trauma of his or her life. The artist must be able to sit with these witnesses/victims, listen to their stories, watch them break down and sob or any of many emotional reactions to trauma, elicit from them as much information as possible, do the sketch and then, when these services are needed again, do the whole thing all over as many times as the detectives call you.

In some ways, you need to be able to think like a cop and understand the kinds of things you need to know if you're going to turn out a sketch that detectives can use, but at the same time, not be "cop-like." By that I mean the artist can and should be more empathetic than a law enforcement officer is able to be, since his or her job description is different. (We'll get more into that later.)

If you go into this field understanding that you have to be able to deal with traumatized people almost every day while, at the same time, *going on to live a normal happy life* and if you are able to realize that your own life will be so deeply enriched by how much you've been able to help those same witnesses/victims—then you've just cleared the biggest hurdle to becoming a forensic artist.

The second most important thing you need to know.

Be prepared, not only in the beginning, but each and every day of your career, to meet resistance and difficulty. Not just from skeptical law enforcement officers—which does fade as your success rate climbs—but from the witnesses and victims themselves.

As I've demonstrated in previous chapters, I have yet to sit down with anyone for a sketching session in which the person does not protest that he or she doesn't think they can contribute anything towards getting a good likeness. People who have been victimized or witnesses will insist that they didn't see the suspect very well or that they don't know where to start to describe him or you'll hear from the cops that the witness is too young or too old or too feeble or blind or whatever to contribute the information for a credible sketch.

I tell my forensic art classes, "Expect a train wreck!"

Expect to hear objections, sometimes even when the sketch is completed. Remember the chapter "Blind Justice," where the witness made me throw the sketch in the trash and the detective not only retrieved it, but went on to solve the crime with it? Remember "A Look of Murderous Rage," when the young victim felt that the sketch, "looks too much like a girl?"

You will get resistance at every step of the way, from all sides. The danger of this is that you may doubt yourself. I had done as many as 2,000 sketches before I began to trust my own ability and to this day, I still have to psyche myself up sometimes and mull over past successes before going in to do what I know will be a difficult sketch.

And yet I've gotten successful sketches from people whose throats have been cut so they couldn't talk, people who only saw the suspect in the dark at a distance, children five years of age, people who'd seen the suspect months or even years before… I could go on and on here, but suffice it to say that if you *expect* resistance and difficulty, you'll be much more able to *ignore it* and go on and do your job.

If someone had only said this to me when I was first starting out, I would not have doubted myself so much for so many years.

Later, we'll talk about how to get the most reluctant witness to give you a good sketch, but for now I want to emphasize another important point.

The third most important thing you need to know.

Have you ever heard that old saying that success is 10 percent inspiration and 90 percent perspiration?

I'd like to flip that around and say that success as a forensic sketch artist is 10 percent talent and 90 percent *persistence, persistence, persistence*.

If you live in an area in which law enforcement officers have not been receptive to forensic artists, you have to change their minds. And the only way to do that is, quite simply, not to give up, to keep trying.

Remember how I first started out? Calling and calling and calling? I called the HPD *dozens* of times before they finally brought me in to do a sketch.

And I proved that a forensic composite could help get the bad guy, didn't I?

In the beginning, if the resistance is very great, you can offer to do the first few sketches without charge, just to establish that you can do it. If it takes three tries to get a hit—and I've known many artists who got major hits on their very first try—then do half a dozen sketches for them. Remind the cops that you will only get better with practice and the only way to practice is to do more sketches.

When it comes time to discuss your fee and they insist that they don't have the money to employ a forensic artist, whip out the grant availability information that you've downloaded from your computer and *show them* creative ways they can, indeed, afford your services.

Offer your services to help with high-profile crimes. Read the newspapers daily, watch for cases that seem to be stumping the detectives, walk in off the street and say, "I would never try to tell you guys how to do your jobs or anything, but I have this skill that I think could be highly useful to you. Let me show you how."

If they use you a time or two and then seem to drop off the radar screen, don't sit around and mope over your hurt feelings. Call them back! Offer to help again!

Cultivate any detectives who have seemed impressed with your work. Follow their cases and offer to help whenever you can.

Call. Call again. Keep calling.

When you're still trying to break into the field, work to hone your skills by working with non-victims. As I've mentioned, my husband Sid would come home from work each day and describe some new guy for me to draw. My friend Diane helped me by describing the gas station attendant for me. Practice like this enables you to do sketches faster, so that when your first golden opportunity arises, you'll be ready.

A quote from Winston Churchill has inspired me and I have repeated it to myself through the years:

"Never give in. Never give in. Never, never, never, never, in nothing great or small, large or petty—never give in...."

Characteristics of a good forensic sketch artist.

The best forensic artists I know have a real passion for the work. In spite of the difficulties and obstacles, they love what they do and remain enthusiastic year after year, whenever they get "hits" on sketches. It's not just catching criminals—though that's part of it—it's the deep personal satisfaction that they feel in knowing that the contribution of their gifts and talents helped a crime *victim* to become a crime *survivor*.

Once a job like this gets in your blood, you can't imagine doing anything else and you can't believe that you actually get *paid* to do something you love so much.

But as I pointed out earlier in the chapter, there are certain characteristics a good forensic sketch artist needs to possess beyond artistic talent and the ability to draw faces well. Some of them include: empathy, patience, sensitivity to others, a good sense of humor and ability to laugh and to make others laugh easily, flexibility and a certain gentle firmness in working with obstructive people.

Faith in God helps a lot, too—or, at the very least—faith in being a part of something much greater than just yourself.

And now, let's get down to the nitty-gritty of compositry.

The three most basic rules of composite sketch creation:

1) Sketch in private with the witness.

Remember one of the first sketches I ever did, in which the victim's best friend sat in on the session and proceeded to dominate—even going so far as to correct the witness's own memory? I'd like to point out here that the suspect was not caught and I learned a very valuable lesson.

I simply have a standing rule, now, that all witnesses work with me alone, in privacy. Certainly there are exceptions to every rule, such as the case of the woman who'd been beaten nearly to death by Theodore Goynes. When I went to her home to do the sketch, her husband insisted on staying in the room and in that particular case, I could see that his presence had a calming effect on the witness.

It's a judgment call and every case is unique.

But in my experience, I have found that, in most cases, most witnesses are actually *relieved* to be doing the sketch without the protective presence of friends, boyfriends, spouses, or other family members. Even children are happy to have their parents out of the room. (Under the age of five, however, I do invite parents to stay.)

As with that early rape case where the best friend took over the interview—sometimes even the most well-meaning friends and relatives can inject a certain tension into the proceedings. (I'll go into that in more detail later.)

Not only that, but legally it does present a dilemma to investigators, who do not want to be accused of having influenced the witness's memory in any way.

Working in privacy vastly improves the relaxation of the witness, helps concentration and avoids any speculation that the witness was influenced by any outside source—even detectives.

2) Use visual aids.

This is such an important point that I'm going to repeat it:

USE VISUAL AIDS.

I emphasize this point so much because there is a very pernicious *myth* making the rounds out there that if a forensic artist uses visual aids to assist the witnesses in creating a composite sketch, then the artist has *contaminated* the witness's memory and thus polluted the sketching process to such a point that it will be impossible to get an accurate rendering.

At least one high-profile forensic artist I know, but will not name, goes on nationally televised talk shows and writes in magazine articles that she is the only artist out there who can get truly accurate likenesses from witnesses.

I feel this would not, in itself, be so bad, except that she then advises all law enforcement agencies *not* to use what she refers to as *police artists*, because she insists that other sketch artists "contaminate" witness memory with such devices as the *FBI Facial Identification Catalogue*.

But despite her high visibility I am certain her claims are not backed up by scientific fact.

I believe such claims are immensely damaging, not just to the entire field of forensic art, but to every other forensic artist who is struggling to break down barriers and put out all these silly little myth-fires that keep popping up.

The bottom line is this: There are thousands of talented artists out there who can learn compositry and who can do it dependably and affordably for all sorts of law enforcement agencies or even freelancing for the families of victims—and who will do it with *no* media attention.

Now, on to the truth about visual aids.

I'm going to show exactly why I believe the use of visual aids is so important, why they DO NOT contaminate ANYTHING and I'll back it up, not just by my own more than 3,000 sketches and almost 1,000 "hits," but by hard science.

First, yes, you can definitely do a composite sketch without the use of visual aids. I did it for the first four years of my career, before attending the FBI Academy. But there are a number of cases where it is virtually impossible to do a sketch without some kind of visual aid—such as in cases where victims are so badly injured that they cannot speak, cases in which there is a language barrier, or cases that involve very young children whose language skills are not yet fully developed.

In order to understand why I believe the use of visual aids is better than not using them, it is necessary to understand a little about how the human brain works.

When we see, say, an attacker's face, that image is recorded in the part of the brain known as the *visual cortex*.

In order for us to come up with the language necessary to describe a face that we saw, we have to use a different part of the brain, known as the *angular gyrus*, which transforms the visual image into a sound pattern, which is then sent by the brain to yet a third part, called the *Wernicke's area*.

Our brains aren't through at that point, though.

In order for us to take that language and then speak it out loud, all of this information then needs to be transmitted to yet another part of the brain, known as *Broca's area*, which issues instructions for the necessary muscle movements needed to create speech.

After that, the part of the brain known as the *motor cortex* orders the muscles of the speech organs to move and alerts the cerebellum to coordinate their movement.

That is, *if the correct words are even known*. With young children, for instance, or people who've suffered head injuries or other incapacitating wounds, the description may not be available for all these various brain transactions to take place, which means that, without visual aids, they would be incapable of working with a forensic artist.

But if, say, we are healthy and we try to provide a usable description without visual aids, I can attest from experience that it can take hours and is an exhausting process for both the crime victim and the artist.

On the other hand, when we are shown a picture similar to what we actually saw, we receive that information in the same part of the brain as when we saw the attacker's face—the visual cortex!

As I demonstrated in the chapter titled, "Some People Just Need Killin'," in which police officer Paul Deason had been shot, run over and dragged down the street and was in Intensive Care when I did the sketch— all the witness had to do was simply *point out* facial features depicted in the visual aid and in no time at all I could get a remarkable likeness.

Still, if that explanation doesn't convince you, then I challenge you to try to describe someone's face without having anything to look at. You could probably come up with hundreds of ways to say "nose."

And if you were giving this description to an artist and trying to help him or her get the drawing right, it would be a trial-and-error process that could take hours.

For victims already traumatized and exhausted by their ordeal, such a process would be absolutely draining. It could even take several days if the witness has to take time off from work for the sketch session.

Meanwhile, law enforcement has to hop around on one foot so to speak, waiting for the artist to hurry up and produce something they can use, while all along, the perpetrator may be getting further away!

All this stress is just not necessary.

For a witness to point out a photo that has a similar feature to the face being described is a much more rapid and accurate method of describing that feature to the artist.

If you do not have access to an *FBI Identification Catalogue*, there are others aids you can use. I will discuss these later.

USE VISUAL AIDS. Period.

Now for the last basic rule of compositry.

3) Be able and skilled and willing to modify the sketch at the witness's direction.

Artists are used to working in solitude and drawing or painting whatever they darn well want or at least whatever the market demands, if they're trying to make a living at it. But a forensic artist is there at the witness's discretion. It's our job to *get it right*.

I compare it to a professional writer, who must do revisions in order to please an editor before their words can see print. Sometimes they have to go back over something they've written and rewrite it dozens of times. This is something they can expect and are willing to do in order to get the piece as good as it can be.

So when a witness wants you to make changes to your sketch, it is absolutely to be expected. It shouldn't hurt your feelings or leave you miffed. You're not there to create a grand work of art. You're there to catch a bad guy. So you must be willing to make any changes they request.

Again, I must emphasize that when you use visual aids, the chances are good that you will not be asked to make nearly as many changes as when you do not.

Later, I'll get into some specifics on quick and easy ways to make those changes to your composites. And trust me, the more practice you get, the fewer changes you'll be asked to make.

This next part is divided into two sections:
1) *The basics of composite sketching*
2) *The interview*

The basics of the actual artwork can be learned anywhere and are, in any event, highly personal to each artist. I am assuming that if you are interested in forensic art, then you already know not only how to draw, but have sketched or painted lots of people's faces. There are, however, certain dos and don'ts particular to this specific art form that need to be addressed.

For instance, different artists often use different mediums in this field. I like to use pastels, but another artist might call me crazy and say they can't work without their graphite pencils. The main point I'd like to emphasize concerning the basics is that you should do whatever makes you most comfortable, because forensic sketching is stressful enough without someone trying to force you to use a medium with which you are not comfortable.

Secondly, an entire section needs to be devoted to the interview. The interview is the single most important aspect of the forensic sketch and the tips I'm going to give you here are not taught any other place of which I am aware.

First, though, let's hit the basics.

The basics of forensic compositry.

1) The medium.

As I said before, it's important that you pick a medium with which you are most comfortable.

Almost every other forensic artist I know uses graphite pencil. In the past those graphite pencil drawings didn't photocopy very well, but today the most basic copy machines have such good duplication capabilities that the copy can come out looking like a photograph of the original. So if you like to use graphite pencils, use them.

Many experienced and successful forensic artists add charcoal to the finished sketch to enhance the darks and shadows—but I would not recommend this technique to a beginner, since complete erasure is so difficult, if not impossible. Some artists also like to add a dot of white paint or even office correction fluid for the dot or shine in the eyes or for shiny highlights on cheeks and other facial high points.

The only reason I like to use pastels is that I sketched thousands of pastel portraits of live tourists/patrons when I worked along the River Walk in San Antonio and later, at shopping malls and other venues, so I feel very comfortable with this medium.

If you have a great facility with pastels, they can save you time, since you can lay the pastel on its side and stroke in large areas in a few seconds. Pastels blend easily to depict smooth flesh and if you need, say, a wet-eyeball shine—you can apply it quickly with a stick of white.

Also, pastels often give a nice three-dimensional aspect to the sketch.

If you're using graphite pencil now, but would like to transition into pastels, one of the best ways to do it is to start with pastel pencils in various shades of gray. These would be pencils that have a "lead" made of a hard chalk-like stick. You can use these pastel pencils for details of eyes, lips, noses and so on and then switch to larger sticks of pastel for features such as hair.

With practice, you'll eventually find that you're learning to control the sticks of pastel as well as the pencil pastels and can switch over then.

But again, stress yourself as little as possible and use whatever medium makes you comfortable.

2) The eraser.

Though many artists like them, I recommend *not* using a kneaded eraser, because that kind of eraser quickly absorbs body oils. Then, when it becomes necessary to make one of those changes we were talking about earlier, the body oils inhibit or make uneven any further application of pigment or other erasures.

In other words, it tends to smear and make a mess.

In my experience, the best eraser is the plain old white plastic kind.

3) Paper.

The best paper for compositry, if you are using graphite pencil, would be a Bristol board with a *vellum* finish. This is an outstanding paper that can withstand lots of erasures and changes.

If you are working with pastels, I recommend you use *Canson Mi Tientes* paper in a middle tone of gray. Keep different shades of gray pastels, from the darkest to tooth-white on hand, for use in making changes quickly and simply.

4) To easel or not to easel.

As with medium choice, artists tend to guard fiercely their choice of whether or not to work with an easel when doing forensic sketches. I like to use an easel and I'll tell you why.

First, when using an easel, I have both hands free. I don't have to use one hand to balance or hold the drawing board.

Second, the easel creates a nice barrier between the artist and the witness, which makes the witness feel more protected from being touched or even from being seen.

Third, the light attachment at the top of the easel is indispensable. It makes the work much easier to do and frankly, makes the drawing look better when the witness views it.

And fourth, with an easel, I can attach my visual aids to the sides of the board while I'm drawing, which keeps them out of the way but readily visible to me. I'm also able to do a better copy of the feature chosen by the witness, which makes a better sketch over-all.

Not only that, but it enables me to draw much faster, which means we get through quicker and the witness has an easier time of it.

I use an aluminum Stanrite 500 easel that can be folded into a four-foot long "T" shape and weighs only seven pounds. This makes it easily portable for packing or for carrying out on house calls.

The light that attaches to the top of my easel has a three-foot long gooseneck, which allows it to be aimed anywhere and is easily adjusted for use in any situation. Remember, you are not always drawing from the comfort of an office. Sometimes you are called upon to go into witness's homes, which may be poorly-lit, or are asked by police to do drawings in odd places like storerooms, where all you've got is a single fluorescent light over-head, or beside a hospital bed where the room is kept in shadow.

Having your own light source is an invaluable aid.

5) Those tricky tattoos.

I could spend two or three pages here describing how to draw tattoos, but I'll confine it to simply giving one invaluable tip: order a catalogue. (The resource is listed at the back of the book.)

Basically, you photocopy the tattoo picked out by the witness, blow it up and sketch it onto whatever body part is needed. For more information than that, you will have to do some studying on your own through a class or from books.

In addition, one good way to find good pictures of vehicles described by witnesses is to subscribe to *Consumer Reports* magazine (also listed in the resources). Each April issue contains photos of all vehicles from that year.

For hats and caps, it's a good idea to take snapshots of someone you know wearing various examples and have the photographs on-hand.

Finally, for eyeglasses and sunglasses—get a catalogue from your local optometrist.

In the resources, because this is a short section, I've listed places where you can take forensic art classes, which will most likely cover all this information in great detail.

6) Most common composite sketch mistakes.

We're getting into territory here where it would help if you had some classroom instruction. Remember, check the resources I've listed including schools where forensic art is taught. Here I can only provide guidelines.

Let me reiterate that it is very possible to provide a sketch that only bears a faint resemblance to the perpetrator that, nonetheless, leads directly to a capture. However, the more realistic your sketch, the better the chance the criminal will be caught.

So it would behoove you to watch for these mistakes and try to train yourself not to make them:

* *Irises too big*
* *Eyes too big*
* *Nose too long or nose outlined*
* *Lips outlined*
* *General lack of three-dimensional look—usually due to poor shading technique*

The main thing you need to realize here is that it is much harder to get facial proportions right when you are drawing from witness memory. It's hard enough to do a portrait from life or from a photograph, but doing it piecemeal from witness memory is really tough.

I advise beginning forensic artists to do everything possible to make their sketches look like normal human faces. Get schooling where and when you can, read and learn from books like this one and practice, practice, practice.

Oh—and don't be too hard on yourself. Sometimes I look at some of my earlier work and shake my head in wonder that the police caught the criminal at all. I have learned that it takes time and practice to get good. Persevere and you'll get there.

How to pull faces from memory and the almighty interview.
Techniques to help a reluctant witness to remember.

1) Relax the witness. Do everything that you can do to put the witness at ease. You start, of course, by projecting a calm and quiet demeanor yourself. If you fidget, glance at your watch, tap or kick your foot, bite your nails, or otherwise act as if you're in a hurry or in a rush to get to the next appointment, this will automatically cause the witness to tense up.

You should have an idea as to approximately how much time you're going to need to get a good sketch and it sometimes helps to schedule a little extra time around that framework, just in case. Then, the trick is to learn to draw very quickly, without looking as though you are rushing.

It helps to tell witnesses that, the more they relax, the easier it will be for them to remember and the better the sketches will be. They'll watch you for cues. If you appear calm and unhurried, it will help them to let down their guard.

Finally, take away the burden of the task from them. Tell the witnesses or victims *you* will do all the work, that the drawing is not *their* problem and reassure them—from the beginning—that they needn't worry that the drawing be perfect or look exactly like the perpetrator. Explain that no one does a perfect sketch, but that the drawing will be good and that anything they can remember would help.

2) Understand what the witness "sees" in his or her mind. When forming a picture of someone's face in the mind's eye, the image appears only for a matter of a fraction of a second or, at most, a few seconds. Then the image fades and must be brought forth again. Even though the witness can bring the image back again hundreds of times, it will continue to fade after only moments.

If you tell witnesses that everyone's visual memory works like that, then they will feel normal and they will understand that their visual memories are not somehow inferior. Reassure them that thousands of successful composite sketches have been produced from this memory process.

3) Never argue with witnesses or victims when they insist that they don't remember. One of the things you must remember is that most crime witnesses are in the throes of one form or another of post-traumatic stress. And one of the symptoms of this stress is obsessing over details of the crime, or something related to the crime. Also, people who have been traumatized become frustrated very easily and tend to lash out or otherwise vent. Some cry, but some just get very angry very quickly.

As long as you understand upfront that this process not only has nothing to do with *you*—the artist—but is an expected and even necessary part of the healing process, then you will be able to sit and let your witness or victim vent.

Many times they repeat statements like, "I don't know why you think I can do this," or, "It was too quick," or, "All I saw was the gun," or, "I was too scared," and so on.

Never argue with these kinds of statements. First, accept in your own mind that what they are saying is highly unlikely. Just don't believe them. Secondly, understand that these objections are necessary for them to be able to relax, which is what you want.

4) *What to say when witnesses or victims insist they did not see the face.* Remember "Blind Justice," when the witness was so adamant that she hadn't seen the suspect that she shouted at me through the whole session? I just remained calm and I said things like, "Why don't you pick out a hairstyle that resembles that of the man you saw?"

Even the most reluctant witnesses will usually comply without thinking and you're on your way.

In the case of Officer Paul Deason, who had been shot, run over and dragged—he insisted that he had only seen the gun. Remember that I dropped the subject after that and spoke of things like how wonderful it was that he had survived, then commented, "What kind of a person would *do* such a thing? What kind of expression did he have?"

When Paul told me that the shooter's eyes had been "empty," and, "It looked like he didn't care about anything," then I knew he'd seen his face.

Anytime a witness or victim can answer the expression question, it means he has seen the face.

Another good tool to use is simply to ask about the perpetrator's hair. The hair—or baldness—is the feature most often remembered. If they can describe the hair, it usually indicates that they have, indeed, seen the face.

Ease up to the subject and when the victim or witness gets upset, back off, talk about other things, then come at it another way. The thing is, their conscious minds have covered over with emotion what their unconscious, rational minds did see and remember. All you have to do is find ways to reveal those glimpses.

I guarantee that the most reluctant witness will be surprised to find how much they *do* remember. And don't forget—many times, even a sketch that does not closely resemble a suspect can still get him caught. Remind the witness of that whenever you can, until they relax.

And remember, when you've managed to coax a usable description from the most reluctant witness, *DO NOT* blurt out something like, "I thought you said you didn't see his face!"

Just be thankful you got a good sketch.

The Interview.

Hundreds of thousands of artists can draw a face. The talent that sets forensic art apart from any other kind is the interview.

The task of pulling information out of sometimes distraught or shut down witnesses is so difficult that most artists won't even consider entering into this profession. Sadly, those who do often limit themselves to doing a few sketches a year, simply because the activity can be so frustrating and uncomfortable for them.

Through the years, I've collected a number of tips on conducting witness interviews in such a way that it can be an enjoyable process, not just for the surprised witness, but for the artist himself or herself.

Some of the information I'm going to give may overlap or otherwise repeat something I've already said—but don't worry about that. If I've already said it once, it's still important that I say it again.

When I get to the end of my own suggestions, I'll include scientific verification for my techniques that were published by the FBI a few years ago. I read these findings some ten years after I'd started using them myself. I consider it a validation for something I knew instinctively.

★   *Empathy is essential.*

In fact, empathy is the single most important characteristic a forensic artist should possess—even more important than highly-trained skills or vast artistic talent.

In this book you've read that I was brutally attacked myself and that when I am in the presence of witnesses, I often draw upon that violent experience not only to help me understand what they are going through, but to offer my own experience as a source of common ground and support.

You may be thinking, *Gosh Lois, that's great, but I've never been attacked! I've never been the victim of a violent crime! I'm glad I haven't been, but what am*

I supposed to do? How can I relate to a traumatized witness and help her to relax and remember?

Don't worry—empathy can be learned and it's not as hard as you think.

Everyone knows what "sympathy" is. When you hear that something bad has happened to someone, you feel bad for him or her.

However, empathy goes deeper than mere sympathy. With empathy, you actually *feel the pain* of the victim. The best way I can describe it is for you to think back to your own "worst day" experience.

How did you feel the day you were in a car accident or your mother died or your child briefly disappeared?

Whatever your own life experience, it can help you to empathize with victims who are suffering, even if you have not had the same experience as they.

Some people mistakenly believe that drawing on their own grief to help another would be too upsetting and stressful, that they're better off burying such experiences. But nothing could be further from the truth. Anytime you use your own pain to reach out and help another hurting soul, you experience healing yourself.

Remember Heidi Guzman, whose own sister was horribly murdered? She drew on that experience to become an activist for the organization Parents of Murdered Children. She would be the first to tell you that every time she reaches out to comfort another bruised soul, she grows stronger and more peaceful herself.

In addition, I would like to reassure any law enforcement people reading this that it is not too traumatic for a witness to participate in a sketch session soon after their attack. It's just the opposite. It's empowering.

This does not in any way mean that a sketching session has to be a weep-fest! Far from it! In fact, that brings me to my next most important point:

★ *The forensic sketching session should be the most enjoyable conversation possible considering what the witness has endured.*

What I'm saying here could also be included in the section on "empathy," but when you are in a session with a crime victim/witness, it is important that you become a bit of a chameleon and change your colors to fit the situation.

It's simple common sense and basic human courtesy. If, for example, your witness has just experienced a terrifying car-jacking, you're not going to ramble on about you brand-new car. If they're high-school kids, well, what are you going to talk about? High school, of course! If they're children, you ask them the kinds of things you know children love to talk about.

And if they nearly died, you don't whisper around the topic like it's forbidden. You can rest assured it's all they think about. So softly say, "You almost died." (This lets them see you know.) Then you can say joyously, "But you lived! Isn't that *wonderful?*"

I've never said those words yet that I didn't see a big smile on a survivor's face.

It's part of helping these survivors relax, it's part of being empathetic, but it's also part of making the interview a pleasant experience.

And sometimes, that can even lead to laughter.

Did she just say, LAUGHTER?

Yes, I did!

Whenever possible, as much as possible, it's important to get the witness to laugh. This is the most valuable tool you can use in a good interview. (Obviously there are some witnesses who have been through too horrific an experience to be brought to laughter. However, I've gotten witnesses to laugh that an outsider never would have imagined.)

Speaking in strictly technical terms, it has been proven, scientifically, that mood elevation aids memory.

In more compassionate terms, look at it this way. You're going to be spending at least an hour in this person's company. He or she has just been through a terrible experience and everyone around him or her usually is grim, worried and unsure what to say. The witnesses often are experiencing depression, anger and a great deal of stress.

The healthiest thing they could possibly do, under the circumstances, is laugh!

I'm not suggesting you whip out a list of jokes or anything. I'm just talking about being relaxed, the way you would when you were first getting acquainted with someone who might become a friend. Remember the drill team member, Emily, the girl who had been savagely raped, but was bravely preparing to go out and perform at half-time? We talked about the dance routine she had learned and she said how she'd practiced and I commented that she would do great that night, that nobody ever died from a drill team routine.

This was a person who had been so close to being murdered that one of her attackers tried to hire a hit man later to finish the job.

So what did she do when I said that?

She *laughed*. Right out loud. Threw back her head and laughed.

Just go with the flow. Don't be afraid to toss out a wisecrack if one occurs to you. Smile as often as you can. Most people will respond in kind.

Even better…they will remember that face and you can draw it from that memory.

Let's recap some of the characteristics of a good interview:

* *Relax witnesses by relaxing yourself.*
* *Tell them how the sketch will be done.*
* *Don't argue when they insist they can't remember.*
* *Take away the task. Tell them it's okay if you don't do a perfect sketch. Let the witness know that HE OR SHE HAS NOTHING TO LOSE—nothing bad will happen if the sketch turns out terrible. Why not just give it a try?*
* *Perform the sketch as quickly as possible without appearing rushed.*
* *Discuss positive things to elevate the witness's mood and, whenever possible, make 'em laugh!*
* *Don't be afraid to bring it up if he or she almost died. Point out how wonderful it is that he or she alive.*

There are some more technical aspects of the interview, such as what kind of chair to use, phone numbers at hand and so forth that I will get into, but now, I'd like to delve into some more psychological aspects of the interview that will help you immensely to understand what your witness is going through and needs to help him or her though the process.

* *Use a soft speaking voice.* For children, especially, it's important not to use a loud voice. Someone who has experienced trauma feels less threatened by a soft voice, which leads to the all-important relaxation.

* *Understand the terrible sense of isolation.* The vast majority of people have never experienced violence and thank God for that. But few people who haven't experienced it really understand how to handle it when a loved one is attacked.

It is sad, but true, that the people who love a victim the most are the ones most likely to make them feel worse! The truth is that a victim's loved ones wish with all their hearts and souls that this terrible thing had not happened; and in their heads, they rewind time, so to speak. A more common term might be, "Monday-morning quarterbacking."

A crime victim's family and friends might say things like, "Well, what were you doing there at that time of night?" or, "Didn't you fight back or scream for help?" or, "I've begged you to quit that night job, but you wouldn't listen and now look what happened." I've known rape victims whose families refused even to believe they'd been raped, or would say things like, "How could you do this to me?"

Blaming the victim is so common in our culture that it is frequently used in court as a defense.

Husbands and boyfriends feel especially impotent that they couldn't stop the attack, whether they were present or not. They feel powerless to protect the ones they love the most and the way many—if not most—men react to such stress is to get angry. They commonly make comments like, "I get my hands on that guy, I'll *kill* him," or, "I'll hunt him down. I'll find him. He won't hurt you again."

They don't understand that such remarks can be deeply distressing to the victim. The last thing this person needs to be doing right then is worrying about whether a loved one is going to storm out and get himself killed or thrown in jail.

If it is a man who was victimized, he may grapple with feelings of cowardice or weakness and shame. He may feel as if there is no one with whom he can talk.

Victims wind up being *re-victimized* by such thoughtless remarks. They may come to a sketching session nursing deep feelings of self-blame, inadequacy and hurt feelings or rage at the person who said such things to them.

It's important to point out to the witness that *the criminal* is always to blame, in any situation, and that comments made by well-meaning friends and relatives are just plain thoughtless and wrong. This nearly always comes as a welcome relief to the victim, helps calm his or her anger and helps him or her come to a point of forgiveness toward those who have been insensitive.

    ★   *Point out that the survivor has much to live for.* One thing victims of violent crime often realize right away is how inconsequential normal, everyday life can seem after having survived a violent attack. Again, other people may be insensitive to this fact, but you can point out to them that having survived the worst, they are now stronger for it. After that, paying bills or interviewing for a job will be a cinch!

★   *Ease their fears.* Many witnesses are consumed with fear of retaliation from the criminal who already hurt them. Almost all these fears are unfounded in reality and you can reassure them on that point. A good tip here is to enlist the aid of a seasoned detective to help put their minds at ease.

Keep in mind that many people think crime victims are dying to hear horror stories about *other* crime victims. This does not help. Let them know you understand their feelings of pain and frustration. They will find it a great relief to talk to someone who does understand and most will find the whole process to be immensely therapeutic.

Again, it will help them to relax.

★   *Remind them that THEY are in control and that THEY are helping to catch the bad people who hurt them.* Most witnesses don't stop to consider how empowering a forensic sketch session can be or how great it will feel if the perpetrators are caught because of it. Tell them that by working with a sketch artist, they have a one-in-three chance of aiding in the capture of the criminals who hurt them. Helping them to realize this can go a long way in assisting their healing process.

★   *You can tell some victims who have been through a savage attack that the more horrible the crime, the more likely your sketch will be effective.* This is because the most traumatized witnesses will have the most indelibly imprinted memory. Plus, the authorities will be more likely to get the sketch out immediately after the crime and law enforcement personnel and the community will be more intense in their efforts to capture the perpetrator.

★   *Praise the detective working the case.* Even if you don't really know the case investigator, if you assure witnesses that the detectives are doing good jobs, it may cause them to work more closely and positively with investigators and increase the chances of solving their cases.

Here are a few miscellaneous technical tips that will help to ensure a successful sketching session:

★   *The witness chair should be as comfortable as possible.* If you are working in a detective's office, have the witness sit in the "power position" in the room. Sit far enough away that, if you reached out your arm, you would not be able to touch him.

★   *If possible, have a separate phone available by the witness's chair. A phone call or two might be crucial to relieving your witness's tension.*

★   *Have tissues, juice and water handy, or soda and soft toys for children.*

★   *If the witness speaks another language, ask what his word for "relax" is and use it.* It also helps facilitate relaxation if you ask the words for such things as "nose," "eyes," "eyebrows" and so on. Even if you have an interpreter close by and the witness can select those features from the catalogue, this is still a warm and ingratiating gesture that can magically soothe tensions.

★   *When using visual aids…* People remember faces by closing their eyes. When a witness is closing his or her eyes, *never* let her open her eyes and catch you staring at her! This is unnerving in the best of circumstances. You can close your own eyes if you wish, or stare off to the side or out the window, or work on the sketch. Give her time and space to *think.*

During this particular part of the interview, be silent.

★   *If you don't have an FBI Facial identification Catalogue…* These catalogues are available to anyone who is employed in any capacity with a law enforcement agency, but if you're just starting out, there are several things you can do to help a witness remember features. In the beginning I would often hand him mug shots to shuffle through and point out features. (Once, the witness sat straight up, held out a mug shot and said, "That's him!" Consequently, the case was solved.)

Alternatively, you can use old high school or college yearbooks. Make high quality copies of the section that features rows of student faces.

★   *Don't show them the sketch until it's roughly finished.* For one thing, this helps you, the artist, work without the pressure of someone watching over your shoulder. It also keeps you from influencing what they are trying to remember. Another good reason not to show them the sketch while you're drawing is that it enables the two of you to talk about pleasant things and thus helps witnesses relax and remember more.

★   *Showing the sketch.* Tell the witness that you are going to show him a rough sketch and will change anything they say. (The more practiced you become, the fewer changes they'll request.)

★   *How do you know you're finished?*

The sketch is finished when the witness says something like, "It's not perfect, there's something not just right, but I can't say what it is."

That's fine. Just say, "We're finished now. We've done all we can. Don't worry, nobody's ever going to do a perfect likeness. You've done a great job! Thanks for your time and trouble."

Sometimes witnesses will shake your hand, sometimes they'll hug you, sometimes they'll be noticeably excited at how much the sketch resembles their attacker and sometimes they'll be doubtful. If they leave the session feeling better than when they came in, then you've done an outstanding job, *even if the sketch doesn't catch the criminals.*

★   *Never ask the witness to "rate" the sketch (on a scale of one to ten) and don't let the detective pressure her into it.* For one thing, such a "rating" only opens the artist up to attack in a courtroom later. Not only that, but I've found through the years that a witness-rating is not a good gauge at all of how good the sketch is.

Some witnesses I've worked with thought my sketch was great, but when the person was caught, turns out it wasn't that good a likeness after all. Other witnesses felt disappointed by the sketch and it turned out to be almost portrait-perfect. Some of the worst sessions I've had, with the biggest struggles, produced the most successful sketches.

The bottom line is, you just can't tell. When the detective asks, "How good do you think the sketch is?" just say, "It's as good as any I've done before," and go on to the next case. You never know; you may have a pleasant surprise.

"Cognitive Interviewing" and the FBI

In the March 1991 *FBI Law Enforcement Bulletin*, Special Agent Margo Bennett, M.Ed. and Special Agent John E. Hess, M.Ed. described a "new" interviewing technique that was a far cry from the old *Dragnet* days of, "Just the facts, ma'am."

They discussed ways of retrieving witness memory that were a bit more *chatty* than what had been commonly used; the old, "How tall was the subject? What color was his hair?" technique.

The new method was called "cognitive interviewing." Technically, Bennett and Hess broke the technique into three phases: (1) reinstating the context of the event (2) recalling the event in a different sequence and (3) looking at the event from different perspectives.

Basically, what this entailed was *letting the witness talk.*

When a shocking event occurs in someone's life, he or she doesn't go home to his or her spouse or parents and say, "I was robbed today. The subject was a white male, approximately 5'8" to 5'10" tall, with brown hair and brown eyes."

Instead, the victim will say something like, "I was running a little bit late to work, so I took the turnpike instead of I-5, only there was a car wreck there, so it made me later than ever and I was in such a rush when I got out of the car that I dropped my purse and spilled my keys and I didn't notice this guy hanging around, but when I put my keys in the lock, he shoved me from behind! I didn't know what to think! I was so scared!" and so on.

The thing is, scientists realized that human memory, frankly, functions better *in context*. We are a culture of storytellers and when we tell the story of a day in our lives, we want to establish setting, mood and background.

Turns out, all this "embellishment" that may have driven old TV detectives crazy is actually an important brain function to facilitate memory.

In the article, investigators are encouraged, among other things, to give the witnesses plenty of time without feeling rushed, let them include all the details they wish (the more, the better) and give them a chance to vent powerful emotions without judgment. Only after the witness has had a chance to pour out his or her story should you *then* go back and ask specific, memory-prompting questions.

The authors point out that in spite of all sorts of advances that have been made in the field of forensics, the truth is that most crimes are solved by *information* and that information is furnished by *people*—crime witnesses.

Good cops and forensic artists have always known that with sufficient empathy, a so-called "cognitive interview" is automatically done! For instance, if you're empathetic and you've given your witness sufficient time for the interview, you will let him or her ramble on, telling all the insignificant details of what happened to the person because you know it is necessary for the witness or survivor to express his feelings. This helps him relax and stimulates their memory.

In the final analysis? Be compassionate and caring.

The rest will fall into place.

I hope this brief overview of the things you need to know to become a forensic artist will answer many of your questions and encourage you to seek more information and instruction.

As I said, it's my goal to get as many forensic artists out there doing compositry as possible, so that we can catch more criminals and empower more crime survivors.

I look forward to seeing more of you in the field and I wish you all the best.

Now… let's go catch some bad guys!

Epilogue

I love my work so much that I don't tell people the depth of my feelings, because I don't want to suggest their own work is less fulfilling or meaningful than a forensic artist's. However, I cannot imagine any occupation where you can get so much fulfillment as mine.

One day recently, I was at the Houston Police Credit Union and a compactly-built, dark-headed cop yelled out to me in front of everybody, "Hey! You're the artist! You gotta be the most fulfilled person in the world! You only take an hour or two to work a case, so you have probably helped bring in hundreds of bad guys. No detective alive will ever get that many bad guys and you're years from retiring! You're great!"

I never got that officer's name, but he absolutely made my day and he expressed so perfectly the way it feels to do what I do.

If I thought only one sketch of mine had made a difference in some crime victim's life, it would mean the world to me, but I can rest in the knowledge that my work has been instrumental or at least helpful in bringing in almost a thousand criminals and helping at least that many victims.

When I sat down to write this book, I had a terrible time selecting cases to highlight. All the cases I've worked on are precious to me and I hope I've shown how much of a difference compositry can make, not just in a victim's life and her family's, but in the lives of the dedicated law enforcement officers who labor hours and days and months and years to find justice for victims.

One of the highlights of my year is, occasionally, when I get to attend the International Association for Identification convention. For a few days I can sit in a room with other forensic artists and know that *they know* how I feel. Of course, I am blessed with a life rich beyond measure outside of work. My husband, Sid, and I have been happily married for more than twenty-two years. To me he's just as handsome now as he was that day we first met and I thought his blond hair shone like a halo.

Our two children have grown up. Brent is an elevator/escalator engineer and enjoys his work. Tiffany is in college and doing very well.

I like to work—almost obsessively, some would say—in my yard. People who don't know me well can't imagine why anyone would choose to labor in the heat and humidity of southern Texas. But the neighbors who are my friends can always tell when I've had a particularly harsh case; they know that when I'm down on my knees, digging in the dirt, smelling the earth and the plants, I'm getting therapy.

Every year, we all take a vacation where our family, including my son, Brent's, delightful girlfriend (whom I adore) and a gaggle of friends rent cabins on the Frio River near Garner State Park. We float for hours in inner tubes in the crystal clear waters of the Frio, with cypress trees towering over us and waterfalls pouring down the rock faces at the edge of the river where the banks are skirted with delicate maiden-hair ferns. The float ends at a beautiful swimming hole. Magical. Heavenly. Then all our sunburnt bodies clamber out of our inner tubes and climb the hundred steps to the cabin, where we take showers and eat a huge barbecue.

Someday, I'd like to take a painting vacation throughout Europe. I've even bought a backpack that can hold a compact set of watercolors along with all my clothes and shoes. I can just see myself on some street corner in Florence or Paris, painting. It's good to dream.

Almost every Sunday, I can be found painting watercolor landscapes, things like the cabin at Frio, places where I have been happy and with each brush stroke, I'm there again.

A few years ago, Sid and I joined the Church of Jesus Christ of Latter Day saints and have found it to be a true blessing.

I teach Sunday School to ten-year-olds and it's a joy, looking out over their sweet, shining little faces... far, far away from the faces of evil.

Resources

BILBIOGRAPHY

Geiselman, R.E., and Fisher, R.P. "Interviewing Victims and Witnesses of Crime," National Institute of Justice, 1985.

Goleman, Daniel. *Emotional Intelligence*. Bantam Books, 1995.

Gordon, Louise. *How to Draw the Human Head/Techniques and Anatomy*. Penguin Books, 1977.

Hammond, Lee. *How to Draw Lifelike Portraits from Photographs*. North Light Books. Cincinnati, Ohio, 1995.

Hogarth, Burne. *Drawing the Human Head*. Watson–Guptill, New York, New York, 1965.

Loomis, Andrew. *Heads/2*. Walter Foster Books, #197.

Peck, Stephen Rogers. *Atlas of Human Anatomy for the Artist.* Oxford Press, Oxford, New York, 1951.

Taylor, Karen T. *Forensic Art and Illustration.* CRC Press, 2000.

TRAINING

Northwestern University Center for Public Safety
600 Foster
Evanston, IL 60204
800-323-4011
www.northwestern.edu/nucps

Federal Bureau of Investigation's National Academy Forensic Art Class
Quantico, VA (Applicants must be full-time employees of a law
enforcement agency)
https://FBIVA.FBIacademy.edu

Stuart Parks Forensic Associates
P.O. Box 73
Cataldo, ID 83810
www.stuartparks.com

Scottsdale Artists' School
3720 N. Marshall Way
Scottsdale, AZ 85251

International Association for Identification (Certifies
forensic professionals)
Joseph P. Polski, Chief Operations Officer
2535 Pilot Knob Rd., Suite 117
Mendota Heights, MN 55120-1120
www.theiai.org

VISUAL AIDS FOR TATTOOS AND VEHICLES

Huck Spaulding Enterprises
P.O. Box 439, Rt. 85
New Scotland Rd.
Voorheesville, NY 12186-0439

Consumer Reports
P.O. Box 2109
Harlan, IA 51593-0298
www.consumer-reports.or/magazine/

EASEL and LIGHT

Testrite Instrument Co.
135 Monroe St.
Newark, NJ 973-589-6767
Or any art supplier